CHRONICLES OF AN AMERICAN MEDIATOR

Preface

A peacemaker, I am informed, was a Colt 45 revolver used to settle the Wild West in years gone by. When I hold myself out to be a peacemaker, I do not want there to be any confusion. My role in life is to bring resolution, peace, conciliation and healing to those in conflict. This is done through friendly persuasion, not the point of a gun. To avoid confusion with gunslingers, let me introduce myself and give you my background so you will know I am a peaceful person.

My name is Richard M. Calkins, originally of Chicago, Illinois. I took the middle initial "M" in 1972, when I started receiving checks made out to another lawyer, Richard Calkins (no middle initial) of Aurora, Illinois. His father was Dick Calkins, who wrote the comic strip "Buck Rogers." Unbeknownst to me, at the time I took the middle initial "M" to eliminate confusion, he took the middle initial "N" and the confusion continued. It was not resolved until his untimely death in 1979.

I attended New Trier High School in Winnetka, Illinois. Little did I know at the time, however, that I came from the wrong side of the tracks. I never sensed the divide between the socially prominent North Shore and the rest of us, because I was active in high school – I played football and track, and was elected to the Tri-Ship board. However, I must confess, most things in life went over my head, because I was a bit immature and very naïve.

I did go to Dartmouth College, against the wishes of my conservative aunt and uncle. Aunt Coralynn and Uncle Harold Hansen identified the college as a hotbed of the liberal eastern establishment infiltrated by radicals and Communists. This was back in 1949 during the McCarthy era. Brainwashed by the Chicago Tribune and its editor, Colonel McCormick, they were conservative Republicans, who were anti-British and anti-everything else. I graduated from Dartmouth with honors in my major, international relations, and truly believed that I was destined to lead the Western world with my classmates and a few from Harvard, Yale and Princeton.

Much to my chagrin, upon graduation in 1953, I was turned down by Procter & Gamble and hired by Scott Paper Company to sell toilet paper to grocery stores in Chicago. My salary reflected the level of my competency, $80 per week, but I did get the use of a company car.

In the army, I rose to the rank of SP3. I was rather proud of this until my son, Tad, in the National Guard, rose to the rank of full Colonel. I received CIC training at Fort Holabird, Maryland and was assigned to

Hawaii, the number one assignment in all the military. I'm not certain I carried out my duties with the right attitude. There is a photograph of my arrival at the airport in Honolulu, Hawaii, carrying my golf clubs, tennis rackets, ukulele, and a single small suitcase. Oh yes, there is a lei around my neck.

I did survive my very sensitive assignment in Hawaii, on the beaches at Waikiki and Makaha, and dreaded my return to civilian life. To avoid going back to Scott Paper, which was required by law to keep my job open, I asked a friend to send me an application to the Northwestern University business school or law school. I didn't care which.

Receiving the law school application, I entered Northwestern University Law school in September, 1956, and graduated in June 1959. I law clerked for federal Circuit Court of Appeals judge Elmer J. Schnakenberg. I then joined the law firm of Chadwell, Keck, Kaiser, Ruggles and McLaren in 1961, and then set up my own law firm with my mentor, George Burditt, in 1969. In 1980, I took leave of absence from the firm to become dean at Drake University Law School (1980 – 1988). It was at this point that I was introduced to mediation, which changed my life.

In reviewing my professional career, my impact on society has been modest at best. I did, however, receive the honor of a roast when I left Drake law school, the only dean so far so honored. However, the master of ceremonies, Dick Smith, summed up my achievements this way: "Dick is a very humble person, but then he has much to be humble about."

It is difficult to explain how mediation has impacted my life, but I will try. In my legal career as a litigator, one case stands out as really being significant, *State of Illinois v. James Harden*. As a newly admitted member of the Illinois Bar Association, I was appointed by the Illinois Supreme Court to represent a black teenager who had been sentenced to 20 years in the State penitentiary for a gangland rape (the victim had been raped 26 times.) He was one of eight defendants tried together, represented by a single public defender. In taking the assignment, I was warned that all defendants sent to the penitentiary say they are innocent, so not to be taken in by any alibis. However, after 1000 hours investigating and combing the West Roosevelt area of Chicago, I was able to establish James' innocence. First, six months before the rape, he had been knifed in the abdomen and had major surgery. At the time of the rape he was so weak he was barely able to climb the stairs to his family apartment. Second, numerous witnesses would testify that he was home in bed before midnight, per doctor's orders, long before the time of the rape. Third, he was in a police lineup and the victim could not identify him, although she did identify three of the other boys. Fourth, the victim told a member of James' family that she could not identify him as one of her assailants. Fifth, police reports, which were withheld at the time of the trial, established the victim could identify only one of the assailants, not James, because it was dark and she was frightened. Sixth, four of the boys were given polygraph tests after the case was reversed and remanded for new trials. Only James passed. And seven, upon reviewing the polygraph test, the state attorney dismissed all charges made against James and he was released.

James was convicted because the public defender refused to offer substantial evidence exculpating him because the other defendants had no alibis. Counsel refused to ask for a separate trial because of a lack of resources. The public defender explained, that if he wasn't guilty of rape he probably did something else deserving the prison sentence. However, James had no police record, had never been arrested and came from a strong family – his father was a Baptist minister.

Upon release we helped James find a job. He got married and now has raised his family to adulthood. And in all those years, James never once complained, even though he served three and a half years in the penitentiary before his release.

Aside from the *Harden* case, the litigation side of my career has been wanting, because in my zeal to advocate, like most advocates, I did more harm than good. The successful prosecution of the Chicago-based Chicken Unlimited franchise on behalf of franchisees, put that fine company into bankruptcy, and a vigorous defense in a lawsuit brought by R. J. Riley against his partners, may have contributed to his early demise due to a fatal heart attack during trial. Or perhaps it was watching so many fellow litigators fall victims to stress, depression and alcoholism, or the antipathy I felt when I saw a lawyer over zealously pursue a client's cause, made me question the career path I had chosen.

There can be no doubt that aggressive "advocacy "has stamped the forehead of all trial lawyers with the scarlet letter "A". It has made the profession the brunt of numerous jokes – Abraham Lincoln once said, the single lawyer in a small rural Illinois town might starve, two will thrive. Even doctors joke about lawyers, which I don't understand. It was reported in the New England Journal of Medicine that some doctors and medical scientists are now using lawyers rather than white mice for the medical testing and experiments – because there are more of them, you get less attached , and there are some things white mice just will not do. Frankly, I don't know why there are not more doctor jokes, but then how can you joke about such a humorous lot, purportedly saving lives (and making so much money doing it). The only doctor joke I know is: what is difference between God and a doctor? God doesn't think he's a doctor. It is clear doctors do not like lawyers and that is because they are the only persons on earth who set a time for their appearance in court and they can't be late.

In spite of this bad humor, the legal profession is honorable and lives by a strict code of professional responsibility. Why there was a lawyer I knew who probated an estate for an elderly widow, which, when the work was completed sent her his bill. In the return mail he received a check from her which was $300 too much. Forthrightly, he faced the serious ethical and moral dilemma – should he tell his partners. Certainly, the Greylord investigations in Chicago, which sent judges and lawyers to jail, including former governor of Illinois Otto Kerner, who was sent to a federal penitentiary directly off the United States Court of Appeals bench, seriously hurt the reputation of lawyers. However, doctors have been jailed for padding Medicaid and Medicare bills, savings loan officers, for making injudicious loans, and stockbrokers for dealing in junk bonds and Ponzi schemes. Still lawyers are held in greater disdain. I think this is because, when people deal directly with lawyers and experience first hand aggressive, overbearing, and many times uncaring persons, they are scarred for life. This was brought home to me when a close high school and college friend went through a very difficult divorce, during which he was cross-examined by the top divorce lawyer in Chicago. My friend could not handle the cross examination and to his utter consternation broke down in tears. Words cannot describe his humiliation. Two years later, I was at the Lyric Opera with him when we bumped into the lawyer during intermission. Not knowing of the prior encounter, I started to introduce them. My friend said nothing, but went to the men's room, got sick, and had to go home.

Much to my dismay, I realize that this antipathy towards lawyers is not limited to this continent nor this age, but has historic roots indeed. One lawyer asked a very holy man, who had just chastised a number of scribes and Pharisees for their hypocrisy, whether he reproached lawyers also. The stinging response given was, "Woe unto you also, ye lawyers!

For ye lade men with burdens grievous to be borne, and ye yourselves touch not the burden with one of your fingers." (Luke 11:45, 46).

The same man advised the people in no uncertain terms to avoid litigation all costs: "Agree with thine adversary quickly, whiles thou art in the way with him; lest at any time thy adversary deliver thee to the judge and the judge deliver thee to the officer, and thou be cast into prison." (Matthew 5: 25) And, again, "if any man will sue thee at law and take away thy coat let him have thy cloak also." (Matthew 5:40) The message seems to be that even the best of lawsuits leaves parties burdened for life with anger, hatred, stress and despair.

Concerned about my profession and my place in it, I developed the philosophy that I would make an effort to get along with each attorney with whom I litigated. My goal was to make them a friend or at least work in a cooperative way. This proved difficult at times because lawyers, gearing up for trial, like to find reasons to dislike their opponents, as a way to hype themselves for the courtroom. It made me look weak in the eyes of some; however, I chose this as the path I would traverse and I did not waiver. I must confess that for this reason my results in court were modest at best. Nevertheless, it did pay dividends, for 75 percent of my referral antitrust business came from lawyers I had previously opposed because they had conflicts of interest and could not represent a particular client.

One incident best illustrates the results of my get-along philosophy. I had two motions to attend in federal court at the same time. I asked counsel in one, as a matter professional courtesy, to request my motion be put to the end of the call because I was in an adjoining courtroom and would return shortly. When I returned to the courtroom everyone but the clerk had left. I inquired about my motion and he explained that it had been dismissed for lack of prosecution. I asked whether counsel explained that I was in another courtroom and would return shortly. He answered in the negative. I returned to my office and called counsel. I read the riot act to him for his lack of professionalism. His comment was that I was a big boy. This made me angrier for now I had to make a special appearance to reinstate my motion. That night I did not sleep well, and the next day I felt ill. I was suffering and I had done nothing wrong. I finally came to my senses and knew what I had to do. I called the attorney and apologized for my rudeness. He accepted my apology but did not reciprocate. However, I felt better and thought that was the end of the matter.

Six months later, I was ensconced as dean at Drake Law School. I received a call from the clerk of the federal court in Houston Texas, informing me that an antitrust case I had was coming up for trial. I asked to have it continued to summer when I would be free to try it. My request was denied. In panic I tried to get someone to cover for me. I could not take a month leave from law school to go to Houston. No one in my law firm was free to cover for me, and I became concerned about malpractice. In desperation, I asked the above lawyer, who was a good trial lawyer and familiar with the antitrust laws, if he would handle it. He readily agreed and won a larger verdict than I would have and the matter was resolved. I'm certain that if I had not apologized earlier he never would've helped me out of a difficult situation.

I think this explains who I was when I embarked on my mediation career in the fall of 1989.

INTRODUCTION

Most American lawyers take great personal pride in the American judicial system, which has stood the test of time for over 200 years. Law students are indoctrinated with the belief that our legal system is the finest yet devised by mankind, that it seeks the truth in all instances, and does justice to all who enter its hallowed halls. How shocked I was when the then Chief Justice of the United States Supreme Court, Warren E. Burger, led a frontal attack on the very foundation of that system and the lawyers engaged in it. In his 1984 Annual Report of the State of the Judiciary, he castigated the court system in these words: "Our system has become too costly, too painful, too destructive, too inefficient for a truly civilized people." And to the lawyers, judges and law professors thriving in it, he had these searing words: "The legal profession, lawyers, judges and law professors, has become so mesmerized with the stimulus of the courtroom contest that we tend to forget that we ought to be healers of conflict." He went so far as to accuse lawyers of being the cause and promoters of conflict and they must reverse course – they must see their role as "problem-solvers, harmonizers, peacemakers, the healers – not the cause – of conflict."

What Justice Berger was attacking was not just the inefficiencies in our courts. It was far more fundamental. He was attacking what he considered to be an archaic system. He stated, that "for many claims [in civil court], trial by adversarial contest must go the way of ancient trial by battle and blood. . ."

At first blush, I was not quite certain why he was likening change in our court system to that which occurred in medieval times. I concluded he was classifying our adversarial system as archaic because the fundamental premise was that the parties had to agree to do battle to resolve their differences. Resolution could be reached only if one party was defeated.

In examining the adversarial approach to dispute resolution, the lowest denominator is war. It attempts to resolve differences in a very destructive way. Sometimes it is successful but most times it is not. In medieval times civil disputes were resolved in the king's courts, where advocates representing the parties, charged each other on horses with lances raised: resolution was reached when one fell to the ground, often fatally wounded – for God interceded on the side of the party who was in the right.

The modern day courtroom is considerably more civilized than the king's court. There is rarely physical combat; however, the battle of words can be just as severe and lawyers representing the parties just as determined. Clarence Darrow ably described the courtroom battle when he said: "A courtroom is not a place where truth and innocence inevitably triumph; it is only an arena where contending lawyers fight, not for justice, but to win." The late associate Justice Antonin Scalia of the United States Supreme Court observed, that Americans "are too ready to seek vindication or vengeance through adversarial proceedings rather than peace through mediation."

An objective examination of the American adversarial system confirms Chief Justice Burger's description of it as being too costly, takes too long, and severely punishes anyone fool-hearty enough to venture into its halls. He felt that American public deserved better.

1. <u>Too costly</u>. The cost of litigation proliferated in the 1980s when $300 per hour for lawyer's time was thought excessive, to in excess of $1500 per hour in the last decade. It is not uncommon for pretrial discovery to cost $40 million, and in the case of the Microsofts of the world, over $80 million. One federal judge stated:

> While we have created the fairest system
> in the world for resolving disputes, it is so

expensive that very few people in America can afford to use it. The court system serves the rich, those with insurance and those who shift the cost of litigation to the rich and those with insurance. I cannot personally afford to use the system that I treasure.

2. <u>Too lengthy</u>. In the 1980s and 1990s, it was not uncommon for cases to languish in the courts 5, 10 and even 20 years. The sheer volume of cases filed each year, over 18 million, brought some court systems, particularly in industrialized areas of the nation, to virtual gridlock. Liberalized discovery, introduction of novel causes of action, promulgation of new statutory and regulatory claims, the backlog of criminal cases, particularly drug-related, which had precedence over civil cases, all added to the mix.

I mediated one case, *Midwest Milk Producers Litigation*, which was in its 21st year of litigation. Lawyers quipped that the fees generated over so many years put their children through college and now their grandchildren. Two individuals asked if I had read the *Bleak House* by Charles Dickens. It is a story of an estate that was in litigation in the Chancery Court of England for 17 years, and when the heirs went to collect their inheritances, they were met by the attorneys leaving the judge's chamber smiling. They explained, the heirs did not have to go any further because there was nothing left – the estate had been dissipated over 17 years by attorneys' fees. The book led to reformation of the Chancery Court in England; that is why it is considered Dickens most important book.

3. <u>Too destructive</u>. Although Chief Justice Burger was concerned about the inefficiencies of the courts, his primary focus was on the destructive nature of the system itself and what it was doing to a wary public – it was "too painful and too destructive for a truly civilized people." One leading jurist, Judge Learned Hand, said in 1926, "I must say that as a litigant I should dread a lawsuit beyond almost anything in life short of sickness and death."

In seeking change, the Chief Justice was seeking something more profound that removing cases from the courtroom to the conference table. He was seeking a basic change in the mindset of attorneys from advocates to peacemakers. He began by redefining the lawyer's obligation to the client. He noted:

> To fulfill our traditional obligation means we should provide mechanisms that can produce an acceptable result in the shortest possible time, with the least possible expense, and with minimum stress on the participants. That is what justice is all about.

This change embraces mediation – it provides an acceptable result because the parties have agreed, it is expeditious because it can be concluded in one day and even before the case is filed in court, its costs are diminimus compared to litigation, and it is user-friendly and accommodates the parties.

To mediate in this new arena, Chief Justice Burger demanded something quite different from lawyers who sought to engage in it. He required them to shed their coats of advocacy and done cloaks of peacemaking. This, he noted, required an entirely different approach to resolution. It required the lawyer to discard his advocacy tools – cross-examination, impeachment, discrediting, undermining, defeating – and add entirely new tools to his tool box, tools which have a positive and not negative impact on the parties. Those tools included building rapport and trust with the parties, not defeating one; seeking common ground between them, not impeaching or discrediting either; seeking to bind the wounds, not deepening them; and, perhaps, most important, seeking to bring healing not hurt.

The Chief Justice set forth a formula for accomplishing the above. He stated lawyers must become

> legal architects, engineers, builders, and
> from time to time inventors as well. We

have served, and must continue to see
our role as problem-solvers, harmonizers,
and peacemakers, the healers – not the
promoters – of conflict.

Unquestionably, lawyers who accept the challenge to become peacemakers embrace the highest calling in the legal profession and are placed on the pedestal with other healing ministries. And most, who have made the transformation to peacemaker, find inner satisfaction, missing in the courtroom contest. They feel so much better about themselves that they describe themselves as "recovering trial lawyers." That lawyer is worthy who lightens the burdens of others.

I am one such recovering trial lawyer and this is my mediation journey and transformation.

———————————————

Mediation was introduced to me in 1989, when I completed my tenure as dean of the Drake University Law School. Anxious to get back into the practice of law, I had no idea of the revolutionary change taking place around me. On a particular dreary day in November, I received a call from Kim Stamatelos, daughter of my good friend and Drake Law School alumnus, Dan Stamatelos. That call set in motion a change in my career path that has impacted my entire life and that of my family. What herein follows is my journey.

CHAPTER 1

A PEACEMAKER IN THE MAKING

It was just another day in Des Moines. The year was 1988. Yet it was a day that would change everything in the world for me. Standing before the mirror, I examined closely the one day growth that had to be removed before showering, dressing and heading to the office. I noticed my puffy eyes, graying hair, and suddenly felt the stiffness in my right knee from Sunday night mixed doubles tennis the evening before, all of which left me slightly discouraged and in a somber mood.

I must confess that I've always been extremely sensitive about my age. When I reached 55, in 1986, I refused to accept senior status and had my wife purchase our movie tickets at the senior citizens discount – I would've paid the full fare. In fact, the one time I did purchase tickets my ego was shattered. The cashier very sweetly asked if I was 55 and thus eligible. "Of course not," I indignantly responded, and paid the full $4.50 to a rightfully embarrassed cashier. I refused to be called grandpa by my grandchildren, so they call me, Dickie. Now some 28 years later, young women regularly give me their seats in a crowded subway train, not only in Chicago, but more recently in Kiev, Ukraine. But that's another story.

In becoming a senior citizen, I adopted the philosophy of Horace Rumpel of the Old Bailey of public television fame, concerning one's wife: "to hear is to obey." And a good wife is, "she who must be obeyed." I subscribed to this philosophy with Anita, that when she asks me a "yes" or "no" question (like, should she keep this new bedspread), she is really giving me a golden opportunity to guess the right answer. Interestingly, when I got the wrong answer she very graciously gave me a second chance. However, it wasn't till I reached the age of 70 that I learned those four magic words which are the cement of a good marriage, "I am wrong again." That raises the deeply philosophical question, is the man who speaks in the forest and there is no woman to hear him, still wrong.

On this dark November day, I also felt melancholy; perhaps it was the empty nest syndrome with Kathie Alice our youngest, off to college for her junior year. I think my melancholy was augmented by Anita's energy and enthusiasm as she greeted another full and challenging day of tennis in the morning, PEO luncheon, and afternoon of stuffing envelopes for the Des Moines Symphony Guild.

Entering the garage, I pressed the door opener (such a luxury from our prior house where we had to manually operate the door) and got into my new 1990 Lincoln Town Car – well it was not new because I purchased it with 17,321 "executive miles." I was pleased with it in spite

lingering doubts we purchased "someone else's problems." These were

not eased during the test run when the front wheels pulled slightly to the

right, and I noted this to Earl, our used-car salesman. He instantly

responded that new cars are built that way to avoid head-on collisions

with oncoming traffic if the driver should fall asleep. Now that's quick

thinking, I thought. Any salesman, used-car or otherwise, who can think

that quickly deserves the sale. So I bought the car and Earl had the front

wheels realigned. He almost lost the sale, however, when he suggested,

after learning that I was a lawyer, "our professions have much in

common." I didn't ask what he meant.

As my car reached I–80 and I–35, I speeded up to merge with the

oncoming rush-hour traffic. I know this is what the law requires because

the one question I missed on the Iowa driver's examination was: in

entering an interstate highway you should, A, stop until the way is clear;

B, yield the right-of-way until you can enter; or, C, speed up and merge. I

chose B, and the clerk very solicitously pointed out that C was the correct

answer.

Heading to downtown Des Moines, I took a cloverleaf to the right

and merged into the traffic heading east on I-235. As I worked my way through West Des Moines, traffic slowed to 40 mph, the extent of the rush hour slowdown. I often wondered what Capt. Jack, who hovered above Des Moines reporting traffic conditions, would do if he had to report just one day of Chicago rush hour. Excitement in Des Moines is for a train to block a railroad crossing for five minutes. But then this is the utter magic of Des Moines, Iowa – 15 minutes door-to-door and not the one hour I used to spend commuting via Northwestern Railroad from suburban Wilmette to my law office at 135 South LaSalle Street (the LaSalle National Bank Building) in Chicago. The relaxed morning rush hour epitomizes the more generally gracious living in that fair city – the people are friendly, more trusting, and women will even greet a stranger on the downtown streets with a smile. Can you imagine the implications of the latter on State Street in Chicago? This is not to downgrade Chicago, a magnificent metropolis which Iowans love to visit, especially Wrigley Field, but to highlight the bucolic charm of Des Moines. As a matter of fact you cannot escape the farming influence in Iowa – it pervades everything from TV ads to the judges sitting on its courts. Everyone lives on a farm, comes from farm, or has invested in a farm, from the governor to the justices of the Iowa Supreme Court. In Chicago, if you want to drop a hint about your success in life, you mention your stocks and bonds portfolio or describe your condominium in Florida or Aspen, Colorado, while in Iowa, you mention how many acres you own in northern Iowa; and I might add, those farms have the richest black soil in the world – more than nine feet deep.

I will remember my first full day in Des Moines, Monday, June 2, 1980. I stopped at a Sinclair gasoline station on my way to Drake Law School. After filling my tank ($1.23 per gallon), I reached for my wallet, which had all my cash and credit cards, only to find I had forgotten it. Facing the attendant with consternation, I explained my unfortunate predicament, expecting the worst; however, the attendant assured me that it was no problem. I could drop by the next day and pay. He refused to take even my name, much less my address, telephone number, social security number and so on, because he thought it unnecessary. (Come to think of it I need to drop by there one of these days and pay the good man.)

There's no doubt that Iowa is different. It took us six months to get used to the farm TV ads selling pesticide for your crops and telling you how to raise healthier pigs. I still remember the TV ad picturing a farmer standing next to his semi -truck loaded with pigs for market. To emphasize a point he slammed the tailgate shut and I expectantly waited for a comic punchline, like on "Saturday Night Live," but it never came. It was then I realized this was for real, this was Iowa.

Somehow, the jokes Minnesotans tell about Iowa and Iowans best describe the place and who the people are. They feel Iowans are a slow and sleepy farming lot. For example, a patient in Minneapolis was told by his doctor he had only six months to live. In desperation he asked the doctor if there was anything he could do to live longer. The doctor said there was: "move to Iowa and it will seem like two years." Out of the Gulf War came the report that a squadron of Iowa Air National Guard jets were sent to Saudi Arabia. As they were approaching the airfield, the commander of the group asked landing instructions, after which he asked for the correct time. The Saudi Arabian air controller asked what state the squad was from, and the commander answered, what difference that made. The controller responded: "if you are from New York, it is 2 PM, and if you are from California it is 1400 hrs. The commander responded with pride they were from the great state of Iowa, and the air controller answered: "in that case, the little hand is on the 2 and the big hand on the 12.

Iowans took umbrage when others laughed at our state motto, "A State of Minds." Minnesotans thought a better motto was Bahá

Minnesota, and Nebraskans liked, Gateway to Nebraska. However, neither could ignore the fact that in the movie "Field of Dreams," which was filmed in Iowa, one of the actors asked if this was heaven, and the star of the movie, Kevin Costner, said "no, this is Iowa."

This is not to suggest that Iowans do not have a keen sense of humor. I became acquainted, through the Drake Law School, with Chief Justice W. Ward Reynoldson, who was instrumental in organizing what is now an excellent judicial system. His outstanding work was nationally recognized when he was elected president of the national organization made up of the chief justices of the 50 states. On one occasion, I attended a dinner at which the Chief Justice of the United States Supreme Court Warren E. Burger spoke and referred to his close friend Ward four times. Afterwards, I asked Chief Justice Reynoldson how it was the Chief Justice of the small state of Iowa, which most people do not even know where it is, could be elected president of such an august body and be on a first name basis with the Chief Justice of United States Supreme Court. He looked me in the eye and said, "they think I'm from Ohio."

I do believe there are many in Iowa who feel that in spite of the jokes, it is as close to heaven as one can get. The schools are excellent, standard of living high, unemployment generally low and the people self-sufficient. One story Iowans love to tell, which they assure me is true, is about the hiring of the president of Iowa State University. He had been offered the presidency at Harvard University with a five year contract, a beautiful mansion, a chauffeur-driven limousine and $1.5 million salary with other significant perks. While interviewing he noticed a white phone in the corner of the president's office and asked what it was for. The provost said it was a direct line to the Lord. Given permission to try it, he spoke to the Lord for 20 minutes. After hanging up he declared that was most wonderful experience of his life. He asked if it cost anything. He was told $1000, which he gladly paid. About to choose Harvard he remembered Iowa State University, and as a matter of courtesy decided to visit the school. He was offered the presidency, but only at half the salary of Harvard, no perks, no chauffeur-driven limousine, and a modest home. About to turn down the offer he spotted a similar white phone in the corner of the office. He asked what it was for and once again was informed that it was a direct line to the Lord. Obtaining permission, he spoke to the Lord for 60 minutes, which was even more inspiring than the first call. When he hung up he asked the cost and was informed it was $.35. He said, "$.35, why at Harvard it cost $1000 for only 20 minutes;

why is it so much cheaper here?" The interviewer responded, "because in Iowa, it's only a local call."

Approaching Keo Drive, I exited the interstate, drove down Keo to Ninth Street and turned south to the just completed Principal building, 801 Grand Avenue. The building is a true architectural gem, the marble coming from South America and cut and polished in Italy. With its eight star decor, it is as fine a building as any in Chicago or New York City. Pulling into the adjacent parking ramp ($55 a month) which is connected to the building via skywalk ramp, I completed the ultimate in commuting convenience. I walked across the skywalk to the third floor of the building (the entire downtown area is connected with over 2½ miles of skywalks – the finest system in the country), down one flight of stairs and then on to the elevator to the 32nd floor. Exiting the elevator, I faced the entrance to my law firm, Zarley, McKee, Thomte, Voorhees and Sease, which just moved into its new space. As I looked at the name, I felt a certain sense of gratitude that this fine law firm had accepted me as a partner two years before, when I stepped down as dean of Drake Law School, and Anita and I decided to remain in Iowa.

Our decision to remain here rather than return to my law firm in Chicago, Burditt and Calkins, was an easy one. Anita announced that if I went back to Chicago, I would go back alone. This was a far cry when we made the decision to go to Des Moines in 1980. Anita was in tears at the prospect of leaving the North Shore in Chicago and go out west. We did not even know where Des Moines was except in Iowa. Looking at an Atlas we first looked along the Mississippi River, which would have been desirable because of its proximity to Chicago. We were dismayed when we found it in the middle of the state some180 miles west of the Mississippi River.

Greeting Linda at the reception desk and Susan my secretary, I entered my newly decorated office and stood for a moment looking out my window facing west. I could see miles and miles of farmland, a magnificent sight. With a sigh, I sat down at my desk and immediately noticed a red phone slip, asking me to call Kim Stamatelos. I called her and she was direct. She said, "I just purchased a mediation franchise for Iowa, Nebraska, South Dakota, and Minnesota. I am setting up a mediation panel, and I want you on it. If you're interested I'm having a training session this weekend."

Kim caught me off guard and I hesitated before responding. Actually, I was looking forward to getting back to the practice of law after just completing my tenure at the law school. I responded, "oh, I just do not have time to attend the training session. I'm not sure I want to be an arbitrator in any event." Actually, I did not know the difference between arbitration and mediation.

"Mediation, mediation," said Kim. "That's different than arbitration. Arbitration is binding and an award is enforceable in court. Mediation is not binding unless an agreement is reached. If there is no agreement, you can still go back to court. Could you come down just an hour or so. I think you will like what you hear."

I hesitated again and then agreed, "but I can only stay for an hour." I stayed two hours and suddenly realized mediation fit my profile perfectly; it's something I could do and be far more successful at than trying cases. I then attended the next training session conducted by Alan Alhadeff and became a certified mediator.

Now, 28 years later, I realize what a right decision this was. I have conducted over 2000 mediations with a 93 percent success rate – that's not the best but it's okay. I have mediated every kind of case imaginable from divorce, personal injury to medical and legal malpractice, antitrust to contracts, construction and so on. I've completed over 900 cleric sexual abuse of children cases. Most important, mediation has given me great inner satisfaction and a far better way to express myself. I feel I am truly contributing to society in a meaningful way.

Hereafter are 59 cases that I have mediated. I hope you will enjoy reading about them. I have changed the names and places in order to maintain confidentiality.

Mediation #1

A Crank Out of Place

On December 16, 1989, I received in the mail my first mediation assignment from Kim, *Rachel Goldman v. Iowa Home for the Aged*, scheduled for January 11, 1990 at 1 p.m. at plaintiff attorney's office. The insurance carrier was Tri-City Insurance Company represented by Jerry Seidel. Plaintiff's attorney was David Wilson. I did not know Jerry but did know David, who was a graduate of Drake Law School, who had gained a reputation of being a good trial attorney. He also had a reputation of being a difficult negotiator, which was enhanced when he turned down a $1 million offer and went to trial and the jury found for the defendant. The plaintiff received nothing. I thought that perhaps this recent experience would work to my benefit in this my first mediation.

On the appointed day I arrived at David's office and was led to the conference room. Jerry was already present. The latter was a tall dark haired man in his mid-30s, who had the lean appearance of a jogger. David immediately walked in and pleasantries were exchanged. He was about 5'10" heavyset with a clean-cut look like all good plaintiff attorneys, and radiated a certain energy and intensity which put opponents on notice that he meant business. As we sat down at the conference table, I asked David where Mrs. Goldman was. He explained that she was in Florida with her son, and because of her age would have had difficulty traveling to Des Moines; however, he explained, he had full authority to settle the case.

As I sat at the table with David on my right and Jerry on my left, I felt definite anxiety as to whether the mediation process I had been taught would work. In front of me I had written notes of what I was going to say by way of opening remarks.

I took a deep breath so I would appear casual and in control. I said: "gentlemen, have either of you mediated before?" Both nodded no, which increased my confidence somewhat – they would never know if I made a mistake. I then continued my canned speech, "as you know this is not an arbitration, and I am not here to make a decision which will bind you. My only function is to bring you together and help you settle this matter. Unless both of you agree, there can be no settlement.

I hesitated a moment to see if there was any reaction. Jerry yawned. I was not sure what that meant. "Gentlemen, let me explain my function." I turned over the page I was reading from. "Because I'm not a judge or arbitrator, I have no authority to make any decisions. As a mediator I am a guest at your settlement table. I will remain neutral throughout the session. In other words, I will favor neither side. Likewise, I'll try to the best of my ability to remain nonjudgmental because if I start giving you my opinion on matters, it will appear that I'm helping one side more than the other. This will undermine my neutrality. Additionally because this is a settlement conference, it is confidential and I cannot later be deposed or questioned as to what occurred, nor can my notes be subpoenaed. I ask you to sign the agreement to mediate which includes a confidentiality paragraph."

At this point I gave Jerry and David the mediation agreement for them to sign. When this was completed, I continued my remarks. "Gentlemen, the way I like to proceed is to have each of you make opening statements, which will give me a better understanding of the case. Then we will go into caucus, that is, I'll meet separately with each of you to learn more about the case. One thing about the caucus is that we can discuss matters which you will not want disclosed to the other side. I assure you, I will disclose only that which I have been authorized to disclose.

I paused again looking at Jerry and then David and asked, "are there any questions? Actually we can conduct our mediation anyway we wish for it is a flexible process – our only goal is to get the matter resolved." Neither reacted, so I added, "David, because you represent the plaintiff, why don't you explain what this case is about from your perspective and then Jerry can respond."

David looked at his notes to refresh his recollection as to what the case was about. This happens in small cases with plaintiff lawyers on a contingency fee, who hope to get a quick settlement without putting in too much effort. This rarely happens on the defense side because the attorneys are billing by the hour.

Remembering the case, David put his notes down and said, "my client, Mrs. Goldman, was 85 years old at the time of the accident, in September 1988. She made one of her regular visits to an elderly patient who was bedridden at a Home for the Aged. On the day in question, she was in good health, articulate, and led a full and satisfying life. The nurse entered the room and pulled out a crank from under the bed, and cranked it up so the patient could sit up. Mrs. Goldman sat in a chair at the end of the bed and talked to her for about two hours. As she rose to leave, she did not notice the crank sticking out – it had not been folded under the bed as required. Mrs. Goldman tripped on the crank and fell fracturing her hip. It's our position the nursing home was negligent in not having the crank in a proper position. We think liability is clear and she's entitled to $70,000 in damages because the pain and suffering she has incurred, as well as a diminution of the quality of her life – she is now confined to a wheelchair and can no longer get around." David stopped.

Jerry, who was taking notes, looked up and looked at me. "Jerry do you have an opening statement?"

Jerry looked at his notes and then said: "There is a big dispute on liability. The crank was only sticking out a foot or so. Mrs. Golden was walking with a cane and we believe that she may have tripped over her own cane. Furthermore, she has fallen several times and her present incapacity is due to a subsequent fall. She incurred $4000 in medical expenses which we've already paid. With a life expectancy of four and half years, her damages are no more than $8000.

I sat there listening intently wondering how I would ever get this case settled because the parties were so far apart. Further, I had tried only one personal injury case and knew little about them or what they were worth. In fact, when they talked about soft tissue injuries I was not certain what that was. In an early mediation, I asked if there were any hard tissue injuries. The lawyers just looked at me for there is no such thing.

Jerry stopped. I finished taking notes and then said, "gentlemen, I'll first meet with David in caucus and then with you Jerry." David got up and motioned me to follow him to his office. Once there I went down my outline of questions to ask in caucus. "David let's first go over the strengths of your case, those things which establish liability."

David explained, "I think the strongest part of our case is that Mrs. Goldman will make a good witness for she is articulate and credible. Furthermore, there will be sympathy for an 85-year-old woman who is now incapacitated. Because the nurse did not see her fall, she cannot testify that Mrs. Goldman tripped over her cane. Furthermore, the nurse in deposition admitted that the crank had not been folded under the bed after it was last used as required by nursing home regulations."

I agreed with David the fact that Mrs. Goldman regularly visited others at nursing homes, trying to comfort them, meant she was a sympathetic and good person and the jury would view her favorably. I asked David what the weaknesses in his case were, if any. I really did not see any so I almost did not ask the question.

He looked at me intently and then said, "will this be kept in confidence?"

I answered, "Of course."

"Well," he continued, "my biggest problem is I don't think Mrs. Goldman can stand the strain of traveling from Florida to Des Moines for trial. In fact, her doctors said she could no longer travel at all. The trial is over a year away and, I'm not even sure she will still be on this good Earth. Her health has been failing. Without her testimony I cannot establish how she fell except by deposition." He stopped speaking.

"Well, David, I will keep this in absolute confidence. What do you think a jury will do in this case, your best case and your worst case? "

David hesitated a moment, contemplating the question, and then said, "best case $70,000 and worst case maybe $15,000."

I then asked what he thought the insurance company would settle for. David again thought a moment and said, "Jerry offered $5000 in addition to the $4000 already paid. But I think his company will offer $8000-$10,000 additional money."

"What are you willing to settle for?" David responded immediately, $20,000 new money. I waited a moment and then ask, "but what is your bottom figure?"

David looked at me intently and then responded, "if we can get $15,000 new money we will settle today."

"David, may I disclose to Jerry that you're willing to settle for $20,000 at this time?" David responded that I should demand $50,000.

I returned to the conference room where Jerry was making a phone call. When he saw me hung up and sat down at the table. I then went through the same question and answer process I had with David. "Jerry, what are the strengths of your case?"

Jerry immediately responded, "first of all, Mrs. Goldman is prone to falling and has fallen three times in the last year, the last time put her in a wheelchair. Second, the bed crank is not inherently dangerous and stuck out only 1 foot or so. Anyone could see it. For her to trip over it she would've had to be walking very close to the bed. Third the nurse will testify that although she was not looking at the moment she fell, she saw her immediately afterwards, and by the way she fell it didn't appear she tripped on the crank, but over her cane. Fourth, Mrs. Goldman has poor eyesight and needed to exercise additional care walking and that she did not do."

I asked, "Jerry, what do you see as the weaknesses in your case?"

Jerry hesitated for he was not prepared to address the question. "Well, I guess you could argue that the crank was a hazard, especially for elderly people in the nursing home. Also, there may be a problem because the regulations specifically require that the crank be folded under the bed. "Jerry stopped, looked out the window, and then said "can I speak to you frankly?"

"Of course. Anything you say will not be shared."

Jerry continued, "quite frankly, we are going to lose on liability; it is just a question of how much."

I asked: "what is your best and worst case in front of a jury."

Jerry answered: "Although the hip has mended, I am sure it was painful for Mrs. Goldman. The jury could easily give her $15,000-$25,000."

"Jerry, what does your carrier wish to settle for?"

He responded, "if we could settle for $15,000, we would be happy. I suppose we would pay more if we had to."

I was very encouraged with his response because both sides indicated a settlement of $15,000. I decided to get everyone back together. When all returned to the room I said, "I have listened to all the evidence and statements of counsel, and I want to make a recommendation that we settle the case for $15,000."

Both attorneys immediately agreed and seemed very pleased. They reached across the table and shook hands and then shook my hand. They made me feel like I was a genius to get the matter resolved. I thought to myself, I like this. Then I thought, I wonder if this was a set-up engineered by Kim just to get me hooked. Well, I was hooked and looking for my next mediation.

CHAPTER 2

MEDIATION AS THE PRIMARY MEANS OF RESOLUTION

After two decades of mediating, I have concluded that mediation is no longer an alternative to the courtroom trial, but the primary vehicle to resolution. It is the courtroom trial that is now the alternative if all else fails. Much of the change taking place is due to the fact that the latter is based on an adversarial system that has significant incongruities and contradictions. We are telling a wary public they must agree to do battle if they want their disputes resolved because resolution can be found only if someone is defeated. It is a battle and it has all the casualties battles cause. Both parties are often scarred for life for that is the nature of combat. I have witnessed two fatal heart attacks and one suicide directly attributable to litigation.

In one case, E.J. Riley wrote a book, *How to Earn a Million Dollars and Not Pay a Penny in Taxes*, which was actually aired on "60 Minutes." Riley sold limited partnerships in real estate in Illinois and as money was received it was transferred to a Panamanian corporation, as a consulting fee, which at that time did not have a corporate income tax. The money was then transferred to a Grand Cayman ten year trust.

Riley got in a legal dispute with several of his partners and legal proceedings were commenced. During the middle of trial, Riley did not appear one morning. Eventually, we checked his hotel room and he was found sprawled on the floor, having suffered a fatal heart attack. However, he won because he paid no taxes on millions of dollars he removed to his Grand Cayman trust, which his young wife of two years eventually enjoyed, although his first wife of 32 years tied up his estate in court for seven long years at a cost of several hundred thousand dollars in lawyer fees.

A. Creating a Process to Meet the Exigencies of the Parties

The genius of a mediation is that it is by contract. You can resolve differences any way the parties wish, even create a process on the spot to meet the exigencies of the parties. What does this mean? Let me give you an example. When Southwest Airlines first came on line it found its trademark was quite similar to one used by a regional south eastern airline, so much so that one would have to give it up. To litigate the matter would cost each airline over $1 million. The CEOs of the two companies decided this was not the road to travel, in that the losing party would only spend $30,000 or so to create a new one. The two decided to resolve the matter by arm wrestling; two out of three. For the cost of a party and fun for everyone, the matter was resolved amicably.

It should be noted that there are six standard mediation formats used in the legal profession. There is the *messenger* format, in which the mediator shuttles back and forth between the parties taking new demands and offers. This format goes back to the ti me of Confucius, but is rarely used today because the mediator is foreclosed from actively participating in the settlement process even if asked. Their only function is to act as messenger.

The next recognized mediation format is the *trial* format in which the mediator acts as a judge or hearing officer. He or she listens to the evidence and then issues a nonbinding award, which the parties can accept or reject, and if the latter, still go to trial. The movie "Disclosure" with Demi Moore and Michael Douglas portrays this format and is an excellent example. This format is also little used because again the mediator does little to bring the parties together to find common ground. Once the mediator provides his nonbinding award his work is complete.

A third example is the *conference* format. Here the parties and counsel all sit at a table and work through their problems. Because all are present it helps open communications between them when previously there was a breakdown. It is particularly effective in family law matters and employment disputes. An example of this format can be found at the beginning of the movie "Wedding Crashers."

The fourth format, *caucus*, is what I use and teach. An opening joint session is conducted at which the mediator explains the process and counsel make opening statements, explaining the case from each side's perspective. Thereafter, the parties are separated and put in separate rooms called caucuses. The mediator then shuttles back and forth between them, taking new demands and offers until the matter is resolved. The mediator is heavily involved in finding creative ways to resolve differences.

The fifth format is *transformative* format. This uses the conference style; however, the parties more actively participate and lead the discussion rather than the mediator, whose responsibility is to keep the parties talking.

Finally, the last format is *collaborative* format. Parties using this format rely entirely on their own attorney rather than an independent mediator. Counsel for both sides are committed to getting the matter resolved. If not successful, the parties are required to get new counsel to file the matter in court.

However, in addition to these established formats the parties can, as noted, sculpt any format they wish. The parties and counsel are challenged to think creatively as the following case studies illustrate.

Mediation #2

Partners Forever

Jim Franklin and Bill Carol operated a repair shop repairing lawnmowers, snowmobiles, snow blowers, and so on. The business was successful and they decided to open a second shop on the north side of town. Bill went to the new shop. Over the next two years, difficulties arose between them, to the point they could no longer get along. They decided to separate with each taking one of the stores. A major problem arose evaluating the two stores because the north store was newer. Their differences reached the point they could no longer speak to each other and their frustration turned to anger and then hatred. Each hired an attorney who recommended mediation. I was selected.

I traveled some 75 miles and arrived 15 minutes before the mediation was to begin. Hank Milton represented one of the parties and Frank Gillespie the other. They were good lawyers and concerned that we would not get the matter resolved because their clients could not agree on anything.

When everyone was together for the opening session, I began my opening remarks. "I have reviewed the file and I want to thank you for allowing me to be your mediator. However, it occurs to me that we have to get this matter resolved today and I will do all I can to do so. So I am asking each of you, attorney and client alike, to work hard and be willing to compromise. To not get this resolved could prove to be a major problem. To go to court is not an option for two reasons: one, it would take months and even a year to get the matter resolved, and I do not believe the two parties would survive working together for such a long time; and two, the cost of litigation would probably bankrupt both of you.

"May I suggest this. That you give me the power of an arbitrator, so that if the mediation fails, I can make a binding decision and the matter is assured to be resolved at the end of the day. To not get the matter done today will push you back into court. By the way, do both of you understand the difference between mediation and arbitration? The latter is binding and concludes the matter. It can be enforced in a court of law. In mediation, the matter is not binding unless an agreement is reached. If one is not reached, you can still go to court."

I hesitated to see everyone's reaction. Then each party met alone with their respective attorneys and agreement was reached that we would proceed as suggested. I wrote out an agreement for me to arbitrate and the parties signed it. Now we knew the matter would be resolved by the end of the day. I then put each partner in a separate room and asked the attorneys to remain in the conference room with me.

"Gentlemen," I began, "with your approval I am going to depart from the usual mediation format and initiate a unique procedure to resolve the problems we face here today. Instead of mediating with the parties present, as we usually do, I am going to mediate only with the attorneys. We will take up each issue to be decided and the attorneys will argue their respective client's position. If you can agree on an issue, that will be my decision. I will then ask you to take the issue to your respective clients for approval. If you cannot agree on an issue, then I will make an independent decision, which will be binding and we will go on to the next issue.

"Gentlemen, one further thought. Both of you know what is in the best interest of your respective clients. However, you are not burdened with the emotional baggage they carry. Because we have to get this resolved, I ask both of you to look at the case wholeistically and not from a win/loss perspective. Whatever we do and say in this room will remain confidential and will not be disclosed to the parties. In other words, if you take a position that your client might not appreciate, it will remain confidential from my perspective. Is that agreeable to you?"

The lawyers nodded assent, so I said, "Okay, let's get to work."

With the lawyers only present, we took up each issue that had to be decided. Ultimately, only one issue was left open. I made a ruling on it and it was resolved. In 8 hours the matter was decided and the parties signed an agreement and separated.

One attorney said to me in jest, "I don't know why we should pay you. You hardly said a word all day." Indeed, he was right. Having set the matter in motion, the lawyers carried on themselves.

In thinking back over the case, I realized that it demonstrated how flexible mediation is. You can use any process you wish. There are no strictures. After completing the paperwork, the trip back home through the Iowa farmland was a real pleasure. I felt good about the day's effort.

Mediation #3

For Motorcyclists Sturgis, South Dakota is More Than a Locale; It is a

Happening

David Browne lived in Indianapolis, Indiana. He owned a manufacturing company and was earning $500,000 per year. He and his wife belonged to the top country club in the city and were active members of society.

One day David came home from work and told his wife to go out to the garage – he had a surprise. Jenny went out and looked inside. David was beaming. There was a brand-new top-of-the-line Harley Davidson motorcycle, glistening in the sunlight coming through the windows. Jenny looked aghast. "David," she said, "you have to be joking. Tell me you're not serious."

David was taken aback by Jenny's reaction. "Don't you like it?" Then he added, "I was prepared to buy you one also, but thought I should ask you first."

"No way," said Jenny. "And, I want you to take yours back and give up this crazy idea."

"But," said David.

"No buts about it. I will not have you riding a motorcycle."

David turned around and walked off, muttering under his breath, "I will ride if I if I want to." And he did.

It wasn't too long until David joined up with some real bikers – unshaven, unemployed, encased in leather jackets. In fact, David spent weekends with his pals rather than with Jenny at the country club. It got to the point Jenny stopped talking to David, but this did not deter him.

Then, one day in July, David announced that he and his buddies were going to ride their bikes to Sturgis, South Dakota, for the international motorcycle rally. Some 250,000 bikers from around the world descend on this small town 30 miles west of Rapid City, South Dakota. It is a true happening, a wild week of Mardi Gras, with women riding around with their tops off. Residents rent out their rooms as well as plots on the front and back lawns for tents. They make over $10,000 for the week. Not only the true bikers attend, but also business and professional people enjoy the affair. Lawyers, like vultures, hover over the town handing out business cards in case there is an accident, of which there are many. The Sturgis affair gives a real shot in the arm to the economy of Western South Dakota, and in particular the legal community.

One business entrepreneur from the Midwest has his bike shipped to the airport in Rapid City. He then flies there in his private jet, picks up his bike, and rides 30 miles to Sturgis.

When David announced his intentions, Jenny was furious and said, "if you go to Sturgis, I'll divorce you." David said, "I'll go if I please." He was clearly captain of his ship. With a little encouragement from his buddies, they left on July 29.

After riding two days, they reached South Dakota. At one point they came upon 25 miles of blacktopping of the two-lane highway they were on. Traveling the side not yet blacktopped they came upon a farmer going 20 mph. One by one they went up on the blacktop and around the farmer to the other side. When it was David's turn, he edged his bike onto the blacktop but did not make a sharp enough angle and his front wheel slipped out and he was thrown to the pavement, hitting his head. Because he was exercising his constitutional right not to wear a helmet, the impact killed him. Now his wife was really angry with him, but at least there would be no divorce.

Jenny commenced a lawsuit on behalf of David's estate against the construction company doing the black topping for inadequate signage and failure to bevel the blacktop already completed to accommodate bikers.

After filing the petition the matter was set for mediation. On behalf of the estate, Jenny demanded $4.5 million, which is what David would have made the remainder of his working career until 65. The insurance carrier, feeling there was no liability or fault, offered $50,000. Little progress was made, and then it was suggested we create a different mechanism.

Rather than try the entire case in a court of law, it was agreed that only the issue of liability would be tried. The parties would negotiate the damages and establish a high and low. Thus, if liability were found, the high would be awarded and if no liability, the low. Initially, Jenny demanded a high of $4 million and the insurance carrier offered a low of $50,000. As Jenny lowered her demand for the high, the insurance carrier raised its low. Ultimately, a high of $2.5 million and low of $150,000 was fixed. The agent representing the insurance company said to me: "We are willing to enter this agreement because it gives us insurance against a run-away jury."

The issue of liability was tried before an arbitrator who found no liability. Thus, Jenny was awarded the low of $150,000.

What is good about this process is that it eliminates the need and expense to prove damages because they are already set by the negotiated high/low. This saves considerable amounts of money in discovery and proof at trial. Only liability must be tried. This can be done through arbitration or even before the original trial judge. They are more than happy to reduce trial time.

Once again, the process was manufactured to meet the needs of the parties. By arbitrating only the issue of liability, nothing was spent in establishing damages.

Mediation #4

A Doctor Breaks Police Officer's Jaw

On a number of occasions, I was asked to arbitrate a case rather than mediate it. The format of arbitration is generally like a bench trial before a judge – the parties question witnesses, offer exhibits into evidence and make opening and closing arguments. However, an arbitrator can be just as creative as a mediator. Because arbitration is also by contract, the arbitrator, with the consent of the parties, can create a format to meet the specific needs of the parties. A good example is the case of a young doctor, Len Paxon, recently graduated from medical school, who was heavily in debt with medical school expenses.

Working seven days a week just to keep his head above water he neglected his young wife, Debbie, and their three daughters. With their wedding anniversary coming up in a month, his wife suggested they leave the children with grandparents and go to the "big city" for a weekend together. Len reluctantly agreed.

When the date arrived the two drove to Des Moines, Iowa and checked into the downtown Marriott Hotel. In the afternoon they visited the State Capitol and viewed the model of the battleship Iowa, which saw action in the Pacific during WWII. They also viewed Civil War battle flags on display in the same building. To non-Iowans this may not seem very exciting, but when there is little else to do in Des Moines, it has to suffice.

That evening they went to The Splash Restaurant on the corner of Locust and 3rd Streets and had a glorious dinner and cocktails. After two and one-half hours and probably too much to drink, they returned to the Marriott. Before retiring, they entered the bar on the ground floor for a nightcap. The bartender brought their drinks and Len said: "This is not what I ordered."

The bartender, who seemed overwhelmed serving so many customers at the bar said, "Yes it is; it's what you have been drinking all night."

The doctor responded, "What do you mean? I just got here."

Debbie said, "Len, please pay the bill and let's get out of here."

Len swore at the bartender and the latter signaled an off-duty uniformed police officer to remove the doctor from the bar. He approached putting his hand on Len's right elbow. Len, who is left handed, without looking, swung and hit the police officer in the face, breaking his jaw.

Those around the doctor wrestled Len to the floor where he was maced. He was taken to a police station and booked, and remained in jail until bail money could be raised. The incident was reported on the front page of Len's town paper, the Nevada Gazette. The Iowa medical board put the doctor on probation requiring him to take alcohol counseling. He pleaded guilty to reduced criminal charges and was given a suspended sentence. The police officer, however, filed a civil action against Len for compensatory and punitive damages.

I was asked to arbitrate the matter. Normally, this would require a trial, the format of which would be like a bench trial before a judge. However, I decided to do it differently. I invited the attorneys to introduce their evidence similar to what would occur in a court of law.

Rather than announce my decision, which would be a binding award, I sat down with the attorneys and parties and reviewed the evidence.

"Thank you," I began, "for presenting your evidence in such a clear and concise manner. Rather than taking the matter under advisement as we normally do in arbitration and then making an award, I am going to depart from that procedure and handle it differently. First, I am going to review the evidence with you and how I am reacting to it. Second, I am going to give the case back to you and give you another chance to settle it yourselves. And, third, if you do settle it, I will enter that as my award. Does anyone have an objection?"

Attorney for the police officer, Carl Sanders, spoke up, "I am not sure we want to proceed that way. We would rather have you simply make a decision."

I responded, "I am only asking that you talk for a few minutes. If you fail, I will decide the matter and enter an award. You have nothing to lose."

After further discussion, the parties agreed to the process I outlined. I then began my analysis of the case.

"May I first thank counsel for your excellent presentations. In reviewing the evidence, it is clear there is liability. Dr. Paxson struck

Officer Mickelson in the face and broke his jaw. However, the bartender bears some responsibility because he provoked the situation by his unprofessional demeanor. Damages have been established in that plaintiff had medical expenses of $7500 and lost wages of $2600. There was pain and suffering and only recently has Officer Mickelson fully recovered. However, I am not going to award punitive damages. Dr. Paxson pleaded guilty to assault and battery and was given a suspended sentence. The matter was reported in the Nevada Gazette, and the medical board put Dr. Paxson on probation, requiring him to receive alcohol counseling. He has, in my opinion, been punished enough. I will award compensatory damages for the injuries caused, only I will not say how much at this time.

"Now, with that review of my thinking in the case, I ask you to negotiate further and see if you can resolve the matter amicably."

I then left the room not too optimistic that the parties could resolve the matter. I had in my own mind decided to award $125,000, if I had to decide the matter.

I waited for one hour wondering if agreement could be reached. Finally, counsel and the parties invited me back in to the conference room. Counsel for the police officer announced they had agreed to settle the case for $45,000. This caught me by surprise. "How did you come to

that figure?" I asked.

Counsel for the doctor said, "it was determined that Len could put

a second mortgage on his house for $45,000. He had no other resources.

Anything above that amount would put him into bankruptcy."

I realized that had the parties not agreed and I awarded $125,000,

this would have put the doctor into bankruptcy, and because there were

several secured creditors ahead of any award I might have made, the

police officer would have received nothing. The process worked better

than I ever anticipated for it assured that Officer Mickelson received

something.

Mediation #5

A Cowboy and Farmer Resolve Their Dispute

I took the above approach to arbitration after I arbitrated several

cases in Rapid City, South Dakota. The first two were straight forward

arbitrations; however, in both I awarded in excess of policy limits much to

the chagrin of the insurance company involved. I concluded it would

never use me again. However, it asked me to arbitrate a third case. It

involved a cowboy and farmer in South Dakota. They drove to a town 75

miles away to hit the taverns. Before they left, the cowboy said he had to be back to go to work in the morning. That evening they went to a number of bars. When starting back, the cowboy asked the farmer if he was too tired to drive. He answered in the negative.

On the way home, the farmer fell asleep at the wheel and the truck left the road and crashed. The cowboy ended up with a cracked rib, a gash above his left eye, which left a scar, and a broken hand. He sued for negligence. The insurance company defended, pleading that the cowboy was contributorily negligent in that he bought the farmer several drinks. It also pleaded assumption of risk because the cowboy knew the farmer had been drinking and might fall asleep yet he was a passenger in the pickup truck when it crashed.

As arbitrator, I listened to the evidence, after which I introduced my new procedure and reviewed the facts with the parties. I noted that although the cowboy bought the farmer drinks, the latter only sipped them so that when they hit the road for the return trip, he was not legally intoxicated when tested by the police. Therefore, I felt the cowboy was not contributorily negligent and I rejected that defense. I also rejected the defense of assumption of risk because the cowboy informed the farmer he had to work the next day and had to return that evening. He also inquired whether he was too tired to drive back. Because plaintiff was asking $30,000 in damages, I indicated that this might be excessive in that plaintiff had had an excellent recovery. Although he previously competed in bronco riding and was no longer able to do so, he was riding his horses again and had in fact broken in a wild mustang.

At this point, I gave the case back to the parties and counsel to negotiate further. After 30 minutes they reported they had settled for $9000. Plaintiff's counsel said to me, "I bet you would have given us more."

I responded, "Look, if your client is satisfied with the settlement, so am I." (I would have awarded $15,000, but did not so inform plaintiff's counsel because I wanted him to feel he had done a good job.)

The legal life of an arbitrator is shorter than a mediator because he must decide a case in favor of one of the parties. The other is not likely to use him again. Not infrequently, both parties are dissatisfied with the award and will not use the arbitrator again. When a mediator fails to settle a case at a mediation, neither party will blame him; instead, they blame the other side. Both lawyers are likely to use the mediator again.

The life of an arbitrator is lengthened if he can get the parties to settle the case without his making an award. It is for this reason I decided to use the procedure outlined above. By discussing how the arbitrator is reacting to the evidence and the defenses raised, it clears the air of obstacles and permits the parties to have meaningful discussion.

Mediation #6

Yellow Pages Does Not Mean They Are Old

Jim Biddle was always on the verge of hitting the jackpot, but never quite. In fact, everything he tried failed. However, he was an optimist and kept on trying. One night he woke up in the middle of the night with another great idea. He had been looking in the Yellow Pages of the regional telephone company and thought, why not have local Yellow Pages for the communities surrounding the metropolitan area. He did not want to wake up his wife, Cynthia, so he waited until morning. He was so excited about the idea he could not go back to sleep.

In the morning he told his wife. She reacted as he knew she would – just another one of his million dollar ideas that was sure to fail. This hurt his feelings; however, he proceeded to develop his idea. Within a year he actually had businesses in several communities signed up and within two years was making money. He was so pleased that this time, as he expanded into other communities, he was going to make it big.

The regional telephone company, however, noted Jim's budding business and decided to enter the market also. Within two years Jim was out of business with another failed business. He was furious and wanted vengeance. He contacted a very successful trial lawyer, Ben Archer, and asked him to file suit. Ben was a personal injury trial lawyer and knew little of antitrust law and the Sherman Act, but was willing to give it a try. He filed suit under § 2 of the Sherman Act, asserting that the regional phone company used its monopoly power to drive his client out of business. The phone company hired the top defense firm in the city and a senior partner, Jonathan Pierpont, took personal responsibility for handling the defense.

After a year of depositions, interrogatories, production of documents, hiring experts, Ben was spending more time and money than he ever anticipated. When motions were filed by Jonathan to dismiss the case, Ben inquired about mediating it. The phone company agreed and I was contacted.

Two days were spent in mediation. I was able to get the phone company to offer $1.2 million; which Jim Biddle turned down "as an insult." He wanted $2 million and not a penny less. Ben tried to talk him into accepting, but he would not. He not only wanted money but wanted to punish the phone company for what it did.

When the mediation failed, Ben pulled me aside and said, "Dick, I have a real problem here. My client won't listen to me and now he wants to go forward with the case. It will cost us another $500,000 to complete pretrial discovery and prepare for a two month trial. I just can't afford the time nor money to continue prosecuting this case. Is there anything you can do?"

I responded, "why don't you arbitrate the matter?"

He responded, "but that will be just as time-consuming and more expensive than trial in court."

At this point, an idea came up. "Why don't we use a summary form of arbitration?"

"How would that work?" asked Ben.

We discussed the matter further and came up with a unique form of arbitration which we called "summary arbitration." It works like this: first, three arbitrators, experts in antitrust law, would be selected and approved by both parties. Second, there would be no more discovery nor depositions. Third, all expert reports would be admitted into evidence. Fourth, there would be no live testimony, only the summary arguments of counsel. Fifth, the arbitration would be completed in 6 days.

The plan was presented to Jonathan who liked the idea. It would save considerable time and money, and he felt he could win on the law. The plan was fine-tuned and the following format was agreed upon. On Monday, the panel would hear all motions. On Tuesday and Wednesday, Ben would present the plaintiff's case in summary form – no live witnesses. On Thursday and Friday, Jonathan would present the defense, and on Saturday the panel would decide the case. No written opinion. If it ruled for Jim, a date would be set for a hearing on damages and attorneys' fees and costs, as provided by law. If not, the case was at an end.

Everyone agreed and signed an agreement. Arbitrators were selected and the hearing was held. The panel ruled for the defendant phone company and Jim received nothing. Another blow to his ego.

Ben called me later and said, "I hate to lose like this, but if that was to be, it was better to do it by summary arbitration and conclude the matter in one week rather than after a 2 month trial and appeal to the Ninth Circuit Court of Appeals, concluding the matter 4 years later.

I sent my bill and Jim never paid his one-half. Oh well, that's the risk of being a mediator. I was not going to sue.

Lawyer Leaves Law Firm

One more example of a creative process aiding parties

to resolve a difficult split up of a law firm is the following:

When a lawyer leaves a law firm, it is always difficult because

of financial considerations. But when lawyers start fighting

over what is owing, the dispute can get quite unpleasant. If

the matter ends up in court, it becomes a public record and it

can prove quite embarrassing for the lawyers, especially when

their salaries are disclosed as well as firm income.

Fred Devonshire was a member of the Poehler, Ruggles, Timkin law firm. He was a contingent fee plaintiffs' lawyer, whereas the rest of the partners in the firm billed by the hour. Complaints arose because significant amounts of money were advanced by the firm in Fred's personal injury cases. A year or more might go by without a case being won in court or settled so there was no income coming in, only debt being accumulated. Still, Fred was drawing a monthly draw as all other partners.

Everything came to a head when Fred lost a major case for which the firm had advanced a significant amount of money. Several partners wanted to end the relationship with Fred because he wasn't carrying his load. Fred, after soul searching, decided it was better if he left. However, the firm insisted he reimburse it for all the advances made on his cases, even the one he just lost. Fred thought this unfair and objected. A heated argument broke out and the firm threatened to sue him.

The day after Fred left the firm, a major case settled and Fred received a substantial check. Rather than depositing it in the firm account, he put the money into a personal account to finance his new operation. Partners in the firm were furious and reported him to the ethics committee of the state supreme court.

Fred came to me and asked if I would mediate the matter and I readily consented. However, the firm said it would not mediate. It finally agreed to arbitrate and Fred agreed. A major benefit of arbitrating was the matter would be kept confidential and no one outside the firm would know how difficult the separation was.

Rather than conduct a regular arbitration hearing, I proposed a different way to proceed. I said, "Gentlemen, I want to thank you for permitting me to be your arbitrator. In thinking about the process, I would like to propose a different way to proceed, which will save all concerned time and money. I propose the following:

"First, like judges in Europe, I will conduct the discovery myself. In other words, I will take all the depositions and request the documents I want to review. In taking a deposition, both sides can feed me any additional questions they wished answered. Also, I will review any documents you wish me to examine in addition to those requested.

"Second, because I will be doing the discovery, it will not be necessary for you to have separate counsel representing you unless you so desire. This will save you a considerable amount in attorneys' fees and costs. Also, I will work at your convenience so as not to interfere in your daily work.

"Third, after discovery is completed, I will prepare tentative findings for your review. I will invite you to make any changes, corrections, additions you wish so long as you both agree. Those facts to which you cannot agree will become the ultimate facts which I will then decide.

"Fourth, because we will need an accountant or CPA we will retain only one both sides must approve.

"Fifth, once the facts are completed we will have a final hearing at which counsel can present closing arguments.

"Sixth, I ask the firm to drop the ethics charges made against Fred."

We proceeded along these lines and before I had to issue an award, the parties agreed to a settlement. The only caveat was that Fred had to take all his cases with him, including a class action lawsuit, and had to reimburse the firm for all advances made in those cases. One of the firm's attorneys expressed concern that Fred would not adhere to the payment schedule agreed upon and they would end up in court. Fred reiterated his intent to make regular payments.

After the matter was concluded, Fred asked me to lunch. He said, "Dick, I have a class action I would like you to help me with." It was one the firm insisted he take with him.

"Fred, I thank you for the invite, but as a mediator, it would be inappropriate for me to get involved in litigation on a matter just arbitrated. (Actually, I did not think the class action had much merit and I did not want to waste time.)

As it turned out he got other attorneys to help him and he eventually settled the matter for $13 million and received $1 million in fees. He then wrote a single check to pay the firm what he owed pursuant to the settlement agreement. The managing partner of the firm called me and suggested some of the settlement should go to it. I reminded the partners that they insisted Fred take the case when he left; therefore, the firm really did not have a legitimate claim.

B. <u>Flexibility During Mediation</u>

Not only can parties be creative in the mechanisms used, but they have total flexibility as to how they conduct the mediation itself. As noted, they can call witnesses on the phone and personally interview them, or continue the mediation so the parties will have time to reflect on the matter and then reconvene. They can interrupt the process to allow the mediator to investigate, have the attorneys research legal points, or request witnesses to appear over the lunch hour.

Mediation #8

Listen To Your Doctor But Not Your Lawyer

Steve Johnson had surgery, during which the surgeon accidentally punctured his colon. This resulted in complications, which left him incontinent and unable to control the escape of gas, which was quite embarrassing. He sued the surgeon and demanded $350,000.

During the course of mediation, Steve lowered his demand to $275,000 and the insurance company raised its offer to $200,000. His lawyer strongly recommended he accept the offer for three reasons: one, it is difficult to win a malpractice case against a doctor in the state in question – 90 percent of the cases are lost; two, Steve looks healthy and his medical problems would not be evident to a jury; and, three, $200,000 is a fair offer considering all the circumstances and the venue.

Steve refused to except $200,000 and stated $250,000 was his final demand. The insurance carrier would not increase its offer. With the mediation failing, I inquired of Steve why he would not move further when his attorney recommended he settle. He responded, "my doctor said the case was worth $300,000."

As a last effort I said, "Why not call your doctor and see what he says?" The call was made.

"Doctor, Steve Johnson and an insurance carrier are in mediation and they have reached an impasse. He is demanding $250,000 and the insurance carrier is offering $200,000. His lawyer recommended he accept but Steve has so far refused. He asked to speak to you."

The doctor responded, "May I talk to Steve alone." I left the room.

Five minutes later, Steve came out and said, "I will accept the $200,000." In other words, he would listen to his doctor but not his lawyer.

The successful mediator must be sensitive to these nuances because they settle cases. Here it took only a single telephone call, which would never have been permitted in a courtroom trial.

Mediation #9

A Fire Extinguisher in Tony's Lounge

Don Cortes walked into Tony's lounge and before sitting at a table conversed with an acquaintance a short distance from the bar itself. The bartender was having an animated discussion with a patron sitting at the bar. Suddenly, without notice, the bartender reached behind him and tore a red fire extinguisher off the wall and threw it at the patron. He ducked and the fire extinguisher hit Don squarely in the face breaking his jaw.

Don was seriously injured, and for two months had his mouth wired shut and could only take nourishment through a straw. Don sued Tony's bar for compensatory and punitive damages. The case was mediated before it was filed.

At the mediation, the insurance carrier took the position that there was no coverage for intentional torts, which throwing a fire extinguisher was, and therefore offered only costs of litigation – $15,000. Don demanded $125,000. I talked to Don and tried to explain why the insurance company was not being more cooperative. Don felt it was being unfair because the owner of Tony's bar knew that the bartender was a hothead.

I asked, "Don, how would the owner of the bar know that the bartender had a bad temper?"

Don responded, "on several occasions the bartender got in arguments with his customers. Six months ago the argument was so violent that a friend of mine reported it to the owner of the bar."

I responded, "you mean, the bartender was reported to the owner and he did nothing to correct the situation?"

"That's right."

"Don, is there any way you can get in touch with this person and encourage him to come down and speak to the adjuster?"

Don made a phone call and reported that the individual would be down over the noon hour. When he arrived he sat down with the adjuster and explained what happened on the previous occasion and that it had been reported to the owner. It was evident the owner had done nothing to correct the problem.

Under the policy, if the owner was negligent this was covered by the insurance policy. Failing to supervise properly a bartender is a negligent act rather than an intentional tort; thus, there was coverage. The adjuster recognized this and offered a fair settlement and the case settled.

Again, the flexibility of mediation permitted us to contact the witness and have him meet with the adjuster and explain what occurred the previous occasion, to which he would testify if the case went to court.

Mediation #10

Reaching 21 Is Not Always a Blessing

I picked up the settlement brochure prepared by plaintiff's counsel to review the case. It was several inches thick in a spiral binder, entitled the "Robert Fillmore case," prepared by Jeffrey Monson, plaintiff's attorney. He was a successful lawyer with offices in Denison, Iowa. The brochure described the accident which left Robert a paraplegic with medical expenses approaching $100,000. The claim against the owner of the car was for policy limits of $1.3 million.

The insurance carrier defending the case was IFS Insurance out of Minneapolis, Minnesota. The adjuster attending the mediation was Chuck Bevington, an adjuster I've worked with on several occasions. I found him to be forthright and desirous of obtaining a fair settlement for claimants as well as his company.

I left early in the morning so that I would be in Denison well before 9:00 AM. I drove from West Des Moines on Highway 141 to Denison and parked in front of Jeff's office. It was well-maintained like many law offices in rural Iowa and look dignified and prosperous.

I was directed to the conference room where Chuck Bevington and Dan Miller, the defense attorney, were already present. As I entered the room, Jeff and the plaintiff, Robert Fillmore, who was in a wheelchair, entered the room. I introduced myself to everyone and asked everyone to be seated at the table. I then began my opening remarks and then turned to Jeff for his opening statement.

In a precise and persuasive voice he explained how Robert, who was living on a farm with his grandparents, drove into Denison on Saturday evening July 18, 2009, about 7:30 PM. He drove to the courthouse in the center of town, where a number young people congregated. Robert turned 21 in February. He did not know too many young people his own age because he only recently moved from California to live with his grandparents. He helped with the farming and worked at a manufacturing plant.

Jeff continued: "While sitting there Robert spotted Kevin Billings, a 16-year-old, who was sitting in his recently purchased second hand two door Buick Regal. Robert went over to Kevin and began talking to him. Shortly after, three girls, ages 16 and 17, parked their car next to Kevin's and the five talked for about 30 minutes. The three girls – Bridget Jones, Betsy Jelson and Jody Bush – asked the boys if they would like to have a party. Kevin suggested they go to Hobbes pit, where they could party. Jody suggested they could go skinny-dipping.

"Kevin stated he had beer in the trunk of his car; however, Robert decided he wanted wine coolers so he went across the street to a liquor store and purchased a four-pack.

"The five got in Kevin's car and drove to Jody's farm to ask her parents if she could stay out later than 12 o'clock. Her parents were not home so they waited an hour, during which time Bridget began drinking some scotch she found in the liquor cabinet. Tired of waiting, the five left for the pit with Bridget driving and Robert, Jody and Kevin in the backseat and Betsy in the right passenger seat. When they arrived at the pit, Robert, Betsy and Bridget went down to the water, but it was too cold to swim in so they sat and drank. Kevin and Jody stayed in the rear seat and partied there.

"Forty-five minutes later they all got back in the car and Bridget insisted on driving, although she did not have a driver's license and she had been drinking heavily. Kevin consented and they drove to Ida Grove where they scooped the loop around the courthouse square. ("Scoop the loop" is an Iowa term, which describes how young people in Iowa entertain themselves on the weekend. The boys start out in one car or pick-up truck and the girls in another. They then circle around the square waving at each other. Later they get in each other's cars or pick-up trucks.)

"After 15 minutes of driving around, a black pick-up truck with KC lights began to follow. Bridget tried to lose it by going down several side streets but couldn't. Because of the hour, they decided to drive back to Denison and proceeded south on Route 59. Bridget was still driving with Betsy in the front seat and Robert, Kevin and Jody in the backseat. As they were driving, the black pick-up truck pulled up behind them so Bridget began going faster. When they came to an intersection, Bridget slammed on the brakes and turned down a dirt road. The truck missed the turn and continued down the highway. Shortly, the pick-up truck pulled up behind them again and Bridget increased her speed to 81 mph. Suddenly the car fishtailed and she slammed on the brakes. The car slid off the road and rolled over three times destroying 27 feet of fencing."

Jeff stopped for dramatic effect. Then he continued, only speaking more slowly.

"The car came to rest upside down and the passengers began crawling out except for Robert, who was penned in the backseat. He felt great pain in his back and yelled for someone to pull the weight off his legs, which were pinned up against his chest."

Jeff stopped again and looked at Chuck and then at me. We knew what was coming next. He explained, "Robert was taken to the hospital in Denison and later flown by helicopter to Methodist Hospital in Des Moines Iowa, where he was operated on.

"To date nearly $100,000 had been spent on medical expenses which includes rehabilitation." Jeff lowered his voice: "Robert is now a paraplegic and will never walk again. He cannot control his bladder or bowels and cannot have sex."

Jeff pulled out a chart which listed the dollar damages suffered in addition to medical expenses already incurred. "There will be past and future pain and suffering, past and future disability, destruction of earning capacity, future loss of enjoyment of life, permanent loss of legs, past and future disfigurement and deformity and damages for humiliation, embarrassment and mental anguish."

Jeff concluded: "Needless to say, gentlemen, we are claiming policy limits of $1.3 million and will not move off this. Robert was an incidental passenger sitting in the backseat of the car. He is a young man with his whole life before him and now every dream, every hope is shattered, and he will live his life in pain and suffering locked in a wheelchair. Kevin owned the car and permitted Bridget to drive it, who had been drinking heavily and did not even have a driver's license."

Jeff stopped and looked down. Robert sat looking at him spellbound by his words, obviously agreeing with what had been said. Dan, the defense attorney, cleared his throat and finally said, with some feeling: "Before I begin I want you to know that we feel great compassion for you, Robert, and we want to help you, but we want to compensate you in an amount that is right and fair."

Dan then picked up his notes and began discussing how the insurance company viewed the accident. "Robert has some responsibility because he was drinking with minors. According to Kevin, Robert bought the beer the girls were drinking."

Jeff jumped up and shouted with anger, "That is a lie. It is not true. If this is where we are going, this mediation is over. The beer the girls drank was already in Kevin's car."

Jeff caught me by surprise. I tried to quiet him down. "Let Dan finish and you can respond. Have you finished Dan?"

"Yes, I have, except for the fact that our defense is that Robert was contributing to the delinquency of minors."

To avoid any further outbreaks, I separated the parties, with Robert and Jeff going to the latter's office. I entered a moment later and expressed my concern with what Robert was facing. I then said, "let's go through your case very carefully because I need all the ammunition we can muster to get the insurance carrier to the level you are demanding."

Jeff sat down behind his desk and Robert wheeled himself to the left side, and I sat down in a chair in front of the desk. Jeff began by saying, "we have a very strong case on liability as well as damages. We should get policy limits on this one."

"Jeff" I said, "let's review the strengths of your case – those things you want me to argue when I meet with the insurance company."

Jeff looked at Robert, and said: "That's my number one strength. Robert is crippled and people will feel sorry for him. More than that he was innocent of any wrongdoing – he was in the backseat. Robert did not realize Bridget was intoxicated. He even offered to drive, but Kevin insisted that Bridget would do just fine. Also, we must remember that the beer that Bridget drank was supplied by Kevin. Bridget also got hard liquor out of the liquor cabinet at Jody's house, and Robert cannot be blamed for that. His only fault is that he, as an adult, probably should not have been with them when they started drinking."

Jeff stopped. I asked: "what do you see as your weaknesses or concerns? I will keep this strictly confidential."

"Probably my biggest weakness is that Robert was with minors and probably should have policed them better when they started drinking. But this may not be too great a problem because Kevin owned the car and should not have allowed Bridget to drive, knowing of her condition. Another weakness may be that a rural jury may be a little slower in awarding a large verdict than a jury in a big city like Des Moines."

Jeff hesitated and then added, "on the other hand, the case is filed in a prosperous county and $1 million will not shock them. I think I can get that much."

I asked, "Do you see a problem in the fact that everyone was drinking, including Robert? Will they blame him for that?"

Jeff looked at me and said, "no, that area of the state is heavily Irish and German and heavy drinking is a way of life out there. They will not hold this against Robert."

"What do you think a jury will do with a case like this – your best-case and worst-case?" I explained how this was for my information only and would be kept confidential.

"I don't care if you tell the insurance company. I think Robert's best case is $2.5 million and worst case $800,000."

"Jeff, I need a figure to begin the mediation, a figure which will show that plaintiff really wants to get this case settled."

Jeff thought a minute and then said, "well, let me tell you where we want to end up and you can tell me where we should begin."

I responded: "Jeff at this time I do not want to know your bottom figure. All I want is something which will give a good signal. You have been asking for policy limits and if you would come down some this would show we're making progress."

Jeff asked me to leave the room for a moment so that he and Robert could discuss the matter. After five minutes they called me back in and Jeff said, "our new demand is $1.1 million but we are not willing to come down too much off of that."

I thanked them and went back to the conference room where Chuck and Dan were patiently waiting.

As I was sitting down, Dan reported that he had called Kevin on the phone and he will testify that after the five decided to party, Robert went to the liquor store across the street from the courthouse. Robert bought two packs of wine coolers – one was Bahama Mama and the other was Purple Passion. Kevin had two 12 packs of beer in the trunk of his car with a lot of empty cans he had picked up on the side of the road. He had intended to turn them in for five cents a can. However, it should be noted that Kevin will swear that Robert bought the beer in the trunk of his car."

Dan turned the page of his notes and continued. "Kevin will also testify that he saw Bridget drink six cans of beer, but he did not remember how much the others had."

"Do you know the ages of the three girls?"

"Yes, I do. Bridget is 17, Jody 16, and Betsy 16. Of course, you know that Kevin was only 16 and Robert 21."

"Dan, can you tell me why Robert would be hanging around with Kevin in the first place, when he is so much younger?"

Dan hesitated a moment and then said, "you need more background than what has come out so far. You see, Robert was born in

Iowa and moved to California with his mother when he was four years old. When he graduated from high school, he began to wander and got in a lot of difficulty with alcohol and drugs. He finally was arrested when he stole some wristwatches and was placed on probation. At this point he went to a rehabilitation center and then came back to Iowa to live with his grandparents on their farm. Everyone believed this new environment would help him straighten out his life.

"Because Robert didn't have many friends he joined a youth group at Kevin's church where he met Kevin. After that, they got together on occasion."

Turning to the adjuster, I asked, "Chuck, is Kevin certain that Robert bought the beer the girls were drinking. This is important because this would constitute contributing to the delinquency of minors, precluding Robert from much recovery."

"Dick, I assure you our client is adamant that Robert bought all the beer because Kevin was too young to purchase it."

There was a break in the conversation, then I asked, "what do you see as weaknesses in your case? I'll keep this confidential."

Without hesitation, Dan stated: "it was a bad accident. Plaintiff is a paraplegic. A verdict in a case like this could go from $200,000-$1 million, so we have a difficult case here."

Dan continued, "you know, Robert is now attending college in the morning, and although his grades are rather poor, should he graduate his chance of ending up with a better job than what he had before the accident is quite high. In other words, because of his injuries he has been more serious and could be better off economically in the future."

"Dan, where do you see this case settling?"

"If it is going to settle, it will have to be in the $50,000-$300,000 range."

"Dan, at this time plaintiff is willing to settle for $1.1 million; I'm certain he will come down substantially. Can you give me a new figure which will encourage Robert to move further?"

Dan immediately responded, $150,000. With this information I returned to Jeff's office where he and Robert were waiting. "Jeff, I think we are making progress, but there is one major issue that must be resolved. May I ask Robert a question?"

"Of course," said Jeff.

Turning to Robert, I said: "Robert, the adjuster has made it clear that there is evidence that you purchased the beer Bridget and the others were drinking. Could you be mistaken when you say that you did not buy the beer when you purchased your wine coolers?"

"Mr. Calkins, I swear to you that I only purchased the wine coolers. I did not purchase any beer. Kevin already had the beer in his trunk. If you call Jody, who lives in town, she will say the same thing. I just talked to her a couple of days ago."

"What will she say, that you did not purchase the beer?"

Robert looked at me with great sincerity, and it was hard not to believe him. He truly appeared to be telling the truth as he saw it. "Mr. Calkins, I am not certain she will say that I did not purchase the beer, but I am sure she will say that the beer was already in the trunk of Kevin's car because she was standing next to the car when we put the wine coolers in. Kevin is not telling the truth."

"Jeff, would you permit me to call Jody on the phone and ask her about what she saw?"

Jeff looked at Robert, and then said, "yes, that will be fine. You can use the phone in my office or the conference room."

I hesitated a moment and then said, "this is really a critical question. Where are the other two girls?"

Robert cleared his throat and said, "Betsy is away for the summer, and Bridget is in Las Vegas working as a chorus line dancer, so we cannot reach her."

"Jeff, Dan has given me his initial offer in response to your demand. This, of course, is just a starter for I am sure he will move up, but I don't know how much. His offer is $150,000."

Jeff turned slightly red in the face indicating displeasure at the figure. "Look, if they're going to play games, I'm going to terminate this mediation. This is bad faith and we will not even consider this."

"Jeff, please understand that this is just their first offer. Give me a chance to work on the case. We will make progress. We'll get the job done."

I left the room and returned to the conference room, and explained what had transpired. A call was made to Jody, who confirmed that the beer was already in the trunk of Kevin's car, but she did not know who purchased it.

After further discussion with both sides with little movement and an apparent deadlock, I asked permission to recess the mediation and meet with Kevin and his family to get a better idea of who was telling the truth on this crucial issue. Both sides agreed and Dan arranged for me to meet Kevin and his parents the following week.

A week later I drove to Kevin's farm. Kevin was a fine looking young man, blonde hair, and a neat haircut. It was clear that he would make a far better witness than Robert. His parents were also nice-looking. I quickly learned that they were Quakers and for that reason there was no alcohol in their home.

"Kevin, Robert insists that you already had beer in the trunk of your car and he did not buy it. He thinks you may be covering up this fact because you would be suspended from football for three games if the coach found out."

Kevin looked at his parents obviously pained to discuss the matter. "That is not true. I told my parents and coach immediately after the accident, and I was suspended three games. I paid my penalty. I can only say that I did not purchase the beer." As he said this he looked me directly in the eye. Then he looked down and would not look at his parents. There was no doubt that he was believable. Yet, one of the two boys was clearly lying.

Kevin gave me more background on Robert which I felt was helpful. He explained that when Robert was 20 he was able to buy beer at a Denison supermarket, they never checked his ID. On a number of occasions he purchased beer for minors. On one occasion, Robert bought the beer for a party attended by high school students, and on his 21st birthday he again bought beer for all his guests, most of whom were underage.

Kevin's father interrupted and told Kevin to tell about Robert's offer.

"What my father is referring to is that Robert offered to pay to fix my car if I would not tell about his buying the beer because he would get in trouble."

"Did anyone else hear Robert make this offer?"

"Yes, a friend of mine, Joel Hinkle, heard him."

Kevin also noted that on prior occasions he got together with Robert to drink beer. As he said this his head was bent down looking at the floor. In fact, they had been together the night before at Betsy's house to watch a video movie and drink beer.

After completing the interviews, I scheduled another mediation session with Robert and his attorney in Denison.

Looking at Robert I said: "Robert, Kevin absolutely insists that you bought the beer at the Regal Liquor Store. Are you sure you did not?"

Roberts seemed slightly agitated. "The only thing I purchased that evening were the four wine coolers."

"But Robert, are you insisting that Kevin is lying? He stated that you offered to fix his car if he said you did not purchase the beer."

Robert looked at Jeff who was about to stop me from making further inquiry. But before Jeff could say anything Robert said, "I swear I did not purchase that beer Saturday night, only the wine coolers." He hesitated again, and then in passing said, "I bought the beer Friday night."

At the moment he said this I was looking at Jeff whose mouth fell open in obvious surprise. There was a long silence.

"Jeff, this is confidential information and I will not disclose it to the adjuster unless directed by you."

"That's fine with me. They will learn this when they take Robert's deposition so he might as well learn it now. "

Jeff asked to put the mediation over for another week because he had to have a serious talk with Robert and reevaluate the case. A week later he called me and said they would accept $400,000. The case settled for $385,000 and all parties under the circumstances felt that this was fair. A large part of the settlement was structured so that Robert now has

tax-free income which will take care of some of his needs in the future.

Any additional income he earned would make life that much easier.

Again, this case illustrates the flexibility of mediation.   None of

this could have occurred if the case were in a courtroom.

Mediation #11

A Lawyer's Worst Nightmare

The story of the Franklins is indeed tragic. Mr. and Mrs. Franklin had a daughter, Jennifer, born February 25, 1996. When one-month-old she was given injections for immunization against diphtheria, pertussis and tetanus (DPT). It is known that a handful of babies receiving the shots have adverse reactions, which in the case of Jennifer left her physically and mentally crippled for life. At 17 years old she spent most of the day lying in bed in the fetal position with the mentality of a six month old baby. As a result of Jennifer's condition her parents have devoted their lives to taking care of her and have refused to institutionalize her. Their love and care has helped Jennifer survive many years beyond her life expectancy.

In 2007, Mrs. Franklin saw Jennifer's doctor, Dr. Harry Random, interviewed on television on the news program "20/20." During the interview, the doctor discussed the possible adverse effects of the DPT shot on a small percentage of infants. Some of the symptoms he described sounded like Jennifer's. Several days later Mrs. Franklin confronted Dr. Random, who concluded that Jennifer's seizures and condition might be attributable to the DPT shot.

The Franklins decided to take legal action in order to ease the financial strain incurred caring for Jennifer. They contacted the firm of Santore and Temple. Benjamin Santore, senior partner in the firm, decided to handle the case himself because it was a very difficult one due to the lapse of time and uncertainty regarding the causal connection between the DPT shots and Jennifer's condition. After investigating the case, suit was filed in early 2008 against the doctor who administered the shots and the manufacturers of the vaccine.

Problems immediately arose in the case: against the doctor because he was dead and his estate had to be reopened; against the manufacturers because plaintiff could not identify which manufacturer produced the vaccine that was used. Santore finally named four manufactures as probable producers of the vaccine.

After a year of discovery the Franklins finally decided to settle the matter and accepted $85,000 in full and complete resolution of their claim. After costs and attorney's fees were deducted the Franklins received $34,500.

Several years later the Franklins learned that in 1986 Congress passed the National Vaccine Injury Compensation Act, which provided an alternative to suing doctors and drug companies in situations like

Jennifer's. The Act recognized that it was very difficult to win a case against the doctor or drug company supplying the vaccine. Under the Act, if it could be shown the child was inoculated with DPT, an award was available to care for the child which could be as much as $2 million.

The Franklins then decided to sue Santore for not informing them of the availability of this Act. Santore was insured up to $1 million. Before much discovery was taken the parties agreed to mediate and I was chosen as the mediator.

Ted Miller, counsel for the Franklins, was an extremely aggressive trial lawyer. He demanded $3 million with little room for movement. Barbara Dutton was there on behalf of Century Insurance, the malpractice carrier, and was extremely skilled at these types of negotiations. She could more than hold her own against Miller.

The mediation commenced with the usual introductions and then plaintiff's attorney presented his case. "Ladies and gentlemen, this is a case of gross malpractice which will permit us to recover punitive damages. First, Mr. Santore settled a case against the doctor, which foreclosed Jennifer from suing under the federal Act – you cannot recover both in a private action and under the statute. And what did Jennifer receive from the $85,000 settlement? Well, the lawyers took one third and, after deducting costs and expenses, she was left with $34,500. Think of it, $34,500 when she could have received up to $2 million under the federal Act."

Miller hesitated a moment. "But you know why Santore brought this private action rather than file under the federal act? It is because you can only recover, I believe, $30,000 in attorney's fees and costs under the Act; whereas, if successful in the private action his firm might have received one third of the recovery plus reimbursements of costs. It's simple, my friends, Santore was greedy. He says he made a mistake in construing the Act, but don't believe that. One of his partners just a few months before the settlement with the doctor filed a claim under the Act for another client. Santore knew this. It was plain and simple greed, and the jury is going to be very unhappy."

I looked at Barbara Dutton and she did not react to the statement. The Franklins nodded their heads in agreement.

Miller continued: "The second act of malpractice was to tell the Franklins that they were ineligible to recover under the Act. Whether this was done intentionally knowing otherwise, or was result of faulty research, it makes little difference. Jennifer is now barred from recovery under the Act. The success rate under the Act is 95 percent; Jennifer would clearly have succeeded. The recoveries under the Act average from $1 million to $2 million with several in excess of $2 million. This is the real tragedy for the Franklin's, to say the least.

"The third area of malpractice is the action against the manufacturers. The reason the case was dismissed was because Santore failed to name all vaccine manufacturers. Santore named only four of seven, and when you are suing on the theory that you don't know which manufacturer is responsible for a generic drug, but one of them has to be, you must name all manufactures as defendants. Well, Santore blew that one also."

Miller stopped, took a drink of water then continued: "My friends," Miller was speaking softly but exuding confidence, "Jennifer is going to recover in excess of $2 million in this mediation or we are going to trial."

There was a long silence. I looked at Dutton, who acknowledged my glance. "Well, I guess it's my turn. Let me first say we are deeply concerned about the Franklins and Jennifer. They have suffered a great deal and we are here today to try to help in some way. However, if this case goes to trial I'm required as an attorney to raise every argument I can in Mr. Santore's defense."

Dutton spoke very calmly. She had a fairly deep and warm voice and her demeanor was such that she appeared to always be in control. She continued: "Let me first point out," she said looking at attorney Miller, "the question of causal connection is not a slam dunk. What I mean by that," she turned to the Franklins, "is that because Jennifer's seizures began one month before she was inoculated, there is a serious question as to whether the inoculation was the cause as you suggest. Dr. Random on "20/20" didn't think so. Someone with his expertise would have identified it earlier as being causally connected to the DPT inoculation."

Dutton hesitated a second and then continued, "In deference to your position, I don't think the jury is going to get angry with Mr. Santore. First, he took on the Franklins' case knowing it was going to be difficult. Mr. and Mrs. Franklin have admitted in deposition that Santore told them this was a most difficult case but he wanted the challenge."

"When he went to sue the doctor he found that he was dead and his estate was closed. Santore, therefore, had to reopen the estate, which required him to go all the way to the Iowa Supreme Court. This cost him a considerable amount of time and money. You must also remember that the federal statute was not funded by Congress until sometime after the case against the doctor was filed."

"Now I will admit that Santore's office misread the statute and that Jennifer was eligible. However, when this federal Act was passed most trial lawyers were highly skeptical of it."

Miller interrupted, "that's because there was a ceiling on what they could recover in attorney's fees and costs."

"Ted, please! Let Ms. Dutton complete her statement, then you can respond," I said.

"Thank you, Dick. I'm not trying to argue with you, Ted. You know we have differences of opinion in this case, and the differences are pretty deep. What I'm trying to say is that trial lawyers looked at the Act with suspicion, and it was not until 2008 it was even funded by Congress. It was at this time that Santore recognized his error, so he called the Franklins to his office. He asked them to bring Jennifer so he could meet her. At that time he specifically told them that they could proceed under the Act, but that the relief sought might not cover Jennifer's needs because most of it was for rehabilitation and training. This was of no benefit to Jennifer, and, therefore, could not be claimed on her behalf. It was the Franklin's decision to continue the suit against the doctor and drug companies."

Mr. Franklin became red in the face, and said, "Santore did not tell us we could proceed under the Act. That was never discussed at the meeting. She's lying."

"Please, Mr. Franklin, Ms. Dutton is simply stating what she believes the facts to be. If they are not true, Mr. Miller will correct them."

Dutton waited a moment for Franklin to calm down then she continued: "At the time the Franklins decided to proceed with their civil suit, they hoped to receive a large judgment against the manufacturers. They can't have it both ways – hope to succeed in their civil case and then when it did not turn out to their satisfaction, turn around and sue the lawyer for not getting the results they wanted.

"Santore knew how to sue the manufacturers. The fact is he couldn't get jurisdiction over all of them and the Iowa Supreme Court did not buy the theory he was espousing, although other states have. In dismissing the action, the District Judge was not willing to pave new ground in the face of the Iowa Supreme Court's ruling."

Looking directly at Miller, Dutton stated, "there is one thing you are forgetting. We have filed a counterclaim against you personally, which we are quite serious about. At the time you took this on, you could have had the settlement with the doctor set aside and proceeded under the federal Act. You chose not to do so, but rather sue Santore. Now it is too late to set aside the settlement and make a claim under the Act."

Dutton stopped and looked at me. "Does that complete your opening statement I asked?" Dutton nodded, and I turned to Miller, who was slightly flushed.

He began in a low voice: "if there ever was a frivolous action, it is your counterclaim against me. I resent what you are doing and will seek Rule 11 sanctions against you for bad faith, I assure you of that." Quieting down slightly he added, "there was no chance that the settlement could have been set aside. That would have had to have been approved by the judge and then the hearing officer appointed under the Act. No one has successfully done this."

"No one has tried," interrupted Dutton.

Sensing another eruption between counsel, I quickly ushered the Franklins and Miller to another conference room for the first caucus. It was clear that this was not going to be an easy mediation. Two hours had elapsed just to complete the opening joint session.

Ted Miller began the caucus by saying one of his strongest points is the Franklins – they'll make excellent witnesses whom the jury will want to believe. Looking at me he asked, "Who would you believe, Santore, who says that he told the Franklins that they could file under the Act, or the Franklins who will testify he never mentioned that Jennifer was eligible to file under the Act.

I did not respond. He continued, stating, "would you believe for one moment that an experienced lawyer like Santore would not put such a matter in writing, particularly when he gave the wrong advice the first time? There is no such document, so believe me, such a conversation never took place."

Ted continued talking about the strengths of his case and the recoveries that had been made under the Act. He mentioned three cases where plaintiffs recovered $1.5 million, $2.5 million and $15 million respectively. The last one is still on appeal.

When we got to the weaknesses of his case he mentioned, first, the fact that the vaccine DPT was an FDA approved drug. Furthermore, DPT normally does not cause permanent brain damage as it did in this case. Finally, he admitted that the fact the first seizures occurred before the inoculation gave him concern in proving the vaccine caused Jennifer's problems. Ted concluded that his best case was $6 million and worst-case $1 million.

He also expected defendants to spend another $150,000-$200,000 to complete discovery and try the case. The new settlement demand I was given was $2 million.

As I left the conference room and went back to the original room where the defense was waiting, I wondered where this case would end up if it settled. It was clear to me that Miller was prepared to try it, an excellent trial lawyer.

After a few pleasantries Dutton took control and made the initial presentation concerning the strengths of her case. She first noted that she did not believe the jury was going to be overly angry at Santore. When he accepted the case it was a longshot because there was no federal statute at the time. So he took the case knowing that it would cost him a great deal of time and money because of the experts that had to be used. Then Santore immediately ran into a roadblock because the doctor that vaccinated Jennifer was deceased. More money had to be spent reopening his estate. So, by the time the case was settled Santore had advanced considerable costs that had to be first reimbursed before the Franklins received anything.

She hesitated and then continued. "Next, he tried to sue the manufacturer, and again this was before the federal statute had been passed. He had to rely on a theory which Iowa has not yet recognized, therefore he knew it was an uphill fight. I submit, he did all this because he felt compassion for the Franklins, and hoped to ease their financial burden to some small degree. Most other lawyers in Iowa would've turned the case down."

Dutton continued: "Now admittedly, Santore's associate made a costly mistake, but it was rectified when Santore met with the Franklins and explained the alternatives under the statute. After all, most of what is allowed is for rehabilitation and training, which are worthless to Jennifer because of her condition."

Dutton added: "That leads to the question, why did not Miller rectify the error when he took over the case? We are quite serious about our counterclaim. Miller could have had the settlement with the doctor set aside and file under the Act. He did not do this and I will tell you why. If he had, his attorney's fees and costs would've been limited to $30,000, whereas suing for malpractice he will get one-third of the settlement. That makes me angry."

Dutton was showing some emotion but this was for the client. She did convince me, however, that she was serious about going after Miller.

"Dick, there is one further point." Dutton now spoke in a low quiet voice." When the federal Act was passed, most lawyers were suspicious of it and were reluctant to use it because if it failed they could not bring a civil action because of the statue limitations. In the context of when the Franklins accepted the settlement with the doctor's estate, the Act had just been funded. It was unclear how it would operate. I repeat, if an action under the Act was so clear why didn't Miller use it himself. He could have. His argument that he could not have gotten the settlement set aside is hogwash. He never tried, and furthermore we have the deposition of the administrative judge who is handling these claims and he testified, under oath, he believes such a prior civil judgment would, on application, have been set aside."

Dutton stopped and looked intently at her notes. She looked up and continued. "Now about damages. We want you to stress with the Franklins the fact that Jennifer started having seizures before the DPT inoculation – it was a congenital problem and not brought on by the inoculation. You can be certain we will have a doctor who will so testify and the medical records establish this fact."

"Thank you, Barbara for summarizing these arguments for me. I have made careful notes. Now would you explain what you consider your weaknesses or concern to be."

Dutton hesitated a moment and then said, "the main problem we have is one of credibility. We maintain Santore told the Franklins they could sue under the Act and they deny it. Wouldn't a careful lawyer have followed the conversation up with a letter or some other written document to protect against malpractice? Further, there will be a great deal of sympathy for Jennifer and the Franklin's. It really is a tragic story and you can't help feeling sorry. That is the reason we are here today. We are willing to pay some big money to settle the case, but we can't give the store away."

"Thank you, Barbara."

Dutton felt the worst case before the jury was a verdict of about $500,000. I do not think the jury is going to want to punish Santore," Dutton added.

I then asked for defendant's first offer in response to the Franklins demand of $2 million. Barbara Dutton said they were willing to put

$150,000 into a structured annuity which would provide $1030 per month for Jennifer's life with 20 years guaranteed. Also she would receive $20,000 on February 25, 2008, another $60,000 on February 25, 2010, another $80,000 October 28, 2012, the final payment of $150,000 on February 25, 2014. They would also pay attorney's fees and costs in addition to the structure. The total package would cost $450,000.

I then returned to the other conference room where plaintiffs were waiting. I gave them defendant's first settlement proposal and Miller was ready to leave. "I consider that an insult and we will not respond to it." Mr. Franklin added, "if that is all they think my daughter is worth after what they did to her, then I think we can leave right now."

"Please," I said in a soft voice. "This is only the first offer. You must be patient and give me a chance to do my work. I assure you I will get the maximum we can. At this point I have no idea what they're willing to do."

Mr. Franklin settled down a little and Miller gave me a long lecture why this was a $2 million case. He then asked me to leave the room while he and the Franklins discussed a new demand. They said they would make a major move to $1.75 million; but he assured me they had little room to move further.

I reported the new demand to the defense and added that I felt that the insurance carrier had to make a major move if it wanted to keep the plaintiffs at the table. Looking at Barbara, I said, "I don't know where the plaintiffs are trying to go but my guess is it is something above $1 million. Let me ask this question, if I ultimately got them down to $1 million is that a figure you would consider? I ask this in strict confidence, but it will give me an idea whether we have even a remote chance of getting this matter settled."

There was a very long pause with Barbara looking intently at me. This pause told me all I wanted to know. I was certain the insurance company would go to $1 million, policy limits.

Finally Dutton said, "I guess we could consider it but we are not prepared to offer that figure. I want you to go back with a package worth $600,000 present value. That includes $400,000 structure and $200,000 cash. The structure will pay $2000 per month for life, 20 years guaranteed if she should die before reaching 37. This is fair and is reaching our limits.

Walking back to the plaintiffs' conference room I realized that we had a good chance to get this matter resolved. By this time it was late in the afternoon, and I was concerned about the parties getting tired and frustrated. When I presented the $600,000 package, Mr. Franklin

snapped back, "that's an insult." He then added, "we will not go below

$1,500,000. That is our final offer.

As he was speaking I was watching Mrs. Franklin. It was clear to

me that she wanted to get this matter resolved as soon as possible. Her

body language told me that she was prepared to accept the offer just

made by the defendant. However, she was not going to speak up and

went along with what her husband was saying.

I then returned to the defense caucus and reported that the

Franklins would not go below $1.5 million. Barbara Dutton did not seem

the least bit perturbed and stated, in confidence, that policy limits were

$1 million and they could not go above that figure for obvious reasons.

Dutton then said: "you have done a fine job. I did not believe you

would get them below $2 million. I'm going to give you one final figure –

$1 million. We're prepared to give $400,000 cash and $600,000 structure.

The structure will provide Franklins with approximately $3400 per month

for their lives assuming they survive Jennifer. If not, the payments will be

made for the rest of Jennifer's life.

I asked Dutton if I could put this offer on the table at this time.

She answered in the affirmative and then added: "let's give them a chance to think about it. We will give them till next Tuesday to respond to this offer.

Entering the plaintiffs' conference room I said, "I have excellent news." I walked to the end of the table and sat down. "Defendants have made a final offer of $1 million. I can give you the details as to how it is to be paid."

Mrs. Franklin broke into a large smile and seemed to be relieved. Miller said nothing but looked at Mr. Franklin. He looked defiant and finally said, "we told you our final figure was $1.5 million. I would breach my principles and integrity if I took less. My daughter is worth more than what they're offering – after what they did to her."

"Defendants have said they will leave the offer on the table till next Tuesday so you will have a chance to talk about it further."

Mr. Franklin said: "there's nothing to talk about. We gave you our final offer and that is it." He then got up and started packing his bag to leave. Mrs. Franklin, as a good wife, followed him to the door saying nothing and the two left. Miller sat there and then said: "I don't know what to tell you. The Franklins are tired. I will talk to them over the weekend and see if I can convince him to accept defendant's offer."

I went to the defendants and reported what happened: "I am certain Mrs. Franklin wants to settle. In fact, I think she would have settled for less." Dutton was a little perturbed at the rejection. Finally, she smiled slightly, and in her Texas drawl said, "I'll tell you what. You let the Franklins think about the offer till Tuesday and you wait-and-see. There's going to be some "pillow talk" going on over the weekend and Mrs. Franklin is going to win out. Sure enough, Monday morning Mr. Franklin called and accepted the $1 million.

What I learned from this case is if you allow the parties time to discuss the matter in a quiet setting rather than push them at the time of the mediation, there's a better chance they will settle. This is particularly true when one of them, like Mrs. Franklin, wishes to settle. Invariably, the one who wishes to resolve the matter wins out, and it does not matter if it is the husband or wife. Pillow talk works.

Mediation #12

Doctor Shakes Nurse and Snaps Her Neck

Jane Meadows was a delivery room nurse in a city hospital. Her doctor, Clifford Roberts M.D., was a difficult person with which to deal and she was somewhat intimidated by him.

On one occasion, he directed her not to permit a father to attend the birth of his child. During the birth, the father walked in and Jane was too busy to try to get him to leave as the doctor had instructed.

After the birth, Dr. Roberts took Jane into another room, closed the door, and grabbed her shoulders shaking her. He screamed at her for disobeying his orders. Something snapped in Jane's neck and she felt severe pain. Jane reported Dr. Roberts to the hospital administration, which, after hearing, dismissed Dr. Roberts from privileges at the hospital. His medical group also dropped him and he was forced to find another hospital outside the state. Jane sued the hospital and the doctor. A complaint was filed. Before much discovery was taken the parties agreed to mediate.

Jane and her second husband of two years, Stuart, attended the mediation along with counsel. The adjuster was present with counsel representing the doctor, who was not present.

During the course of mediation, Jane demanded $500,000 and the insurance carrier offered $50,000. Over several hours, I was unable to make much progress primarily because Jane was so angry and just wanted to punish the doctor even though he was not footing the bill. During the course of the caucuses with Jane, Stuart remained very quiet. His body language suggested he was uncomfortable with what was occurring. My hope was that maybe he was concerned about how angry Jane was. This might be affecting their marriage. If that be the case, I decided I needed to give them time alone so that they could "pillow talk" the matter.

After six hours I suggested we take a break and get back together on Monday. Jane was simply too angry to be reasonable. Jane and Stuart needed to talk over the weekend. Hopefully, Stuart would calm Jane down and we could get this matter resolved on a reasonable basis.

Monday morning we got back together again and it was apparent the pillow talk worked. Jane was much more reasonable about getting the matter resolved so that she and Stuart could go on with life. The case settled for $280,000, a fair figure.

When the mediation is bogging down, a question arises as to whether the mediator should keep the parties late into the evening and literally wear them out until they capitulate. I do not subscribe to such an approach because I think it is unkind. I prefer to put the mediation over to another day when the parties are rested and in a better frame of mind.

Those who contend that the parties should be kept in session while the iron is hot express concern that the parties will make their position worse if they go home and think about it. In all the thousands of mediations I have done, when the mediation was put over to another day, the parties may not have changed their positions but they did not make them worse. And more times than not they were more flexible.

Allowing parties to sleep on the matter and approach fresh another day has two benefits: first, the more the parties talk and think about the matter the easier it becomes for them to compromise. It is the used-car salesman approach – let the prospective purchaser take the car home overnight or take it for a spin, for the more they handle it the easier it becomes to close the deal.

Second, when there is a member of the family who wants to get a matter resolved, they invariably work on the party to settle. They many times just need a quiet setting to do this. With a husband and wife, if one wants resolution and the other is holding out, the former will win out if given quiet time. They will pillow talk the matter night and day until resolution is reached.

C. Flexibility as to Matters Included in the Settlement

By contract, the parties can not only use any mechanism they wish, and conduct the mediation as they find expedient, but the parties have the flexibility to include anything they wish in the settlement agreement, even matters arising outside the dispute itself, so long as the parties agree.

Mediation #13

<u>You Can't Teach Old Dogs New Tricks</u>

Elmer Linden worked at the Guibal Manufacturing Company for 29 years, when he was fired two years prior to his pension vesting. He was chief accountant for most of those years. New owners sought to computerize the accounting department. Elmer tried to learn to use a computer but could not become proficient enough to run the department. New owners hired a young woman at considerably less salary, who set the system up and operated it. Elmer was devastated by the loss of his job, for he loved the company and devoted most of his working life to it. (As an aside I must confess that I greatly empathized with Elmer. I am also one of those "anachronisms" that is computer challenged. In fact, I take pride in being a purist and doing it the old-fashioned way, pen and paper.)

Elmer brought a lawsuit under Title VII of the Civil Rights Act of 1964 for age discrimination. He claimed that he and two other employees, also in their 50s, we're forced to leave in violation of the Act.

Within six months he died from other causes, but his widow, Anne, felt it was from a broken heart. She took over the lawsuit to honor his name.

The matter was mediated, and Anne, on behalf of the estate, demanded $200,000. The new owners offered $50,000. She eventually came down to 125,000 and would move no further. The new owners went to $100,000 and said they could afford no more – there was no insurance. As mediator, I tried to reach a compromise, but failed.

The widow was quite emotional and it was clear to me that the $125,000 was an arbitrary figure, that she was trying to send a message to the new owners. When it looked like the mediation was going to fail, counsel for the widow asked to speak to her alone. Five minutes later I was called back into the room and they said that the widow had terminated the mediation.

As an afterthought, while the parties were packing their bags to leave, I said to Anne, "Would an apology help?"

Anne answered, "Yes it would, and it would also help if the new owners would agree to take sensitivity training so that they would know how to handle employees properly in the future."

This was presented to the new owners and they readily agreed to both conditions. The case then settled for $100,000. As it turned out, the widow would have settled for $50,000, for what she wanted was recognition of her husband's dedicated service over so many years. The written apology satisfied this need.

In a court of law, the judge or jury would have no jurisdiction to award an apology or even consider it. They can only award money damages.

Mediation #14

<u>Bank Worker Gets Letter of Recommendation</u>

Trudy Arnold was very intelligent, a hard worker, and enjoyed her job at the Wilkin National Bank, Wilkin, Texas. There was only one problem, she was prone to having epileptic fits. For the most part, Trudy was able to mask this. However, at the annual summer picnic for bank employees she had a serious attack, which required her being taken to a local hospital for care. Many of the employees became frightened. The bank decided they could not risk such an attack in front of bank customers and decided to terminate her employment.

Trudy was devastated when she received a termination notice. She consulted a lawyer and decided to bring a lawsuit under Title VII of the Civil Rights Act of 1964, Americans with Disabilities Act. Before discovery commenced, the parties agreed to mediate.

At the mediation, Trudy asked considerably more than these cases were worth and she would not compromise. When the mediation seemed to be failing, Trudy observed how embarrassed she was at losing her job and she was having difficulty facing her friends and other bank employees. At this point, her attorney suggested that maybe a letter of recommendation or commendation would help ease the pain Trudy felt. She immediately broke into a smile and said this would help immensely. I presented the idea to the bank and it was more than receptive. It had no difficulty preparing a letter of recommendation, because Trudy had been an efficient and faithful employee. With this completed, the case quickly settled.

Trudy's goal in this matter was not money, but recognition that she was a competent person, as much as any other person at the bank, and that she had been faithful to the bank over the seven years she worked there. She was then able to show the letter to others, which gave her a sense of dignity and respect.

Mediation #15

A Novel Resolution

Bill and Sandra Willoughby lived in a gated community in St. Louis, Missouri. They hired Malcolm Chandler, a home improvement contractor, to work on their home, including installing a new kitchen. The contract price was $75,000. When the work was completed, Malcolm submitted a bill of $100,000, which included $25,000 for additional costs and expenses incurred when Malcolm had to make trips to St. Louis to check out the work. The Willoughby's refused to pay the $25,000 on the ground that none of the amount had been approved in writing as required by the contract.

At the mediation, it was obvious to me that the Willoughbys could write out a check for the $25,000 without thinking twice. So it had to be a matter of principle that they were holding out. For Malcolm it was a matter of economics. He had already spent $3000 to prosecute the case and he had to get something out of it. His construction company was struggling to make ends meet.

In caucus with the Willoughbys, I asked counsel: "We are only talking about $25,000. How much will it cost the Willoughbys to defend the case?"

Attorney Jeff Anderson said: "We could spend $15,000 to $20,000."

Bill Willoughby interrupted: "Costs are not the issue. Malcolm did not adhere to the contract and charged us for items concerning which we had not approved." There was a long pause, and Bill added, "Chandler needs to be taught a lesson if he is going to stay in business."

In a later caucus with Chandler, he felt he was being taken advantage of because by the time litigation ended he would have spent most of it in attorney's fees and costs.

In a latter caucus with the Willoughbys, Sandra spoke for the first time. "You know, Malcolm did a good job in remodeling our home, and I realize we can afford this lawsuit and he cannot. What if we did this. Twenty-five thousand dollars is owing. We will pay $10,000 now, and I will recommend to my friends that they use Malcolm for work they might want done. If in 2 years I cannot generate an additional $25,000 for him, then we will pay the remaining $15,000."

Sandra obviously caught her husband off guard. "Why would we enter such an agreement?"

Sandra gave one of those stern wife looks and said, "Bill, don't be so cheap. Malcom is struggling and there is no reason not to help him a little. I am certain I will generate $25,000 more business for him."

Bill knew when to remain silent and keep peace with Sandra. He said nothing and folded his arms.

Malcom accepted the proposal and the matter settled. Such a resolution would be unthinkable if the matter were in a courtroom.

Mediation #16

Plaintiff Receives a Letter of Recommendation

Plaintiff, Ted Martin, worked for Titan Real Estate Company as superintendent of janitors for some 7 housing complexes. One day a worker complained to him that he was receiving more work than others and he felt this was unfair. An altercation followed and the individual, Steven Ashworth, threatened plaintiff that he would beat him to a pulp and kick him in the a _ _. He said he had been in jail and knew how to take care of someone like plaintiff. Plaintiff complained to his supervisor and was told to file a complaint with the police. Seven days later plaintiff called the police and had Ashworth arrested. Plaintiff's supervisor became furious and fired Martin on the spot for having an employee arrested without permission of the company.

Plaintiff then sued the company for retaliatory discharge and under the state's Whistleblower Act. The matter was mediated. After opening remarks, I asked plaintiff's attorney, Devon Anderson, for an opening statement.

"Thank you Mr. Calkins for agreeing to mediate our case. We feel we have a very strong case. There is no question that a criminal assault was perpetrated on Ted when Ashworth threatened him with physical harm. Ashworth is over 6 feet tall and 220 pounds. He makes a very threatening appearance especially to Ted, who is 5'6" tall and 145 lbs. Further, Ashworth is 32 years old and Ted is 60 years old. Added to this is the fact that there is no question, Ted had Ashworth arrested. Under the law we are entitled to lost wages of $150,000 for the last 2½ years Ted has been off work, as well as future lost wages until Ted gets a new job. He is also entitled to recover for mental distress because he has been concerned about his safety. Finally, we are entitled to get our attorney's fees and costs which will exceed $100,000 by the time this gets to trial."

Devon stopped, and there was a long lull. Finally, Dorsey McMillon, defense attorney, began her response. "First, let me thank everyone for agreeing to mediate. We tried once before but were unsuccessful. We are, of course, sorry this matter ever got to the point of a lawsuit, Mr. Martin was a good employee, however, we do not feel he has any cause of action for what Mr. Ashworth did. Mr. Ashworth was wrong in getting into an altercation with Mr. Martin, but this was not an actionable wrong. He never touched him, and further the company took appropriate action to punish him. Mere words, even threats, are not enough to trigger an actionable wrong. That is our position. However, we are here to get this matter resolved and I think we have sufficient funds to do so."

"Thank you everyone," I said. "I think we have gotten off to a good start."

I then met with plaintiff first. Plaintiff's counsel, Devon, felt he had a very strong case. I asked for a demand, and he said they would settled for $500,000 without reinstatement and $400,000 with reinstatement.

"Devon," I asked, "has the defendant indicated it would take Ted back?"

"Yes," he responded. "They have said it numerous times."

"What has been their offer to date?" I asked.

"They offered to pay $75,000 if he returned to work, and $100,000 if he found work elsewhere."

I caucused several times with both sides and Devon informed me they would go to $300,000 if plaintiff was rehired; otherwise, their demand was $400,000.

Dorsey McMillon stated there was no way defendant would pay $400,000 or even $300,000. Their top figure was $100,000 if plaintiff returned to work and $150,000 if he found employment elsewhere.

At this point a more creative solution had to be found. Ted was a member of a union so Dorsey suggested they contact the union and see if it would help Ted find a new job. This was done and the union representative said he liked Ted and would do all he could to get him a comparable job. He felt sure he would succeed in doing so.

I asked the defendant whether it would write a strong letter of recommendation to help Ted find a new job. Counsel said they would and Dorsey drafted a letter. It stated:

> "Ted Martin has been employed by our company for 10 years with the last 4 as a supervisor. During this time his work has been exemplary. He is efficient, respectful and a positive member of our team. We highly recommend him for employment with whatever company he selects."

With this letter and the assurance of the union representative, I returned to the plaintiff caucus. Ted was quite pleased and felt we were making real progress. As it turned out, he wanted to move on but was concerned about whether, at his age, he could find another job. With the union assurance, this eased his mind.

At this point, I put a mediator's number on the table for settlement purposes. I suggested the case settle for $250,000 and Ted working elsewhere. Both sides agreed. In addition to Ted's concern about getting a new job, the lawsuit was worrying him and he was feeling very stressed. He simply wanted to get the matter resolved and go on with his life.

Once the case settled and the papers signed, both sides seemed very pleased with resolution of the matter.

This case illustrates how a letter of recommendation and the assurance of the union representative turned the tide and led to settlement.

Mediation #17

A Mother is Not Necessarily a Daughter's Best Friend

When Julie was born, she was crippled through negligence of her doctor. Her mother, Mary Sue, sought a lawyer to bring a malpractice case against the doctor. Five lawyers turned her down, saying she had a questionable malpractice case. (In most jurisdictions 70 to 80 percent of such cases are lost by the plaintiffs at trial and the outlay of costs is more than what most lawyers can sustain.)

One lawyer, Sam Benson, said he would take the case if he could bring in his cousin, Julius Spencer, an excellent trial lawyer, to prosecute it. Mary Sue consented. Thereafter, Spencer was able to get a settlement of $1.2 million. The funds were disbursed, one third to counsel, one third put into a structured annuity for Julie, and one third deposited in a bank account to pay living expenses for the child. The mother was made guardian ad litem for Julie and Sam Benson was appointed counsel for the estate.

An order approving the deposit of the $400,000 in the bank account provided that any expenditures had to be first approved by the court. Two weeks after the deposit, application to the court was made to withdraw $32,500 to purchase a van with a lift to accommodate Julie. The court approved the expenditure.

A problem arose because the court's order requiring approval of all expenditures from funds held by the bank was never submitted to the bank. Knowing this, Mary Sue went to the bank and withdrew the remainder of the $400,000 and moved to Hawaii with Julie. There she purchased a home on Maui and she and her boyfriend moved in. Funds were dissipated with a trip to Paris with her boyfriend, investment in his business which failed, and a car.

Mary Sue failed to file the required annual report, and the court investigated the matter. Finding that Mary Sue had been derelict in her duties, a new guardian was appointed. The guardian then sued Sam Benson and Julius Spencer for failing to submit the court's order to the bank. Sam had no malpractice insurance and no money – he was judgment proof. Therefore, the guardian concentrated on Julius, arguing that he could not delegate his duty to his cousin to file the court's order with the bank. He sought recovery of attorney's fees ($400,000), and loss of the money deposited with the bank ($400,000 less the price of the van).

Spencer's malpractice carrier defended on the ground that when the case was settled Spencer turned the funds over to his cousin and was no longer in the case. It also contended that Mary Sue, as guardian, had committed a felony against her own daughter in pilfering the funds in question for her own benefit and not for the benefit of the child.

As the mediator, I confess I lost my objectivity. I became incensed that the new attorney representing the guardian ad litem, Phil Masterson, would sue Julius, a fellow attorney and friend, when the latter obtained such an excellent result in a case other attorneys turned down.

"Phil", I said outside the presence of his client, "why would you sue Julius Spencer? He successfully prosecuted the case when no one else would take it. Now you're seeking his fee, part of which went to Sam Benson, who has no money, as well as the $400,000 dissipated by Julie's mother. That is not right."

"Richard," responded Masterson, "this is business, you know that. It is not personal."

"How are you going to get around the fact that Mary Sue stole her daughter's money. She's a intervening cause. If you recover this money, she will benefit a second time, and if her daughter dies, which is not out of the realm of possibility, she is in a position to squander it a third time."

"That's —" (using profane words), responded Masterson. "Both lawyers had a duty to submit the court's order to the bank, which required court permission to withdraw any funds."

I could feel the redness rising in my neck. The pitch of my voice rose and I committed the cardinal sin for a mediator. I argued the defense's case as though it was my own.

"That doesn't make sense. Sam Benson was appointed counsel for the guardian and had the responsibility to submit the order to the bank.

Go after him. When Julius turned the $400,000 over to Sam, his duty to the estate ended."

"Wait a minute," responded Phil, "Sam Benson and Julius Spencer were partners for the purpose of this matter, and Julius had just as much a duty to comply with the order as Sam."

"Where did you go to law school?" I asked, "to come up with such an argument. I challenge you to submit the question to a neutral party for ruling on the issue."

"I'm not going to be bound by any arbitrator," responded Masterson. "I'll have the issue submitted to a jury as a question of fact."

Cooling down somewhat, I proposed that we submit the issue to an ex state supreme court justice for a nonbinding ruling on the question. Then I added let's also submit the question whether Mary Sue embezzled the money and this was an intervening cause, which would eliminate any claim of negligence against Julius. Phil said he would think about it.

By now I had recovered and was calm.

Outwardly I was disgusted with Masterson for pursuing this matter. There was simply too much of lawyers suing lawyers. I felt it wasn't just an insurance matter, for most lawyers like Julius we're insured, but a matter of honor in the profession. (I had one mediation where a party was suing its attorney for legal malpractice. The law firm being sued was suing the plaintiff's attorney in another matter for malpractice. And one month before I settled a malpractice action against the defense attorney in this case. Maybe there was no longer any honor among lawyers, even here in Iowa.)

Phil and the insurance carrier covering Julius agreed to my proposal and an ex Iowa supreme court justice was chosen to review the matter. Much to my disappointment, he ruled that, indeed, Sam Benson and Julius Spencer were partners for purposes of the lawsuit and Julius had a duty to be certain the court's order was carried out. He also ruled that the mothers conduct did not negate this duty.

I was dropped as the mediator, which I expected, because I lost my impartiality and objectivity so I should not complain. Shortly after, through continued negotiations, the case settled for $400,000. Julius had insisted his carrier settle the matter and not leave him exposed. He did keep his attorney's fee so that was something.

D. Structured Annuities

One of the common settlement tools mediators use is the structured annuity. When a plaintiff potentially will receive a substantial amount of money, the mediator might propose the person consider investing it in a structured annuity. The person has to invest it somewhere. The major benefit of the structured annuity is the person does not have to pay federal income taxes on the interest earned while invested. In other words, any other investment that earns income is taxable. This tax free benefit can only be utilized in a settlement of the matter; if the case goes to trial, the tax benefit is lost.

Mediators use the structured annuity as one benefit in getting a matter settled. In setting up the annuity, it can pay out a set amount per month for a fixed period of time, or for the life of the plaintiff. It can be held until the person reaches retirement age and then pay out like a pension. There is total flexibility as to how it is structured. There are many benefits in addition to its tax-free basis:

1. No brokerage fees are charged.

2. Once structured it cannot be altered. This means brokers cannot change the investment and charge an additional fee. They cannot "churn" the account.

3. The annuity is not subject to market fluctuations. Once fixed it pays out as directed by the annuity contract.

4. Annuities are placed only with top rated companies in the field. The investment is secure.

5. There is no opportunity for the annuitant to dissipate the funds because the investment cannot be altered.

6. Family and friends cannot get their hands on the money invested.

7. It is not subject to bankruptcy; therefore, creditors cannot reach the corpus if the plaintiff files bankruptcy.

8. The annuity is particularly beneficial for children. Responsible parents do not want their child to receive a large sum of money when the child turns 18 because they are vulnerable at that age. The annuity can be set up so the child will receive a fixed amount to go to college with lump sum payments made later when reaching 25, 30 and 35, for example.

Likewise, the annuity can be used to protect the child from irresponsible parents who might gain control of the child's money and dissipate it for their own benefit. The next mediation illustrates this.

A Structured Annuity Helps A Little Girl

Janie Dunlap was 3 years old. She and her mother lived in a low rent housing complex. The janitor, John Hinkle, a man of 70 years, lived in a basement apartment. He sat in his underwear with the door open and enticed little children to enter the apartment with an offer of candy. On one occasion Janie entered and he sexually abused her causing injury.

Suit was brought on behalf of the child by her mother against the owner of the housing complex and Hinkle. A check of the records before Hinkle was hired would have revealed that he was a registered pedophile.

The insurance company handling the claim was not willing to pay very much because it feared Janie's mother would get control of the money and quickly dissipate it. She was addicted to drugs and had a different man sleeping in her bed most every night.

With this scenario I suggested that a structured annuity be set up and the settlement invested in it. The attorneys and insurance representative readily agreed and a settlement of $75,000 was agreed upon. The annuity did not begin to pay out until Janie reached 18 years of age. She would then receive $2000 per month for the rest of her life. The insurance company also agreed to pay Janie's mother $5000 for agreeing to the settlement. She accepted and the matter was resolved.

In this case, the insurance carrier was willing to pay considerably more, knowing that the child would be protected from her mother and would have something when she reached majority. This could never have been accomplished if the case had gone to trial.

Mediation #19

Structured Annuity Puts Plaintiff's Life Back Together

Debra Colton, 22 years old, had had a difficult life. She and her divorced mother and five siblings struggled to survive. They lived in a small rundown house in rural Iowa. They survived on state and federal aid, as her grandparents had. At 16 she ran away from home with her boyfriend, Tim. They married and had three daughters by the time Debra was 20. Tim then abandoned the family and left for California with a girlfriend and was never heard from again. Things got so bad that Deborah and her girls had to move in with her mother.

Debra was not lazy and looked for work. She finally was hired by a small concern that augered the kernels off of corncobs. Workers placed corncob in bins, put a screen over the top, and turned on an auger. The kernels fell through the bottom of the bin which were collected in baskets.

Two weeks into her job a decision was made by management to leave the screens off because vibration of the augers made the screens come loose. Time was wasted continually tightening the screens. Management, however, put a big red warning sign not to pull stalks out of a bin without first shutting off the auger. Debra, on one occasion saw a small cornstalk and reached to pull it out without shutting off the auger. The physics are such that her hand was pulled into the auger faster than she could let go. She lost her hand cut off at the wrist.

Suit was filed against the manufacturer of the bin for a defective product. After the case was filed and some discovery taken, the parties agreed to mediate. I knew all the attorneys involved, particularly plaintiff's counsel, Ken Richter, a personal friend. He was very successful and made a fortune in propane gas explosion cases. In fact, he just completed a burn case and the jury awarded plaintiff in excess of $3.5 million. Coming off such a victory, I knew Ken would be difficult, however, I did not realize how difficult.

On the appointed day, we met at Ken's office for the mediation. In addition to Debra, Ken and myself, Harrison Millard, counsel for the manufacture of the auger bin, retained by Sun Insurance Company, and Ruth Bateman, the adjuster for the carrier, were present.

After everyone settled in, before I could make my opening remarks, Ken Richter stood up and announced, "I want to make this clear. We did not ask for this mediation, and if the Sun Insurance Company wants to get this matter resolved it will have to pay north of $1 million."

I thought to myself, not this again. Why did Ken take such a hard position at my mediations. It just makes my work that much more difficult. I said nothing. Harrison Millard then responded: "if that is the case, you are right, this will be a short mediation."

I said: "Now ladies and gentlemen, we have not even gotten started so let's not state what our final positions are. Much can happen in a mediation that will give us guidance. All that I ask is that you give me an opportunity to do my job."

We got through my opening remarks and counsels' opening statements. Plaintiff's counsel informed me that a workers compensation action was pending against Debra's employer. Another lawyer was handling this. We then went into caucus, first with the plaintiff.

Ken immediately took over the caucus. He likes to be the alpha dog in any situation in which he is involved. He described the negligence of the manufacturer of the auger and how it created a difficult life situation for Debra and her family. He went on at some length without stopping for a breath of air. Finally he came to a halt. There was silence for a long moment.

Debra sat in silence looking at Ken. I could not decide if she was pleased with Ken's aggressive manner or not. She looked older than her 22 years. Three years of trying to survive was taking a toll. She wore a sleeveless blouse, I'm sure at the insistence of Ken, so that the stump on her right arm would stand out. The last thing Ken said was, "we want $1.5 million and we won't move further until the other side makes a significant offer."

I entered the defense caucus and everyone looked at me intently. I suppose they hoped I would have good news. Harrison spoke first, "well," he said, "what is their new demand?"

"Harrison," I responded, "let me cover a few matters first and then we will get to the numbers. First, what are the strongest points in your case, those things you would like me to argue to the other side that will get their attention."

Harrison Millard was obviously well-prepared as most top defense lawyers are. Without hesitation he said: "Ken has some real problems in this case: first, product liability cases are difficult to prove. I know they are arguing that the screens kept coming off the bins because of the vibration caused by the augers. However, we were never notified of this problem and if we had we would've fixed it immediately.

"Second, Debra's employer took it upon itself to leave the protective screens off. She should look to her employer and not us. In fact, we will bring her employer into the case because it has a substantial percentage of fault.

"Third, there's no way Debra is going to get $1 million in rural Iowa for a lost hand. This is farm country and every farm has accidents. She will get along just fine with her prosthesis. We want to get this matter settled but it has to be within reason, okay?" said Harrison.

I then asked what concerns he had about the case. He candidly admitted that Debra would make a sympathetic plaintiff with three small girls and being abandoned by her husband. Also, the accident was rather shocking and will raise concerns that this nice lady needs help.

There was more discussion and then I mentioned Debra's demand of $1.5 million.

"$1.5 million!" said Harrison in disbelief. "We can't even respond to that."

"Don't be discouraged, Harrison. You know this is how all mediations begin. We will still get the matter resolved. Give me a response which will get negotiations started."

"It's hard to respond to this. I guess we'll go up $25,000 to $100,000. However, we will not go beyond this until plaintiff goes below $1 million."

"Thank you, Harrison. I will convey that."

I went back and forth several times with Debra lowering her demand to $1.1 million and defendant raising its offer to $150,000. Both sides said they would go no further – plaintiff, because it had to settle north of $1 million and defendant because it would not get serious until plaintiff went below $1 million.

At this point, I used another approach to break the logjam called "bracketing." Speaking to Debra and Ken I said, "both sides have dug in so I am going to take another approach. One thing is clear to me: the defendant will not pay $1 million; so if you want to keep the mediation going you will have to commit to go below $1 million. Now if this is not possible, I understand and I wish you the best of luck. But if you want to get this matter resolved in the next few weeks and not four years from now, and get on with life, you'll have to give me this commitment."

Ken did not respond but asked to speak to Debra alone. I then went to the defense side and gave them the same presentation, only I said you have to go above $500,000 to keep the mediation going. Harrison immediately said this would work.

Returning to the plaintiff caucus Ken said, "Richard, we have talked this over and we'll go to $999,999.99."

"Thank you, Harrison. That is all I asked." I knew that going below $1 million Debra would accept $950,000 or possibly $850,000. So at least I narrowed the gap. This had taken most of the day so I suggested we put the mediation over to another day. All agreed, and I set a date to have a separate caucus at Ken's office.

On the day set, I arrived at Ken's office. He was gracious and we talked about golf while waiting for Debra to arrive. When she arrived, I got down to business.

"Debra, I had a structured annuity put together to see what it would look like based on what I think we can get from the other side. If we take $650,000, and . . . ."

"Wait a minute," interrupted Ken. "We are not going to settle this case for $650,000. Don't even suggest that. Go no further."

"Ken, all I'm doing is taking a hypothetical figure that I think they will pay and show what can be done with an annuity. We don't have to agree to that figure." I stopped and Ken seemed very suspicious of my explanation.

I continued: "if you take out attorney's fees of $217,000 (you always pay the lawyer first to get their attention) and take $300,000 from the balance and put it into a structured annuity, it will generate $3100 per month for the rest of Debra's life with 20 years guaranteed, that is, if she dies in less than 20 years, payments will continue to be made to the children for the remainder of the 20 years. Also, at age 55 she will receive a lump sum payment of $40,000; age 60 an additional $52,500; age 65, $70,000; age 70, $147,000. Also the girls, when each reaches age 18, $15,000 per year for four years to go to college or use otherwise, $35,000 age 25, $50,000 age 30, $62,500 age 35. Additionally, there will be enough left over to purchase that house you wanted for $75,000, and you can also purchase that used pick-up truck you so desperately need."

I stopped and there was a long moment of silence. Ken started to speak; however, Debra interrupted him. "May I talk to my lawyer alone for just a minute?"

"Of course," I responded and left the room.

An hour later I was called back into the office and Debra said, "I will take your offer."

I could see from Ken's expression that he was not pleased with the decision. I think he felt that I pulled a fast one on him; however, I was certain of the reasons for Debra's decision. First, the most she or any member of her extended family had ever earned was $1200 per month and now she would receive $3100 per month for the rest of her life. Second, $3100 per month would permit her to raise her daughters even if she didn't go back to work. Third, she no longer would have to depend on government assistance to survive. Fourth, this gave her a sense of dignity which no one in her family had ever known for several generations. By using the structured annuity approach it showed Debra the value of money and what could be accomplished tax free.

She thanked me.

CHAPTER 3

<u>LEARNING WEAKNESSES OF EACH PARTY</u>

One of the primary reasons caucus mediation is so successful is that you can ask questions of counsel which have never been asked before in legal jurisprudence. The mediator in strict confidence can ask each party what the weaknesses are in their case. A judge, opposing counsel, jurors, arbitrator could never ask such a question, but the mediator can because he pledges the response will be kept confidential. When both sides respond, the mediator has an understanding of the case never before enjoyed in legal jurisprudence. He or she is in position to work out a strategy to get the matter resolved.

The following case studies illustrate this:

Mediation #20

<u>A Parent's Worst Nightmare</u>

Darcy Townsen graduated valedictorian of her high school class, was head cheerleader, president of the student body, and recipient a full scholarship to an eastern woman's college. She was everything a parent could ask. She was driving west in a car given to her at graduation on a main thoroughfare in Chicago, when she came to a red light. She pulled into the turn lane to go south. She then proceeded through the intersection and was broadsided by semi-truck and killed.

In opening statements at the joint session, the attorney for Darcy's estate, Ron Jeffries, contended that the semi-truck ran a red light. Max Anderson for the trucking company contended that Darcy was turning on a red light and his trucker entered the intersection on a yellow light.

In the first caucus with the plaintiff, I first asked what the strengths of the plaintiff's case were. Ron responded, "There will be great sympathy for Darcy's parents. Darcy's death was a terrible blow, a parent's worst nightmare. As you know she was everything in high school and had a full-ride scholarship to a top women's college out east. Further, nobody likes a trucker, especially one in a hurry running a red light."

"Thank you, Ron," I responded. "Now in absolute confidence would you disclose to me what you feel are weaknesses or concerns you have in the case, if any. This will not be shared with the other side, of course."

Ron hesitated a moment and then said: "We have one major concern – when Darcy pulled into the turn lane to go south, she was facing west at the time, and a car pulled in next to her who was continuing west. He will testify that out of the corner of his eye he saw Darcy start her turn. Because the light going west was still red, Darcy had to have turned on a red light. In other words, the green turn arrow does not come on until the light going west turns green. He was looking at the light and it was still red."

"Does the other side know of this witness?" I asked.

"No, but we will have to disclose the witness shortly if we don't get the case settled."

Ron gave me a new demand, and I went to the defense caucus. They were waiting expectantly and seemed relieved when I walked into the room. I initially asked what the strengths of the defendant's case were and then asked the key question, "what are the weaknesses or concerns, if any?"

Max Anderson was expecting the question, but before answering, he asked about confidentiality, which I assured him covered everything said in caucus.

"Well," he began, "these death cases are always difficult to defend especially here in Chicago. And when such a promising young woman is killed, it makes it even more difficult. There is another concern however. The driver was speeding when he came to the intersection. As you know, every semi-truck has a black box which records its speed at all times. The black box in the defendant's truck shows he was traveling 50 mph in a 40 mph speed zone 15 seconds before impact. The tape shows him slowing down to 42 mph and then speeding up, and then it goes blank at the time of impact.

"However, we have a more serious problem. Our trucker had to be running a red light. When the lights are red going west they are also red going east. North and south traffic then proceeds through the intersection. Then, when the light going west turns green, the green arrow comes on to go south. Darcy either turned on a red light or green arrow, but it makes no difference. Either way the light going east was still red. He was entering the intersection on a red light. With these facts I am deeply concerned that a Chicago jury will award a substantial amount of money. We need to get this matter resolved."

Thereafter, the case did settle for a substantial amount.

Mediation #21

A Ponzi Scheme With Banks

Philip Fissler was, to all appearances, a very wealthy business entrepreneur. He had several mansions in Illinois, a mansion in Naples, Florida, a 50 foot yacht on which he entertained business associates and friends, several limousines, chauffeur, maids and gardeners, and so on. He also generously contributed to many worthwhile charities over the years. To all intents and purposes, he had it all – except for one thing. His apparent wealth was a house of cards – a Ponzi scheme. His Ponzi scheme, however, was borrowing from banks rather than defrauding private citizens. He borrowed millions of dollars from one bank, then borrowed from a second bank to pay the first, a third to pay the second and so on.

Fissler borrowed $3.5 million from a downtown Chicago bank, Primo Western, his sixth bank. He signed a note and pledged $8.8 million in stock in his Smith Barney account as collateral. The bank required his wife also sign the note and the security agreement pledging the stock.

In 2005, his house of cards crumbled and his Ponzi scheme uncovered. Overnight he was bankrupt and facing criminal charges. Unable to face the future, he committed suicide, leaving his widow to face the music.

Primo Western sued Fissler's widow, who was the beneficiary of a $3 million life insurance policy, which Fissler took out on his life. (It was incontestable in that it had been in effect over two years and therefore had to be paid out even though he took his own life.) Primo Western pled the fraud committed against it and that his widow knew of Fissler's financial dealings. It also contended that there was no Smith Barney account, that this also was a fraud.

When Primo Western did its due diligence check on Fissler as to whether there was a Smith Barney account, he gave it his own e-mail and telephone number, and when inquiry was made pretended to be the managing partner of Smith Barney. He affirmed the existence of the account both in the email and on the phone.

Fissler's widow counterclaimed against the bank, alleging that the bank had violated a federal statute, the Fair Debt Collection Act, which provided that it was illegal to require a spouse to sign a loan agreement unless the bank was relying on her credit to make the loan. Hearing was held on the counterclaim and the trial judge found that Fissler's widow had no credit or assets of her own, that she signed the note because directed to do so by her husband. In fact, she had no understanding of any of her husband's financial dealings. The court then set a date for hearing on damages – the widow was permitted under the statute to collect damages for any injuries she suffered, as well as general damages and attorney's fees and costs. At this point the mediation was held.

At the mediation, the bank demanded the $3 million and the widow offered $100,000 just to get rid of the case. In caucus with the widow, when asked about any weaknesses or concerns, counsel looked at me and said, "we have no weaknesses and there's nothing we are concerned about." Almost pleading, he added: "if we have a weakness please tell us what it might be." He said this with such sincerity. Frankly, I saw none and so stated.

Working with the principle, there is no perfect case, I began to research the law. I found a case written by Judge Posner, a very excellent judge sitting in the federal Seventh Circuit Court of Appeals in Chicago. In that case, the judge stated that the Fair Debt Collection Act is intended to provide protection to spouses who are required to sign notes intended for the benefit of their spouses. However, when a spouse also signs a security agreement, this is outside the scope of the Act. In other words, when a spouse signs a security agreement which pledges stocks and bonds, for example, she represents that the account exists and has the stated value. In this instance, to contend she did not know that it was nonexistent is no defense. She knew or should have known before she signed.

When counsel for Fissler's widow examined the opinion, he realized his client had exposure for signing a false security agreement. A weakness was found in the case and it settled at a figure both sides felt was fair.

Mediation #22

<u>You Can't Fool the FAA</u>

Many times the weakness in a case is not apparent to the lawyers representing the parties. It is a fact that the mediator looks through a different prism than the lawyers and sees things counsel is missing. It's not that the mediator is more intelligent, rather he is not burdened with albatross the trial lawyer has called advocacy. He is not trying to win the case for a client. He is dedicated to settling it for all concerned.

Another example where a weakness was spotted that counsel for the plaintiff failed to identify initially, involved Mary Jane Hellman, a first officer, who flew international flights for a major airlines. She was traveling from O'Hare airport to her home in Schaumburg, Illinois, when she was rearended while stopped at a red light. She felt immediate pain in her neck and back. She went to the hospital, but was later released.

The next day, she was in considerable pain with a severe headache. She went to her family physician, who prescribed medicine for the pain. A year later she was still suffering and was given a steroid injection, which helped for a short period of time. During all this time she continued flying and just suffered through the discomfort.

Prior to filing a lawsuit, Mary Jane's attorney requested mediation. I traveled to Palatine, Illinois for the session. Upon entering the conference room, I was introduced to Mary Jane. She was an attractive woman, professionally dressed and was articulate. In caucus, she explained how much she was still suffering from the accident. Her attorney made an initial demand of $150,000 and the insurance carrier offered $10,000. It admitted liability and only damages were in issue.

After several hours, the defense stated that Mary Jane would have to go well below $100,000 if the case were to settle. Mary Jane's attorney stated they would move slightly under $100,000, but they were not willing to move too far. The carrier then raised it's offered to $20,000.

I was becoming concerned because neither party was willing to make a major move. Then, a major item came to light. In Mary Jane's documents that were to be turned over to the defense if the case did not settle, there was an innocuous looking physical examination form, which Mary Jane had filled out. Looking at it, I inquired what it was. Mary Jane responded: "every six months, as a commercial airline pilot, I have a physical and have to fill out this form so I can fly. This form was filled out one month after the accident." Looking it over, I quickly realized Mary Jane had to settle: she could not file a lawsuit nor proceed with the case. And I relaxed.

Looking at Mary Jane, I asked: "Do you realize the implications of this document? It asks, do you currently use any medications? And the box indicating "no," is marked. It asks under medical history a number of questions and for each box no is marked; they include the following: frequent or severe headaches, no; neurological disorders, no; other illness, disability, or surgery, no.

"This would indicate that you are not currently having any problems. Is there a reason you answered the questionnaire as you did?"

Mary Jane hesitated and finally said, "if I answered yes to any of those questions, I would have been grounded. You have to understand that becoming a captain on intercontinental flights is my dream. If I get grounded now, I'll be passed over. There're so few women who are captains on such flights I did not want to let the others also seeking their captaincy down. This is the reason I have toughed it out."

Turning to Mary Jane's attorney, I read a "notice," which stated

Whoever in any manner within the jurisdiction of any department or agency of United States knowingly and willfully falsifies, conceals or covers up by any trick, scheme or device a material fact, or who makes any false, fictitious, or fraudulent statement or representation, or entry, may be fined up to $250,000 or imprisoned not more than five years or both. (18 US code section 1001, 3571.)

I also read the signature line which states:

I hereby certify that all statements and answers provided by me on this application form are complete to the best of my knowledge, and I agree that they are to be considered part of the basis for issuance of any FAA certificate to me.

Counsel remained thoughtfully silent. I asked if the document had been turned over to the defendant, and counsel stated it had not. And he said, "could I talk to my client alone for just a minute." I left the room.

The implication of the document was clear. Either she had a full recovery and was not suffering as indicated by the medical form, which defendant in the case would use to reduce the claim for damages, or she falsified her medical condition and she risked losing her FAA certification to fly and possibly be prosecuted for falsifying her medical condition. At a minimum, she would have been grounded.

I noted that just filing the complaint put Mary Jane at great risk because the complaint would plead she was still suffering. The FAA could easily pick this up and end her flying career.

When Mary Jane and counsel returned to the room, they made a much lower demand and the case readily settled to the relief of Mary Jane.

CHAPTER 4

PROVIDING PARTIES WITH A REALITY CHECK

There are times when a mediation comes to a halt and neither side will compromise further. If they return to court and try the matter, at least one of them is going to be shocked and greatly disappointed by the jury verdict. However, there are other steps that can be taken to give the parties a reality check. The mediation can be suspended and the parties given polygraph tests, or a summary jury trial or focus study can be conducted. The parties can even conduct a mock trial to determine which party, or both, is not being realistic.

A. Polygraph Test

The courtroom, whether civil or criminal, will not allow use of polygraph tests. This is because they're not totally reliable. However, in mediation they can be used with great effect to consummate a settlement. There are two scenarios when they are effective: one, when two people are saying opposite things and only one can be telling the truth. And, two, when a person seeks to establish his or her credibility that the person is telling the truth.

In the first scenario, the issue in dispute must be clear. It cannot be a yellow light, red light issue. Because only one person presumably can pass both are offered the test. The one who cannot pass will generally refuse, explaining that they get nervous, they're sick, or such tests are unreliable, or are inadmissible. The prevaricator almost always declines the test, while the person telling the truth welcomes the opportunity.

In the second scenario, it is used to verify that the person is telling the truth. A person claiming they were sexually abused might take the test to prove credibility.

Mediation #23

Nothing More American Than Baseball

Julie Olsen and her husband Dan attended a local health clinic for a 30-day cleansing. They felt they had become too involved in social drinking and using social drugs. At the completion of the program, they were outpatients for a six-month period. Their assigned counselor was Devon Hastings, (not his real name). Pursuant to clinic rules and ethical standards, he was not to socialize with the Olsens for any purpose during the outpatient period.

Devon, an African-American, had been a professional baseball player who won the Cy Young Award. When the Olsen's 14-year-old son learned who Devon was, he begged him to coach his baseball team. He finally gave in and the boys were thrilled beyond words.

Julie, who was Caucasian and blonde (this is relevant), stated that she met with Devon on several occasions. On one occasion, she went to his apartment seeking financial advice. They began having an affair, which continued for a year until her husband found out. She identified Devon as the respondent. At her husband's insistence she retained an attorney and threatened to sue the clinic and Devon. Before suit was filed, the parties agreed to mediation.

I traveled to Omaha for the session. Both sides had lawyers in attendance. After the usual opening remarks, I met with Julie and her husband and attorney, Matt Simpson. He made a matter-of-fact presentation as to the strengths of their case. He said he had no concerns because Julie was very credible and would never make up such a story. Plaintiff made an opening demand of $200,000.

I then met with the defense. I asked what strengths Devon and the clinic had, and Andy Fillmore, defense counsel, responded, "we have one major strength. He did not have an affair with Mrs. Olsen."

I interrupted him and said: "Wait a minute. Are you telling me this lady is lying? Why would she do this and face the shame? No amount of money is worth that. A jury will never believe this baseball player's word over this lovely mother of three, who looks all-American."

"Hold on," said Andy. "Don't get excited. Simple fact is he took a polygraph test given by the Omaha Police Department and passed."

Andy showed me the report and he was correct. The right questions were asked and Devon's answers truthful. He denied the allegations.

The clinic was not insured and could afford to pay only $75,000. It offered to pay $30,000. After several rounds, plaintiff came down to $120,000 and defendant offered the $75,000.

The case clearly involved credibility of the only two persons who could speak to the issue – Julie and Devon. There was no doubt in my mind whom the jury would believe, the All-American mother. After some thought, I said, "let's take a different tact. Let's offer Julie a polygraph test. Based on Devon's results it is clear she can't pass. I am sure her attorney, who undoubtedly believes her, will push her to settle if we approach this the right way."

I then suggested: "Let the clinic pay the $125,000 if she takes the test and passes. If she fails, the clinic should pay her $25,000 – there needs to be an incentive to encourage her to take it. Or, if she declines to take the test, the clinic should still pay her the $75,000 already offered. If you end up owing the $125,000, this could be spread out over a period of months or even years to make it more palatable." There was extensive discussion. Finally, Fillmore said they would follow my suggestion.

I then returned to the plaintiff caucus. "Friends, I have great news. The case is settled. The clinic has agreed to pay the $125,000. The only condition is that Julie must take a polygraph test which she will of course pass."

Matt responded, "great work. I knew you would be fast but I didn't expect you to get the case settled this quickly. We will arrange to have Julie take the test. Let me speak to Julie and Dan for just a moment."

I left the caucus room. Forty-five minutes later, Matt came out. He looked quite serious. He said, "Julie will take the $75,000."

I said nothing because nothing had to be said. Papers were signed and the matter concluded.

As I got into my car to drive home, I asked myself, why would the clinic pay anything knowing that Devon was innocent. I answered my own question. It had no choice. First, whom would a jury believe, an American housewife with three fine children and a loving husband, or an ex-major league baseball player? It wasn't even close. Second, the mere filing of a lawsuit and the publicity generated because of who Devon was, would probably force the clinic to close.

The lingering question in my mind, as I crossed the Missouri River on the Mormon Bridge, was, why did Julie make such a charge against

Devon? She did not appear to need the money inasmuch as Dan made a good living. There had to be a different reason.

Two months later I found out. Andy Fillmore, defense counsel, called me one day. He said Julie had an affair with an African-American and Dan found out about it only he did not know who it was. In actuality, it was someone at work. To save her marriage, Julie identified Devon hoping her husband would feel he took advantage of her because he was her counselor.

I hung up the phone stunned.

Mediation #24

When A Woman Says No, She Means No

Thousands of cases have been brought under Title VII of the Civil Rights Act of 1964. Many of those cases are brought by women for sexual harassment and abuse in the workplace. To say that men are not very bright when it comes to sexual harassment is putting it mildly. I have mediated many cases under the Act and the man loses almost every time. Yet the harassment continues unabated. The following case came out a little differently than I expected.

Pauline Jeffries was a very attractive woman in her mid-40s. She was very intelligent and a CPA. The Temkin Manufacturing Company out of Waterloo, Iowa hired her as their chief financial officer. According to her, the CEO of the company, Randall Smith, was infatuated with her and wanted her to travel with him when he went on business trips. Both were married; however, Randall made it clear he wanted to have an affair. To keep her job Pauline consented.

After a year and one-half, Pauline felt the affair was undermining her marriage and she informed Randall that it had to stop. He persisted and she finally quit her position. She contacted attorney Travis Hinken who contacted the Temkin Company, threatening to file a lawsuit under Title VII of the Civil Rights Act for sexual harassment. The parties agreed to mediate before the case was filed.

The mediation was held at Travis Hinken's office. I started the mediation with everyone introducing themselves. In addition to Pauline and Randall, their attorneys were present. I gave my usual opening remarks and Travis Hinken, plaintiff's attorney, took the floor. He stood up when he outlined Pauline's case. He made it clear that this poor woman entered the relationship in question in order to save her job. He stated that Randall Smith threatened termination if she did not consent. When he concluded, he stated their demand was $800,000.

Defense counsel, Frank Waters, then began. He remained seated. First thing he said was, "I agree with everything Travis said, except he left out one important fact. Pauline and Randall began the affair two years before she was hired by Temkin. The affair was consensual, and not imposed upon her as a condition of employment."

When this was said, Travis jumped up and said, "that's a lie. I will not sit here and listen to such garbage. This mediation is over." He grabbed Pauline by the arm and led her out of the conference room. Fortunately, we were in his office so he did not leave the premises; he retired to his private office.

Frank and Randall sat stunned. Frank said, "now what do we do?"

I responded, "Randall, would you take a polygraph test to establish that the affair existed before Pauline was hired?"

"Of course I will," responded Randall.

"Let me talk to Travis and his client," I said. "If she is lying like you say, she will refuse to take the test." I went to Travis's office and asked to speak to him alone. Pauline went to the waiting room.

"Travis, I know how strongly you feel about your case. I'm sorry Frank upset you. There is a way to resolve this matter, however, which might keep the settlement process going. We could give both polygraph tests. One of them is clearly lying. What do you think?"

Travis hesitated and then said, "let me talk to Pauline. I don't have a great deal of faith in polygraph tests, but it might just work in this instance."

Travis conferred about half an hour. Then he came out of his office and said, "Pauline has agreed to take the test. What do we do now?"

"Let me talk to the other side to confirm that they're willing to go forward with the test. Perhaps we can set it up with the same operator." Frank confirmed that Randall was prepared to go forward with the test. Frankly, I was surprised that both agreed to take the polygraph test because almost always one will refuse. At this point I couldn't tell which one was telling the truth. This is going to be interesting I thought to myself. Frankly, there was no question in my mind that the jury would find for Pauline.

The date and operator were set and we waited for the tests to be taken. There was only one problem. One of the parties backed out the night before, sending an email to the attorneys, explaining that she was ill and that in any event polygraph tests are not reliable. She declined to take the test. With this Travis was satisfied that Pauline had been untruthful to him.

At that point Travis talked to his client and told her she had to settle or she could get another attorney. He would not allow a client of his to perjure herself on the witness stand. Pauline got the message and the case settled for $350,000. Randall was willing to pay this because when Pauline sought to end the affair, Randall was required to honor this. He did not, and therefore Pauline was entitled to some compensation, just not what she would have received if she was required to have the affair to maintain her employment.

Mediation #25

A Question of Credibility

Over the years, I have completed over 900 sexual abuse cases, mostly charging clerics with sexual abuse. I have often been asked what is the worst case I have handled. It is the following, which involved six children from the same African American family. The family was literally destroyed by the abuse. Had it not settled and the matter made public, it would have done untold damage to the church.

Attorney Jeremiah King, a black attorney, contacted me and asked if I would mediate a very difficult sexual abuse case. He explained that an

African-American family of six children had been sexually abused by a white cleric. Three of the children were male and three female.

I indicated I would be interested in helping out if the church would agree to use me. It did, and a date was set for the mediation. In reviewing the material, it was alleged that the cleric raped and sodomized all six siblings when they were children. He encouraged the children to have sex with each other while he watched. And he had a group of Latino boys have sex with the three girls. One of the girls, who was 14, became pregnant. She had a baby boy with strong Caucasian features, and everyone assumed the cleric was the father.

Mediation was set for the entire family. However, one week before the mediation, the church had a DNA test conducted and it established the cleric was not the father. The church then concluded that the entire claim was a fraud and refused to offer more than costs of litigation.

This came as a shock to the family and counsel. I contacted counsel and suggested he have polygraph tests taken of the claimants to establish their credibility. Only four were tested, however, because one was in prison on felony charges and one of the girls was bipolar and could not be tested.

The following questions were asked.

1. When you were a minor (under 18 years of age) did you have any type of sexual encounter with cleric Gilbert (not his real name)?

2. When you were a minor (under 18 years of age) did cleric Gilbert ever encourage you to have sexual intercourse with your sisters (brothers) while he watched?

3. While you were in contact with cleric Gilbert, did he tell you that sexual encounters with your sisters (brothers) were "natural?"

4. When you were a minor (under 18 years of age) did cleric Gilbert have sexual intercourse with you?

All four siblings answered, yes, to each question. The examiner concluded the oldest male and two females told the truth, and the youngest did not. The latter's test came out inconclusive; however, this result gave more credibility to the testing as a whole.

The test results were turned over to the church, which then concluded the charges were valid. It offered several million dollars and the matter was settled. Except for the polygraph tests the matter would never have been resolved and the utter destruction of the family assured.

B. Summary Jury Trial

When a mediation is failing and neither will move further, the mediator might consider offering the parties opportunities to conduct a summary jury trial as a reality check on the parties. After this is completed, the mediator restarts the mediation until settlement is reached. The summary jury is usually conducted in one day with the two attorneys presenting their cases in summary form as in closing arguments. A jury is impaneled and hears argument, is instructed by the judge or person presiding, and deliberates until it reaches a verdict. The verdict, which is non-binding, is announced and each party is permitted to confer with the jury alone to determine why it reached the verdict it did. Or, if the jury deliberations were videotaped, the parties can review it. The verdict then provides the parties with a reality check because it indicates what a real jury might do under similar circumstances.

Mediation #26

A Plaintiff Is Not The Star She Thought She Was

During the flood of 1993 in Des Moines, Iowa, when the downtown area was all but closed down, buses going to the bus depot had to use an alternate route. In one case, a bus was traveling down the middle of a three-lane street. Plaintiff, Gloria Stevenson, was driving in the right lane behind the bus. When the bus made a right hand turn,

Gloria banged into the rear wheel of the bus (the bus driver did not see her in her Volkswagen Beetle). She banged her head against the driver side window and began suffering migraine headaches. Two years to the day, her attorney filed suit and the case was submitted to mediation.

Gloria had made a fairly good recovery but complained of periodic headaches for which she wanted $150,000. The bus company ultimately offered $65,000 and would move no further. Gloria complained bitterly but would not compromise unless the bus company went above $100,000. It would not.

Rather than give up and send the case back to the court for trial, I suggested the parties submit the matter to a summary jury trial. They agreed, and the judge, who was to try the case, conducted the proceedings. Each attorney was given one and one-half hours to present their cases, the jury was instructed, and it deliberated for 3 hours. Ultimately it came back with a verdict of $35,000.

Gloria was shocked for she thought the jury would love her and give her more than $150,000. What she learned was the jury felt she was exaggerating her condition and in any event was a whiner. With this result her lawyer recommended she accept the $65,000 the bus company had offered. Using most of the 48 hours allowed to decide, she finally acquiesced and the bus company's offer was accepted.

C. Focus Study

Another reality check is the focus study procedure. In this instance, the party conducting the study will retain a psychologist trained in the process. He will review the pleadings, depositions, documents and present the case in summary form to a specially selected jury made up of individuals from the same jury pool as would make up the petite jury hearing the case at trial. The jury is supposed to represent a cross section of persons in the venue as to age, sex, education, ethnicity, employment, etc. After summarizing the case and answering all questions the jurors ask, the jurors are polled as to the verdict each would reach. The entire process is videotaped. The videotape is often used in the mediation to buttress a party's position.

Mediation #27

Wife Killed in Head-on Collision

Kerry Madison met her husband, Dan, in town for dinner. They lived in a rural area. In driving home, Kerry was the lead car and Dan followed her. Defendant, Bobby Michelson, was intoxicated and was driving 104 mph in the opposite direction down the two-lane county road.

He came up over a crest and lost control of his car and hit Kerry's car head on. She was killed instantly, Dan rushed to her car and saw her mangled body.

Dan sued Bobby and the company he worked for on behalf of Kerry's estate and on his own behalf as a bystander. He sought $2 million. The county in which suit was brought was very conservative and had never returned a verdict of $1 million. Knowing this, Dan's attorney, Kim Jacobson, had a focus study done of the case. He hired a psychologist to conduct it. A jury of 10 persons was selected, which represented all segments of the jury pool that would hear the case if it went to trial. The eight hour session was videotaped.

At the mediation, knowing that the insurance company would want to settle for less than $1 million, Kim used a segment of the video as his opening statement. It was 30 minutes long and showed the jurors discussing what they felt a verdict would be in the county. Of the ten jurors, one said $600,000, another $1.3 million and the rest $2 million up to $10 million.

The insurance carrier asked to see the entire 8 hours of the video as well as interview the psychologist. When this was completed, it offered to settle for $1.5 million and the case was resolved. Again, the process was used as a reality check during the mediation itself.

4. Mock Trial

Another method to provide the parties with a reality check is to hold a mock trial. This is conducted by one side for its own benefit. The law firm conducting the process will use its own lawyers to represent the other side and may even hire an actor to play the part of the other party. The trial can take several days and is conducted before a jury. Some law firms even have a courtroom set up to conduct the process. The entire case is then tried, with the jury receiving instructions and deliberating to reach a verdict. The verdict is then used as a measuring rod of what an actual jury might award if the matter went to trial. It can then be used to guide the party during negotiations or the mediation.

Mediation #28

A Farmer Shows His Cows

Jon Johanssen was selling 20 cows to a neighbor, Wilbur Meadows. During the negotiations, Jon took Wilbur out to the pasture to view the cows. They rode out on two All-Terrain Vehicles (ATVs), with Wilbur following Jon. On the return to the farm house, Jon traveled through a wooded area and then up a steep hill. When Wilbur negotiated the hill, he was not leaning forward enough and it flipped backwards on top of Wilbur, breaking his back.

Because of the accident, Wilbur claimed he could no longer farm. He sued Jon and the manufacturer of the ATV on the ground there was inadequate signage warning of the hazards of traversing up a steep hill. Jon's insurance carrier settled with Wilbur and mediation was conducted between the ATV company, which was self-insured, and Wilbur. Ultimately, Wilbur demanded $650,000 and the carrier offered $300,000. Neither would move any further.

I suggested to plaintiff's counsel that he mock trial the matter to find out if Wilbur's demand was in line with what a jury might do. The law firm conducted a mock trial, using some of its own people, to fill in for the defense. The jury came back with a verdict of $150,000. When questioned, Wilbur found the jury did not believe that he was so incapacitated that he could no longer farm. Another thing Wilbur learned was that farmers are bad jurors for plaintiffs. They will not give a lot of money away.

With the results of the mock trial, Wilbur lowered his demand and the case settled for $350,000.

CHAPTER 5

BUILDING RAPPORT AND TRUST WITH PARTIES

Over the years as a mediator, I have learned many valuable lessons. A primary goal is to build rapport and trust with the parties. If this is properly done, it is difficult for a party or attorney to turn his back on you and walk away. They will walk the extra mile and generally get the matter settled.

Building rapport and trust can be done in several ways. First, the mediator can inquire about family, schools, sports teams and hobbies, anything that will create a bond. Second, rapport and trust can be established by giving the parties an opportunity to vent, tell their story to someone who will listen. Many times they have not had this opportunity and a responsive mediator can provide it. Third, the mediator can show interest and concern by identifying hidden agendas or special needs of the parties. Many times parties are not even aware that these needs can be addressed and included in the settlement.

This chapter discusses the ways rapport and trust can be established.

A. Inquiring About Family and Interests

Mediation #29

Chicago White Sox Come Alive

Teddy McFarland was sexually abused as an altar boy by a cleric at his church. At the mediation he said nothing, sitting with his arms folded and looking down. When I spoke to him, he would not look at me. Frankly, I was becoming frustrated especially when his lawyer was asking considerably more than the case was worth. Finally, I said to Teddy, "Teddy, what do you do in your spare time?"

Teddy answered, "I work at White Sox Park in the evenings. I work in the score board at the end of the field that shows the innings and scores.

"White Sox Park!" I exclaimed, "I have been a White Sox fan since they were in the World Series in 1959. I can name every player on the team – Al Smith, Jim Landis, Jungle Jim Riveria, Nellie Fox, Luis Aparichoo, Billy Pierce, Sherm Lollar . . ."

Teddy's face lit up and with enthusiasm we talked about the White Sox chances of making it to the World Series for the first time since 1959. We talked for 30 minutes, no longer really interested in the mediation.

Teddy asked, "I can get you some tickets if you would like to go to a ball game."

"That would be wonderful," I responded. "Let me look at my schedule and we can set a date. I would like to go on one of the upcoming dates with the Cleveland Indians."

At that point, the mediation was almost an afterthought and the case quickly settled for a fair price. We had bonded.

B. Opportunity to Vent

Mediation #30

Getting To The Heart of the Matter

John Feldon, from all appearances, was a successful business executive, vice president of one of the major car manufacturers. He lived in an affluent suburb of Detroit, belonged to the country club, drove a limousine, and married a woman who was a prominent member of society. He had it all. However, there was a dark secret which affected his married life and his feelings of self-worth, something he told no one. He had been sexually abused as an altar boy when he was in the sixth and seventh grades at a parochial school.

When other victims finally came forward and commenced legal action against the church, John finally spoke of the matter to his wife. She insisted he get professional counseling, which he did. He was advised to join the legal action, which the therapist felt would help the healing process. John contacted a private attorney, who was handling such cases. He was advised that a first step in the process was to participate in mediation. John agreed.

John was invited to attend the opening session of the mediation in which he was to be given an opportunity to tell his story to the bishop, an opportunity to vent.

John flew from Detroit to Chicago for the session. He appeared at the mediation site in a coat and tie and looked quite professional. His attorney, Tom Oliver, briefed him as to what was going to occur. They entered the room together. Sitting at the table were the current bishop, two attorneys, and myself as mediator. I welcomed John and explained, "I want to give you an opportunity to say whatever you wish. The bishop is here to listen and not comment. You can take as long as you like."

John looked at some notes and then raised his eyes looking at the bishop. He began speaking slowly: "I was raised a good Catholic and taught to respect the priesthood. My eight brothers and sisters are all good people, intelligent, successful, all with families of their own. I started out as a workman in an auto plant, rose to foreman and then management. I will admit I have been quite successful in life, marrying into a wealthy society family, which was beyond my wildest expectations."

John then stopped. He choked and seemed embarrassed. He tried again.

"I want you to know how the abuse has affected my life. I have fought depression most of my adult life. To block out the depression I began drinking heavily." Then he stopped and began to weep, "my dear wife has had to endure hell at times. I have been aloof, indifferent and angry, not at her, but at the church, which she could not understand. And my two daughters, "now he was sobbing, "have not received the love they deserved from their father."

He stopped again and asked for a drink of water.

I said, "let's take a break. Get a breath of fresh air, John, and then we can resume."

Thirty-five minutes later John came back into the room. He was composed as he sat down. He looked at me and I nodded he should continue.

He stared at the bishop for a long moment. Then he said, "do you want to know how angry I still am at you and your church?" Before the bishop could answer, he added, "I will tell you."

He reached for his briefcase and pulled out an 18 inch plastic tube. Then he pulled out a smaller 6 inch tube and attached it to one end of the longer tube. He then took tape off the other end of the larger tube and he was holding a dagger, which he pointed at the bishop. "This is how angry I am," he shouted.

He was too far from the bishop to attack him, but we were ready to restrain him just in case. To say the least, we were shocked by this display of anger and frustration; however, we continued with the mediation and got the matter resolved. I also convinced John to surrender the weapon. Had he been caught with it on an airplane, he would have been charged with a felony. Later in the afternoon he caught a plane back to Detroit.

Two days later his wife called John's attorney and told him how the mediation session had helped. "We're not out of the woods yet, but there has been real progress," she said. "He definitely is showing more warmth towards me and our daughters. I'm hopeful. Thank you for your help."

Mediation #31

Don't Alienate the Affections

Most states used to have a claim for alienation of affection. If a person seduces another's spouse to break the marriage covenant, the victim can sue the third party for damages. Because the claim was so difficult to prove and so destructive to the family relationship, the claim has been repealed in all states except South Dakota.

Chris Pearson was 43 years old and knew his marriage of 20 years was in trouble. His wife, Ginger, was indifferent towards him and they were arguing over the smallest things. He did not touch her, but he had to confess he was verbally abusing her, and this was not good, especially in front of their 16-year-old daughter, Madison.

One day, Chris got the shock of his life. Ginger was having an affair with a family Friend, Todd Hamilton, who also lived in Sioux Falls. Chris and Todd had been close friends since they played football together in high school.

Chris exploded and went over to Todd's house with the intent to do him bodily harm. Fortunately, Todd was not home, but his wife, Megan, was. She also was unaware of the affair and went into shock. Chris went home and decided he would sue for alienation of affection and expose Todd to the community. He would have his vengeance in the newspapers.

Before the case was filed, Chris's attorney, Joseph Riordan, convinced him to mediate the matter. He agreed; however, one week before the mediation, he cancelled, saying he wanted to go to trial. Counsel finally convinced him to at least try the process, so the mediation was rescheduled.

At the mediation, I was introduced to the participants. Chris was a rather large man and still looked the football player he once was. He towered over Todd Hamilton, who was slim and hardly looked the role of a paramour. Todd's attorney, Fred Melton, was a well-respected trial attorney in Sioux Falls, South Dakota with whom I had worked before. He was a no nonsense attorney and practical, and one who I believe would be constructive in finding resolution to this difficult matter. I didn't know Chris's attorney except that I could see he was young, and I presumed inexperienced in matters of the heart.

I made my opening remarks and the attorneys waved opening statements because of the delicacy and volatility of the subject matter. In the first caucus with Chris, he broke down and wept. He proclaimed his love for Ginger and explained that he opposed divorce, which was pending at the time. As the caucus progressed, I learned the following: first, Chris stated under oath in his deposition that Ginger was just as much at fault as Todd, that it was 50/50. Under the law of South Dakota, this pleaded him out of court, because the paramour must be more than 50 percent at fault. His case would be dismissed.

Second, he recognized his wife would testify that she pursued Todd and initiated the tryst. Again, to have a claim against the paramour, the latter must have initiated the relationship which broke up the marriage.

Third, if the case ever got to the jury, he would lose every Catholic, particularly women. When he and Ginger were seniors in high school, he got her pregnant and insisted she have an abortion. Without the consent of her parents, she went to Omaha and the abortion was performed.

Fourth, if Ginger continued with the divorce proceedings, he was prepared to show that she had been unfaithful during their marriage. On one occasion, she and four female friends took a girls' weekend in Phoenix, Arizona. They hooked up with some salesmen attending a convention and slept with them. This exposé could jeopardize the marriages of Ginger's friends. Of course, most of this was irrelevant but this would not stop Chris from putting it in the complaint, which the local newspapers were sure to pick up.

The bottom line was Chris did not care what happened in the lawsuit. He just wanted revenge and to punish Ginger, Todd, and their friends. He demanded $300,000 to settle the matter and would not agree to confidentiality. Todd simply did not have that kind of money, although he was able to pay something.

After five hours mediating, we were getting nowhere. Finally, it occurred to me that Chris's daughter, Madison, was a junior in high school and attended the same high school as Todd's daughter, Martha, who was a sophomore. I said to Chris, "have you ever weighed the consequences to Madison if you pursue your claim? Classmates will be merciless in teasing and laughing at her. The same thing is true of Todd's daughter."

Chris went silent. After long pause, he said, "I did not think about that."

We took a 30 minute break, during which time Chris went outside to get a breath of air. When he returned, he looked different, like a load of bricks had been lifted off his shoulders. He said, "last thing I want to do is hurt Madison. She is innocent in all this, and I can see what a lawsuit would do. I will settle the matter, but I ask two things: I want a chance to meet alone with Todd, and I need to be paid something in recognition of the wrong done."

I left the room very pleased. Todd and counsel were waiting. "Todd," I said, "I made great progress in the other room. It came after I pointed out that filing this lawsuit would make the whole matter a public spectacle, hurting both families. The persons to be injured the most would be Chris's and your daughters. Both would suffer great humiliation at high school. Girls at this age can be quite cruel."

"I agree," said Todd. Then he continued, "how can we get this matter resolved?"

"Chris will settle with two conditions: one, he is given the opportunity to meet alone with you, and, two, you pay him something in recognition of the wrong done."

Todd said, "the first condition is easy. How much does he want? I very much want to get this matter resolved."

I answered, "I do not know. What would you pay?"

Todd responded, "could you get him to accept $10,000?"

"That is a fair figure. I will do all I can to get him to accept it." I then met with Chris.

"Chris," I began, "we're making excellent progress; we are going to get the matter resolved. The only issue is how much must Todd pay to end this. He has agreed to meet with you."

I hesitated to allow what I said to sink in. Then I continued, "if I could get Todd to pay $10,000 would you feel he recognized the wrong he has done?"

Chris thought a moment and then responded with a simple, "yes." The matter was resolved except for the meeting. I had the papers signed first and then invited Chris and Todd into the conference room without the attorneys. I was prepared to interject myself only to avoid violence.

At first the two just stood there. Chris tried to speak, but choked up. He tried again. "Todd, I want you to know I love Ginger very much, and I'm so sorry this terrible mess occurred. However, Ginger loves you and I must accept this as much as it hurts."

Chris lowered his eyes. There were tears. "Todd," he continued, "I know you're getting divorced, and I only hope you intend to marry Ginger. Please promise me, if you do not intend to marry her, tell her now because I don't know what she might do to herself physically if you string her along."

Todd said nothing, weighing the enormity of Chris's request. There was a lull. Todd finally said, "I hear what you are saying. Thank you for your concern. Ginger is a beautiful and delicate person, I know that."

The two spoke for 15 more minutes. Chris then went over to Todd and gave him a bear hug, which Todd reciprocated. Both had tears in their eyes. The matter was resolved. Both found relief in venting.

C. Hidden Agendas

Mediation #32

Keep Your Eyes Open and Mind Alert

Probably my most important, yet smallest mediation, was venued in Rochester, Minnesota. I was informed that it was rather small and not worth traveling the 185 miles to Rochester to mediate. Still I agreed to do so because I enjoyed getting out on the highway and enjoying a nice fall ride through Iowa and Minnesota farmland.

When I received the papers, I realized it was indeed a small case, a "fender bender" as we say in the profession, only worth $8000-$15,000. I arrived at about 9:30 AM for the 10 AM mediation. Tony Stewart, plaintiff's counsel, welcomed me into his office and introduced me to the plaintiff, Keda Mombac, an African woman, who was obviously pregnant. Tony pulled me aside and said, "Keda was very shy and will be difficult to talk to. For that reason she probably will not fair very well in front of a jury, although she is a delightful person when you get to know her. I want to get the case settled," he added.

I learned that Keda was born on an island off the west African coast, previously a British colony. She was taught never to look a man in the eyes, always keep your head down, and speak only if spoken to. She had been injured when a car turned in front of her and she ran into it causing physical damage to the vehicles and soft tissue injuries to herself. Although pregnant, there were no complications.

Keda worked at Mayo Clinic as a cleaning person. She was not married and had a six-year-old son. At the time of the mediation she was off work because of complications in her pregnancy unrelated to the accident. Her attorney made a demand of $20,000 and the insurance carrier offered $5000. The insurance adjuster, Ted Middleton, was a long-time adjuster and had done hundreds of mediations. He took pride in being tough and rigid in his negotiations.

In the first caucus with Middleton, he announced that he would pay $10,000 and no more. By noon this was offered and Stewart lowered plaintiff's demand to $15,000. I then suggested we settle for $13,000. Plaintiff accepted but Middleton would not budge. Because the lunch hour had arrived, I suggested we take a break to get a sandwich. All agreed and started leaving the office.

Keda just sat there saying nothing. As the others walked out the door, I said, "Keda, please get a bite to eat." Still she said nothing. I finally determined she had no money. With difficultly I learned that she did not have money to buy food for herself and her little boy that evening or, for that matter, the rest of the week until she could get food stamps on Friday. However, she was not complaining. I also learned that she was three months behind in her mortgage payments on her little house and this was bothering her.

"Keda," I said, "here is $20. I want you to go next door and get a sandwich. You need to take a break. When everyone gets back from lunch, we will continue and we'll get the case settled."

She accepted my $20, but said nothing and left the office. I then went across the street to a hotel restaurant. After eating, I went to the washroom. I was very deep in thought.

In entering the washroom, I noticed the colors were pink and light green with flowers, which I thought was odd for a men's room. On entering a stall I suddenly realized there were no urinals along the wall. I panicked questioning where I was. Then I heard click, click of another person who entered the stall next to me. There was a little noise which confirmed my worst fears. I pulled in my feet to avoid any possible

detection.

The next five minutes where the worst of my life. I started

sweating profusely not knowing what to do. How could I possibly explain

to the police such a stupid mistake? I waited till I thought the coast was

clear and dashed for the door, opened it, and darted into the men's room.

No one saw me and I began to relax. I asked myself, how could I have

possibly made such a mistake. Then, knowing me, it was easy to fathom.

I had become so engrossed in the mediation that everything around me

became obscure and irrelevant.

Returning to Stewart's office I met alone with the adjuster Ted

Middleton. "Ted," I said, "Keda has to settle. She has to accept your

$10,000 because she has no money, not even for food tonight for herself

and her little boy. In fact she has no money for food until Friday when she

can get some stamps to purchase the necessities she needs. However,

you have a priceless opportunity to help someone in dire need, who is

truly worthy of help. She's an honorable person who does not complain,

and is not asking for a handout. Just a person living in a foreign land,

alone, as a single mom.

"If you would pay the $13,000, this would make a major difference in Keda's life. She would have enough to feed herself and son until she can go back to work. And she could bring her mortgage up to date."

I stopped and looked intently at Middleton. I could see he was listening and now weighing my words. However, he said nothing. Then I added, "don't let this golden opportunity slip by, for an adjuster rarely has an opportunity to really touch a person's life and make a profound difference."

At this point, Middleton looked at me with a pained expression and said, "don't do that to me. Alright, I'll pay the $13,000 and write out a check immediately."

The transaction was completed and an important matter resolved. The case illustrates how a hidden agenda uncovered became the basis for a successful mediation.

Mediation #33

The Sudden Acceleration of a Vehicle Was a figment of the Beholder's Imagination

Mike Gallagher was one of the top trial lawyers in Iowa and the Midwest. He asked me to mediate a difficult case involving a 1991

Chrysler Jeep which slammed into a car filled with eight Vietnamese immigrants, killing two, and injuring several others.

The owner of the Jeep had taken it to a Jiffy Lube shop to have the oil changed. After the work was completed, the worker asked if he wanted his air filter changed because it was dirty. When the owner answered in the negative, the worker got into the Jeep and started driving it out of the shop. Without warning it suddenly accelerated and drove into the street striking the plaintiffs' vehicle.

The insurance company insuring Jiffy Lube wanted to get the matter settled; however, Chrysler Corporation would only offer $100,000, claiming that it was not at fault. It contended there was no such thing as "sudden acceleration," that the worker had put his foot on the accelerator rather than on the brake.

Mike and Jiffy Lube's insurance carrier became quite frustrated with Chrysler because there were 84 similar cases filed throughout the nation against Chrysler. And some had actual video tapes of Jeeps suddenly accelerating and crashing.

To counter Chrysler's position, the insurance carrier spent a significant amount of money in engineering costs proving the viability of the sudden acceleration syndrome. Still, Chrysler would not raise its offer above $100,000.

At the mediation I decided to take a different approach, something Chrysler may not have thought of – the hidden agenda. I asked Mike to list the last 10 cases where he recovered more than $1 million. My intent here was to impress Chrysler with how good a trial lawyer Mike was. Then I wrote Chrysler a memo that explained several things: First, there were 84 pending cases raising the same issue, and plaintiffs' attorneys in those cases were communicating with each other.

Second, Mike's case was scheduled to be tried first and the courtroom was in Des Moines, Iowa, Mike's backyard. Lawyers from New York City might not fare so well. I listed his million-dollar plus successes so Chrysler would know that he was not a farm boy in the courtroom.

Third, Chrysler was up against not only Mike Galligan, but also Jiffy Lube's insurance carrier, whose defense was there is a sudden acceleration problem and Chrysler is responsible. And it was prepared to call its engineering experts.

Fourth, if Mike won and established that there was a phenomenon called sudden acceleration in the Chrysler 1991 Jeeps, Chrysler was foreclosed from trying the issue a second time. In other words, all the other 83 cases could rely on this first determination and the issue of a defect in the Jeep was established. All they had to do was try the issue of damages. This is called, in legal terms, issue preclusion or collateral estoppel. I asked Chrysler if it wanted to risk having Mike try the case with the insurance carrier supporting his position.

Chrysler got the message and settled, putting a substantial amount of money on the table to resolve the controversy. Here, the hidden agenda moving Chrysler was the skill and success of Mike Galligan and the effect a first trial of the matter would have on all subsequent cases. Chrysler did not want to roll the dice.

Mediation #34

Even Attorneys Have Hidden Agendas

The following case was mediated in Kansas City, Kansas, about a 3 hour drive from Des Moines. It involved an African-American boy, Devon Anderson, who was out for football at a local high school. He was a big boy, 6'5" tall and 250 lbs. It was pre-season in August and the weather was hot and humid. Suddenly, he collapsed on the football field. When he did not revive, he was rushed to a local hospital. It was then determined that he had a bad heart and would have to have a heart transplant. He was then moved to another hospital, which was a heart transplant center. He was hooked up to a thoracic pumping machine.

While waiting for a transplant to become available, he was hooked up to a

second machine when the hospital began having difficulties with the first.

During the connecting process, the nurse got the wires crossed, hooking a

blue line with the red line and the young man was dead in two hours.

The young man's mother, Jasmine Anderson, represented the

estate. She was raising seven children as a single mom. She worked

earning $2000 per month; however, she was barely able to make ends

meet. They lived in the worst area of the city.

During the course of the mediation, Jasmine's attorney, Jud

Friedman, demanded $2 million and the hospital offered $400,000.

As the mediator, I looked for hidden agendas, which would give

me some leverage to get the matter resolved. I quickly learned what the

hospital's was. First, the hospital was attempting to build a reputation as

the leading heart transplant hospital in the region. The filing of a lawsuit

would damage its reputation. Second, the hospital was under

investigation for criminal negligence, which it felt would be dismissed if

the matter was settled in civil court. Therefore, the hospital pushed its

insurance company to offer $1 million. The carrier made this offer in confidence, stating it was only offered if I, as mediator, knew the plaintiff would accept.

Meeting with Jasmine and her attorney, it was more difficult uncovering the hidden agenda. I inquired, "Jasmine, how many children do you have?"

She responded, "I have 6 children in addition to Devon."

I asked, "are any of the others out for sports?"

She responded, "Oh yes. Donald and Jesse are out for basketball. Donald is 16 and Jess 14."

I turned to Jasmine's attorney, Jud Friedman, and asked, "how long will it take to take this case through trial and possible appeal?"

He responded, "four to five years. The trial docket here is backed up with criminal cases, mostly drug related, which must be tried before civil cases."

I then turned back to Jasmine and asked, "how are the children doing in school?"

She responded, "they are doing alright. I would like to see them challenged more because I want them to go on to college."

Suddenly, I saw Jasmine's hidden agenda. I wondered if she had identified it yet? She needed to settle now and not in 4 or 5 years so she could move the children to a better school district where they would be better prepared for college. To allow the case go through the courts, at least 3 would be denied a better education. I wondered if I should point this out. Then I learned what Jasmine's attorney's hidden agenda was, and I realized they were quite aware of the school question.

Attorney Jud Friedman said to me, almost casually, that "we have already picked out a house in my son's school district," (which was the best in the city). Upon further inquiry, he explained, "son number 2, Donald, is an excellent basketball player and we want him on my son's team. With him they will win the city championship and possibly the state title."

Jud hesitated, and then added, "Jesse is even better and will be a high school freshman next fall. He has the touch of a 'Chris Webber.'" (Chris Webber was a professional basketball player out of Michigan who had a very soft touch when he shot the basketball.) As he said this, he held his right hand up as though he was making a basketball shot. So even the attorney had a hidden agenda.

With the hidden agendas uncovered, the case quickly settled for $1 million and Jasmine's family moved.

CHAPTER 6

EARLY LESSONS LEARNED

Over the years as a mediator, I have learned many lessons. For example, do not ask lawyers what they will settle for, for they rarely give you an honest answer in the hope they can do better. Also, invariably, the "final figure" is not enough to settle the case. There will have to be further movement to resolve the matter. Therefore a mediator cannot accept the statement of counsel that there is no further room for movement. Lawyers are always saying this and even begin packing their bags. This is a tour de force and cannot be taken seriously. There is always room to move.

A second lesson I learned is do not put the attorney and his or her client on the defensive. Many ex judges , who become mediators, feel they still wear their judicial robes and can dictate to the parties for what they should settle. They often play devil's advocate. In doing this, the attorney will respond defensively and defend his or her position, thereby having a stronger commitment not to move, feeling that movement is a sign of weakness and uncertainty. The mediator can only build rapport by being supportive and work with, not against, each side.

Another important lesson I learned is not to mediate unless the decision-makers, particularly plaintiffs, are attending. When the mediator arrives at a mediation and is informed that the plaintiff is not attending but is available by telephone, it means one of three things: one, the plaintiff will not present well and counsel does not want the mediator to know this; two, plaintiff and counsel do not get along and the latter feels he or she will have better control without the plaintiff present ; and, three, counsel is concerned that the mediator will push the plaintiff to settle for less than what counsel feels the case is worth at trial. However, it is difficult to mediate over the telephone. You cannot build the rapport and trust you need to get compromise.

A final lesson is be cautious supporting the lawyer when the client is not listening to his advice. So many times, the client has inflated expectations for what the case should settle. The temptation for the mediator is to jump in on the side of counsel to help explain his reasoning. This has the effect of isolating the client and making her feel that counsel and the mediator are "ganging up" on her.

The following several case studies illustrate the lessons I learned.

Mediation #35

Do You Trust Your Anesthesiologist?

Peggy Meyer was over nine months pregnant and her doctor decided to perform a cesarean section. Peggy had taken time off her two jobs – a beautician during the day and cocktail waitress in the evenings at a local bar in the riverfront town of Keokuk Iowa. She had to work both jobs to make ends meet, and loss of income the past few weeks weighed heavily on her mind. Her husband, Jim, partially disabled by a car accident two years before, felt he could not work. He took care of the two-room bungalow, located on the outskirts of Keokuk as well as warm a barstool at a nearby tavern.

As Peggy rested in the waiting room before the operation she realized that adding another mouth was going to strain their already meager income even more. And she thought of her husband, Jim, and became angry. He would not even try to go to work because of his soft tissue back injury. He rarely worked before the accident, so what else was new?

"Are you ready, Mrs. Meyer?" A friendly nurse inquired. Peggy said nothing but turned her head to the wall. "Dr. Panjab is your anesthesiologist, and you know your doctor, of course."

Peggy was wheeled into the operating room and Dr. Panjab went to work. Peggy became unconscious and the cesarean section performed, and a beautiful healthy little girl was born. Peggy , however, never regained consciousness and died.

Six months later a lawsuit was filed by Peggy's husband on behalf of her estate, on his own behalf and the baby, Nikki, against Dr. Panjab, alleging that he improperly ventilated Peggy resulting in cardiac arrest and her death.

Michael O'Malley, plaintiff's attorney, sat comfortably behind his desk as I walked into his room prior to the mediation. He smiled but said nothing.

"Good morning, Mike," I said, "I appreciate your giving mediation a try."

Mike looked at me intently and then said, "this is the kind of case I like to try. A foreign trained doctor, with a foreign name, who speaks with a decided accent who killed the decedent through an act of wanton negligence: a malpractice death case at its best."

"Mike, I thought you were going to mediate the case, not try it. By the way, is the plaintiff here?"

Mike had a self-satisfied smirk on his face showing that he had absolute confidence in his case and what he could do in front of a jury.

Mike was an excellent trial lawyer who lost few cases. He did make one major mistake of judgment when he took on some 500 asbestos cases and almost went bankrupt prosecuting them. Because the asbestos industry went bankrupt it was almost impossible to collect a money judgment after a successful prosecution. For example, he won a multimillion-dollar verdict after a difficult trial, but collected not one penny from the bankrupt defendants. With costs and expenses mounting each week his firm almost did not survive. This was typical of many plaintiff firms throughout the nation, which got involved in some thousand or more asbestos cases.

Mike looked at me and said, "the plaintiff will not be here, but I can reach him in Arkansas by telephone. However, I have full authority to settle this case, but I'm rather confident they will not give me the $1 million I am demanding."

I did not realize it then, but I quickly learned, never go into mediation without the plaintiff and the insurance adjuster, who makes the decisions, present. Much of what occurs in mediation is for the benefit of the parties, who will decide whether to settle or not. Having them a telephone call away means they will not observe opposing counsel and hear his or her opening remarks, nor hear their own attorney discuss the weaknesses of the case, and what a jury might do. Likewise, the mediator cannot communicate directly with the party and use the art of persuasion to gain compromise. Whatever the mediator says or does will be filtered by counsel so that the party will only hear what counsel desires.

During the opening remarks Mike described in considerable detail how Dr. Panjab's negligence killed Peggy; it sounded bad. Mike kept emphasizing that the jury is not going to like the doctor because he is arrogant and speaks with the decided accent. Further, he got his medical training on the island of Granada in the Caribbean and failed his medical boards first time. It was clear what kind of an appeal Mike was going to make and frankly it gave defense counsel concern. When Mike mentioned the name of his expert witness, a member of the medical faculty of University of Iowa, this gave the defense even greater concern.

Phil Durkin, defense counsel, did not make a detailed response because plaintiff was not present. He merely said they would do all they could to get the matter resolved.

During the first caucus with Mike, I asked him what the weaknesses in his case were. He looked me square in the eyes and said, "there are none." He added, "I will nail the doctor and recover over $1 million. You must remember, Dr. Panjab lied under oath during his deposition – did I mention that to you?"

I indicated he had not, so he explained: "the doctor had put the incorrect blood pressure on the medical chart and when questioned about it tried to cover it up. When I prove he lied, the jury will give me even more."

I was getting concerned about the mediation because Mike was not showing any signs of compromising – he just kept telling me how good his case was and how much the jury would give him. He instructed me to tell defense counsel that the last three medical malpractice cases he tried came in at $750,000 to $1.5 million, and that was without the 10 percent prejudgment interest from date of filing which must be added.

"Mike, I need a demand to take to the defendant to show that we want to settle his case. I don't want your best figure, I just want an amount that will keep them at the table and give me a chance to do my job."

Mike looked out the window and then at me, and said, "look, I offered to settle this case for policy limits of $1.25 million and they never responded. I think they must make the first offer. I am simply not going to bid against myself."

"I thought they made an offer of $250,000," I responded.

Mike's Irish face became slightly flushed and then he said: "I consider that offer an insult and not worthy of a response. If they're going to play that kind of game, this mediation is at an end."

"Please, Mike, give me a chance – we have just started the mediation. I was hoping you would give me a new figure just to help us get started."

Mike looked at me intently, and then started to smile. "No offense, Richard. I'll tell you what I will do. I will drop my offer to $1 million, but I don't have much room to move – I hope you understand that."

"Thank you, Mike. That's a good start, but please don't dig your feet in until I've had a chance to do my work."

I left Mike's office and went to the conference room where the insurance adjuster and defense attorney, Phil Durkin, were waiting. As we discussed the strengths and weaknesses of the case I quickly realized that they had little to say on the issue of liability, but intended to defend the case on the amount of damages to be awarded. What would Peggy have accumulated over a lifetime, and what was the value of the loss of her mother to baby Nikki, and the loss of consortium or companionship to Jim?

In discussing what a jury might do, it was clear that emotion and sympathy would play a big part in the case. Durkin was concerned because, as he put it, the verdict would be a big one, but he could not say how big – perhaps $700,000. Durkin then said, "we have one piece of evidence we do not want you to disclose to Mike at this time, and that is Jim is dating a woman in Arkansas and is going to marry her as soon as this case is over. As a matter of fact, she has already moved in with him and the child, and I question how that will be received by an Iowa jury." (This was 1989.)

"Why don't you want me to disclose this to Mike; it might help me in negotiating with him, for he sees no weaknesses in his case." After further discussion it was decided that I had discretion to use this information if I thought it would help.

"Mike has reduced his demand to $1 million, and I am reasonably certain he will come down further. How much I do not know. I need a new offer from you."

The adjuster, who had been silent during the caucus, answered, "we will go to $350,000."

I took the new offer to Mike who only laughed. "I told you they were not serious. I dropped $250,000 and they raised their offer only $100,000. I just don't just don't see how we are going to get anywhere."

"Mike, they will come up more; this is just the first round." We discussed the case further and Mike finally agreed to drop his demand to $900,000, but that was about as far as he would go. I took the new demand to the defense and they agreed to raise their offer to $450,000.

After taking some notes, I asked the adjuster: "Would you feel uncomfortable giving me your top dollar? I will keep this absolutely confidential, but it will give me a chance to determine if we have a chance to settle. Right now the parties are so far apart, I don't know if we have any chance whatever. I will ask Mike the same question and then I can determine if we should continue."

I was asked to leave the room while the adjuster and counsel conferred.

When I was invited back, Durkin said: "We will give you our top dollar, but this is to be kept confidential. We will go to $600,000 with a structured settlement. With the structure it will give Jim $35,000 per year for 15 years and then it will go up to $40,000 per year for the rest of his life. It will also provide a college education for Nikki, or, if she doesn't want to go to college, cash will be available to her when she reaches 21 years of age. Please understand that this is three times more income than Jim ever saw in a year and it's tax free."

I took down notes and then added: "this sounds like a good settlement figure. I have to return with an official offer, however. May I give $500,000?" This was agreed upon and I went back to Mike's office.

"Mike, because the parties are so far apart, I asked the insurance company in confidence, where they are willing to go in order to help me determine if we have a chance. I need to get your best figure and then I will see what the spread is. Rest assured I will keep it confidential."

Mike hesitated only a moment, and then said, "my bottom figure is $800,000. I will go no lower."

"Mike, I hope you're not digging in now because I need more compromise if we are to settle. The insurance company is going to give Jim and Nikki an annuity which provides yearly income many times more than Jim and Peggy ever earned."

"But, Richard, this little baby will never have her real mother to care and comfort her like only a mother can do. Don't you think that is worth more money than the insurance company is offering?"

"That assumes, Mike, that Jim does not have a female friend that could step in and become a mother to Nikki. What if such a person is already with Jim and the child?"

Mike didn't blink an eye and said, "the defendant will never get in such evidence, but if they do, it will have little impact on a jury. No, my final figure is $800,000, and you can give that figure."

"If the defendant increases its offer substantially providing excellent security for Jim and the child, would that not be worth something?"

"Richard, read my lips. My bottom figure is $800,000.

I thanked Mike, and returned to the conference room. "Mike has authorized me to give his final figure and it is $800,000. He will not go any lower. I think he's making a mistake, but is the best I can do. I'm sorry."

The adjuster then said, "we can't go that high. We think that we have made a fair offer."

"Let me talk to Mike once more. In fact, I will take him to lunch to see if I can get any further movement. May I give him your $600,000?" They consented and I met Mike for lunch, but he would not alter his position and the mediation failed.

Mike O'Malley ultimately tried the case and received a jury verdict of $655,000, which greatly disappointed him. However, with the prejudgment interest the judgment entered was over $700,000. However, not being structured, his income per year was less than what he would have received from the settlement offer. This assumed he invested the entire amount after attorney fees and costs were deducted.

There is, however, an important caveat to this case. Within two years of receiving his money, Jim and his girlfriend had spent every penny on trips to Paris, the purchase of two new cars and gambling at a local casino. Had he participated in the mediation, he might well have accepted the carrier's settlement offer, which included a structured annuity which would have paid him $30,000-$40,000 per year for life, tax-free. It would also have provided income for his daughter when she reached age 18. Because this is not what counsel wanted the proposal was never conveyed.

This leads me to a second mediation where plaintiff was not asked by counsel to attend.

Mediation #36

Look Out For Lawyers Who Are Cowboys

I was asked to mediate a matter in Duluth, Minnesota. It involved a secretary who worked in insurance office. As happens, the sales agents and female secretaries started telling dirty jokes, posting lewd photographs and exchanging sexually explicit gadgets as Christmas gifts. Plaintiff became upset with this inappropriate conduct and complained to management, but nothing was done. Once the other others realized she was uncomfortable with their conduct they turned on her and made her the brunt of their antics. She finally could take it no longer and quit her job and retained a lawyer to pursue legal action.

I boarded a plane at 6:30 PM at the Des Moines International Airport. I often wondered why they call it "international" inasmuch as none of the planes fly further than Chicago, Minneapolis, St. Louis or Denver, where one has to transfer to fly further. Maybe it just sounds more important.

We sat for 30 minutes and finally we're directed to leave the plane as it was too foggy to fly out that evening. In fact, it was worse in Minneapolis, our destination. I returned home with the intent of catching the same flight the next morning.

The next morning the plane left on time, although it was still foggy, and arrived in Minneapolis on time. I ultimately arrived at the

Duluth airport at 10:00 AM and took a cab to downtown to Duluth only one half hour late for the mediation.

The area is fairly flat from the airport to the edge of Duluth. There, the road suddenly descends several hundred feet into the center of the city. Looking back, the city is framed by a high ridge against Lake Superior. Although the day was January 17, 1990, it was not bitterly cold as I anticipated, being so far north. It was, however, cloudy and trying to snow. If it did snow, I wondered if I would be able to get back to the airport because vehicles had difficulty negotiating the steep incline when covered with ice and snow.

Exiting the cab, I entered the building where defense counsel officed, and took the elevator to the 10th floor. There I was directed to the conference room where I met Raymond Erickson and a representative of Eastern Insurance Company, Dominic Fielding. Five minutes later, plaintiff's attorney, Phil Deeter, entered the room and we were introduced. He was alone, and when I inquired where the plaintiff was he responded that she was at home, but could be reached by telephone.

"Phil, it's very difficult to mediate a case without the plaintiff present," I said.

Phil responded: "That's alright, I have full authority to settle the case. In any event plaintiff is available by telephone."

"How long would it take to get the plaintiff here? I hope that you will trust me that we need her at the mediation."

"It will take her over 45 minutes to get here," insisted Phil.

"That is alright, Phil, we can wait." When Phil realized that I was not going to proceed without the plaintiff, he got on the phone and called her. Fifteen minutes later she walked into the conference room.

Joyce Helton was rather thin, 5'4" tall with long brown hair. She was not terribly attractive but did have a kind and gentle look. Her husband, David, followed her into the room. He looked very much the blue-collar laborer he was. His greatest joy was watching the Vikings play football at a local tavern with a beer in his hand. I introduced myself and they barely acknowledged me. When everyone was seated, I gave my introduction and asked Phil to give his opening statement.

Phil said, with some annoyance, "I didn't know we were to give opening statements. Give me a moment so that I can pull things together."

It was evident to me that Phil Deeter had not reviewed the case, but intended to "wing it" at the mediation. After all, this was just one of so many cases he had, and as a single practitioner could not devote too much time to any one case until he had to prepare for trial.

"Alright, I have my notes together. Joyce has five children by a prior marriage, ages 15 through 25. She did not graduate from high school but did receive her GED at Duluth Technical Institute. Throughout the years she has been a homemaker, a cocktail waitress, and a cashier. She moved to Duluth in 1980 from Chicago with her prior husband, who was stationed at the Duluth airbase.

"Her first full-time employment was with Bill Hand and Brad Townsend, both of Eastern Insurance Company, as a secretary in their local office here in Duluth. Later, Cotton Trevino joined the office as a salesman. Joyce was hired through a Minnesota program whereby disadvantaged persons are trained and then given a job opportunity. The individual is, in part, paid by the state as well as by the employer for a fixed period of time. This job, therefore, meant a great deal to Joyce and she was determined to make good."

Deeter hesitated a moment realizing that he really wasn't getting to the substance of the mediation. "Our claims of sexual harassment are that Bill Hand, her boss, and salesman Brad Townsend and Cotton Trevino repeatedly told dirty jokes in her presence. This was unacceptable and she asked them to stop. Her husband called the office and told Bill that if this didn't stop he was going to call the home office.

"Well, it didn't stop and it got worse. Although other women in the office thought the jokes were cute, Joyce did not and continued to complain. The dirty jokes led to pornographic pictures and the exchange of sexually explicit gadgets between the two salesmen and other secretaries. After six months of this, Joyce was forced to resign from her position and seek other employment. She has been looking for a year and a half without success. She has had to see a psychiatrist and have therapy because she cannot sleep at night. She is depressed and is entitled to recover for mental distress as well as lost wages."

Deeter stopped and looked at me. Then he said, "we are demanding $150,000 and if this is not agreed to immediately we are terminating the mediation."

Ignoring Deeter's last comment, I turned to Ray Erickson and asked for his opening statement. He stated: "We do not feel there is any liability whatever. Joyce quit her job voluntarily not because of anything the men in the office were doing. Oh yes, there was joking around, but Joyce was a willing participant and even told a few dirty jokes herself."

"That's not true," interrupted Deeter. He was angry and ready to argue his point.

"Please, Phil, let Ray continue, and then you can respond," I said.

Ray looked at me, obviously annoyed with the interruption. He continued: "Joyce even brought cucumbers to the office and made comments, comparing them to Cotton's anatomy. I don't need to go into any details except to say Joyce was a willing participant in the sex discussions.

"The real reason Joyce left the office was because the office was moved to the west side of town, which was 30 minutes from her house. Because she did not have a car she would have to take public transportation and that she did not want to do. The bottom line is that there was no sexual harassment – no one touched her or made obscene gestures."

Ray stopped, and before Phil could respond, I suggested we go to caucus where Joyce could explain her side of the story.

Ray and the adjuster left the room and the instant door shut Joyce blurted out, "I did not invite their disgusting sexual comments. Everything that lawyer is saying is untrue. I was disgusted and ashamed and could not take their antics any longer. I will admit I laughed at first but that was because I wanted to keep my job, and I was afraid if I looked offended I would merely attract more attention."

After Joyce calmed down I turned to Ray and asked him to discuss the strengths of his case. He looked over his notes and began explaining his case to me. But the more he spoke, the more I realized that he was not prepared. He was even asserting a claim which was already barred by the applicable statute of limitations.

When I asked him for his weaknesses, he immediately stated that he had none. When asked the range of possible jury verdict he stated his worst case was $75,000 and his best case $275,000. He also stated that Joyce's last demand for settlement was $150,000."

"Phil, I need to go back with a new settlement figure to signal that we want to settle this case. I don't want your final figure but one well within what you're willing to do."

Phil immediately responded, "$200,000."

"But Phil," I said, "that's going the wrong direction."

"Look, Mr. Calkins, we offered the $150,000 a year ago and we have incurred a lot of time and expenses since."

For the next 15 minutes I tried to convince Phil we would lose the mediation if he raised his demand. He finally agreed that I could go back at $150,000 and I considered that a victory.

I walked into attorney Erickson's office where he and the Eastern Insurance Company representative, Dominic Fielding, we're waiting. Also present were the individually named defendants Bill Hand, Brad Townsend and Cotton Trevino. They did not attend the opening session for fear their presence might upset the plaintiff.

Erickson immediately took charge. He was prepared and had great confidence in his ability as an advocate. I started the conversation: "I'm not certain where Phil Deeter is coming from. He wanted to raise his demand from $150,000 to $200,000, and it took all I had to keep him at $150,000."

Ray responded, "Phil is a cowboy and runs a one man operation out of his home. He has a terrible reputation, for he is rarely prepared and tries to settle his cases rather than go to trial. When he goes to trial he normally loses. Need I say more?"

We went through the strengths and weaknesses of the defense and Ray was well prepared. "No weaknesses, he said: "First , Deeter will not be prepared for trial; second, this lady, and I say lady advisedly, was in no way offended, but invited the attention she received; and, third," continued Erickson, "the real reason Joyce quit is because she didn't want to travel across town to a new office on public transportation. She doesn't have a car. And, fourth, we don't think that the jury will like Joyce. She will not make a convincing witness."

I noted that Eastern offered $5000 and I needed a new settlement offer from them. Ray immediately responded, "we're not going to bid against ourselves. Joyce was at $150,000 when we offered $5000. She must move first." Then he added, "the most we are going to pay in any event is $10,000."

This caught me off guard because the way Ray said $10,000, I knew he meant it. I asked if I could take that back to the plaintiff and explain that this is all the further the defense would go?

After a 10 minute discussion outside my presence, Fielding approved the $10,000. I then returned to the plaintiff's caucus and relayed what had just transpired.

Deeter looked at me with anger in his eyes. "That's an insult," he declared. "My client has truly suffered and a jury is going to give her at least $150,000. We will not respond to that offer. This mediation is over." And he turned to start packing his bags.

"Phil, please don't give up. We can get this matter settled if we just keep trying."

Phil stopped packing his bag and turned to me and said "alright, I will give you our final drop dead number, $75,000, take it or leave it." I looked at Joyce and then her husband and neither would look at me. Joyce's husband finally said, "that's our bottom number. We are ready to go to trial."

I returned the defense caucus and presented the new demand. Ray responded, "well, that should pretty much wind it up for we are not going above $10,000."

As he said this, I was looking at Dominic Fielding and noticed, very subtly, that he was not necessarily agreeing with him. Finally he said, "Ray, I think we can go a little higher."

"But Dominic, there's no way she will receive even $10,000, and we will more than likely receive a defense verdict. I am certain I can beat Phil 10 out of 10 times in the courtroom."

Dominic responded, "that may be true, but I think it would make sense to settle this matter before the case is filed."

Immediately I saw a ray of hope. Fielding was concerned about publicity. That's the weakness in the defense. All that sex talk would be picked up by the newspapers and even carried on CNN news on a slow Sunday evening. That's why Fielding, a senior vice president of the insurance company, flew all the way in from New York City. He intended to get the matter settled.

I immediately said: "We can make one of the conditions of settlement that the agreement will be kept confidential. I'm sure Joyce would want confidentiality to avoid embarrassment."

I asked for a new offer and Dominic said they would go to $15,000. As I walked back to the plaintiff's caucus I wondered how I could separate Phil Deeter from his client. Walking in I said, "good news. Eastern has moved up to $15,000 and I am certain they will move further. We need to respond."

Phil said: "not a chance, Mr. Calkins."

"Please, Phil, call me Dick," I responded. I knew I was becoming irritated and was doing everything I could to restrain myself from making a sarcastic remark that I would regret. My feeling was that Phil had no idea how bad his case was and he was denying his client a chance for a meaningful settlement.

I asked Phil to go into the hallway with me. As we left, I said to Joyce, "a little lawyer talk. You know how lawyers always have to talk." She smiled.

In the hallway, I told Phil that I sensed his client wanted to get this matter resolved because she was embarrassed about it. I asked him that if she was willing to go below $75,000 would he permit her to do so. He responded that he was professional and if that is what she wanted he would not interfere, but it would be against his strong recommendation.

We reentered the caucus room and I said, "we have been talking and I explained to Phil that if we wanted to get this matter resolved, we would have to go below $75,000. I don't know how far below, just below."

Joyce immediately responded, "why that is what I was thinking. Can I go below $75,000?"

Phil responded, "you can if you wish but it is against my advice."

Joyce turned me and asked, "what do you think our response should be?"

I responded, $55,000 would send a strong signal," and Joyce approved. Her husband spoke up for the first time and said that it was too low, but Joyce insisted.

Through this last exchange, Joyce seemed more sympathetic and likable. She made it clear that she wanted to resolve the matter today not three years from now; $15,000 was a lot of money that would help the family budget.

I returned to the defense caucus and announced the new demand of $55,000. Fielding seemed pleased with the move and said he would go to $25,000. This was relayed to Joyce, and after two more rounds, the case settled for $38,500. Both parties seemed very pleased with settlement; however, both attorneys were unhappy with it, Phil out of ignorance, and Ray out of greed (he wanted to try the case for he was certain he would win and this would gain him a handsome fee.) I was happy with it because I worked through a difficult situation with the attorneys. It reaffirmed my conviction, never mediate without the decision-makers, particularly the plaintiff, present. Without them you will never know if there is a different agenda between the client and the attorney.

Oh yes, the snow held off and my cab was able to get me to the airport on time.

Mediation #37

Counsel and the Mediator Gang Up On Plaintiff

Connie Jefferies was 52 years old, single, athletically built, an avid bowler and a person who was always in the right. One winter day, with new snow on the ground, Connie exited her building to walk a block to the mall for lunch. As was her custom, she exited the rear door and walked down the driveway, a shortcut to the mall.

Snow removers had not yet removed the snow in the driveway, although they had completed the front steps and walkway. Connie stepped on a patch of ice under the snow and fell breaking her ankle. She sued the owner of the building (not her employer) and the snow removal company, for not clearing the driveway.

At the mediation, Connie's attorney contended that the owners of the building knew that employees used the rear door to go to the mall over the lunch hour. There was a duty to clear the area to accommodate them. In the alternative, he contended that the owner should have put up a sign directing employees to use the front door and walkway.

The insurance carrier insuring the building contended that Connie was responsible for all injuries because she could see the snow, yet chose to walk in it rather than exit through the front door and walk down the front walk which had been cleared, which would've taken her two minutes longer to reach the mall. He also pointed out that it was very difficult for plaintiffs to win slip and fall on ice cases in a northern climate. Over 70 percent of the cases are defense verdicts.

Connie demanded $100,000 and the carrier offered $10,000. At the end of several hours, Connie came down to $60,000 and the carrier offered $35,000. Connie said, "$60,000 is my final figure. If they don't pay, I want to go to trial. After all its insurance money and they have lots of it."

Up to this point I had remained silent. Finally, I said, "Connie, I agree with your attorney. It is difficult to win a slip and fall on ice in a northern climate. Over 70 percent of the cases are lost."

Connie cut me off. "How many slip and fall cases have you had?"

I responded, "very few."

"There," she said, "you don't even know what you are talking about. The jury will believe me."

Getting a little irritated with the affront I said, "Your attorney is an excellent trial lawyer, and he has tried many cases like this one. You should listen to him because he is giving you good advice. You will regret it if you don't settle."

Connie sat quietly for a moment, and then said, "Whose side are the two of you on?" Why don't you help me? I will not go below $60,000."

She went to trial, and as we warned, the jury returned a defense verdict, and she received nothing. Her parting words were, "I wonder how much they paid the judge?"

It was clear that in her eyes, we had "ganged up" on her and were pushing her to accept something she opposed. After this case, when disagreement arises between the attorney and the client, I hold back and say nothing. By remaining neutral between them, I am able to speak to the plaintiff in a more quiet setting and have better success in encouraging the person to accept an offer when it is a fair one. Also, when the split between the attorney and client becomes a serious one, by remaining silent I am able to step in and save the mediation even when the lawyer's services are terminated by the client.

Mediation #38

Client Fires Her Attorney Slamming Her Purse on the Table

Hilda Hinkle was raised on an Iowa farm. She was married to Burrell for 37 years, when he died in surgery. She retained counsel and sued the surgeon for medical malpractice. The matter was settled and she received net $750,000, which she used to purchase an insurance policy.

A friend of Burrell, who was an insurance agent, Montgomery Kindle, talked her into switching insurance companies and purchasing a Universal Life policy from him at a higher rate of return. At the end of the year, the IRS informed her she owed a substantial income tax on the sale of the first policy, which the insurance agent never mentioned. She was furious because she lost a lot of money when she paid the tax. She hired Henry Johnson, a local attorney, to sue the agent for fraud. Henry informed her she could possibly recover over $1 million in the case, as an insured in Texas had involving similar facts against in the same insurance company.

Well into the first caucus with the plaintiff, I asked Henry what he thought was Hilda's best case in front of a jury. He said, $150,000, which their expert had said was her loss. When he said this, Hilda jumped up and slammed her purse on the table and swore at Henry. "You told me I would receive $1 million. You lied to me to get my case. You – – – !"

Remembering the broken ankle case, I said nothing as the two fought it out. I could easily have jumped in and explained the difference between this case and the Texas case. There, the agent knew of the tax, but purposely held back and said nothing. The jury awarded substantial punitive damages. In the instant case, it was established that the agent did not know of the tax. He was merely negligent for which there were no punitive damages.

Plaintiff was about to storm out of the caucus room when I pulled counsel into the hallway for some lawyer talk.

"Henry," I said, "Hilda is really upset."

"Are you trying to tell me something I don't know?" Henry said.

"Look, I know you're upset because your client is not listening to you. Do you want me to continue with her and try to get the matter settled?"

Henry immediately responded, "I'm sorry I was sarcastic. I'm just upset with the turn of events. Of course I want you to continue. She will sue me if we don't. Although a frivolous complaint, I would still have to report this to my insurance carrier which will probably raise my rates."

"With your permission," I said, "I will take her to lunch and try to calm her down."

Henry interrupted me saying, "Hilda fired another lawyer and sued him. Now, no one in the county will represent her. I was her last chance. Whatever you can do is fine with me. I will even cut my fees."

I reported what occurred to the defense, which included a vice president from the insurance company, who flew in from Connecticut. I asked consent to take Hilda to lunch to calm her down. They consented.

At lunch I avoided talking about the case. We got better acquainted, and when we returned to the mediation, Hilda agreed to lower her demand to $500,000. Much to my surprise, the defense seemed to be pleased with the move off $1 million. It responded at $100,000.

I returned to Hilda and presented the insurance company's offer. She immediately became angry again, and I explained to her, "this is just their first offer, that they will move up further. Please remain patient."

"Are you saying, I am not patient, Mr. Calkins?" Hilda asked.

"On the contrary," I assured her, "you have gone through a great deal, but I'm concerned about the stress it is causing in your life. I'm going to do everything I can to get this concluded. You deserve to find peace of mind."

Hilda calmed down and then said: "I will go to $400,000, but expect them to make a substantial move."

I weighed whether I should mention to her the fact that her expert had limited her damages to $150,000. I decided not to discuss this because it might trigger another outburst. Instead, I took her new offer to the defendant and they responded by going to $150,000.

I reported the new offer to Hilda and she thought long and hard. Finally she said, "look, I will go to $300,000 that is my last offer. If they reject it, I'm ready to go to trial."

Again, I thanked her and presented her new offer to the defendant. They asked if I would leave the room. While in the hallway, I could see the receptionist board that they had put a call in presumably to the home office in Hartford, Connecticut. They finally called me back in and announced they would pay the $300,000.

To say that I was surprised is to understate my reaction. With the case settled I learned why the defendant had doubled the actual loss of Hilda. The company had seven cases like this around the country and they did not want another Texas result. They therefore instructed their representatives at these mediations to settle at whatever cost was required. Defendants were merely following directions.

CHAPTER 7

IDENTIFYING CASES THAT MUST BE SETTLED

Mediators look through a different prism than the attorneys representing the parties. Often they spot matters which counsel may be overlooking, which signals the case cannot go forward because of the consequences to one or both of the parties.

It is most difficult to convince an attorney that circumstances are such that to proceed further with the case in the courts cannot be justified. Costs may be too great or confidentiality must be maintained, or the law is simply against the party. The following cases illustrate this point.

A. Costs Too Great

Mediation #39

Fee Shifting Provisions Can Be Costly

There are those cases where fee shifting provisions require the defendant to pay all costs and attorneys' fees if the plaintiff establishes liability. Potential costs are such that the defendant must settle.

In one case, plaintiff, Jaimon Crosby, was a highly skilled diesel mechanic who worked on over-the-road diesel trucks. At his shop he claims his supervisor gave him more janitorial work than the other mechanics because he was black. He also felt he was not receiving pay increases in line with the white mechanics. He complained to his supervisor but nothing was done to correct the situation. At this point some of the other mechanics retaliated against him making racial slurs. He reported this also but nothing was done.

Finally, Crosby contacted a lawyer who threatened to bring action against Crosby's employer pursuant to Title VII Civil Rights Act 1964. He demanded $30,000. When the defendant was served with the complaint it was shocked and highly incensed at what Crosby was asking.

In caucus with defendant and counsel, I asked: "Is there liability in this case?" Counsel responded, "as to the cleaning duties and promotions, there is no exposure. Plaintiff was in line with the white mechanics, no more, no less."

"What about the racial slurs," I asked.

"To be honest, there is some exposure, but damages are minimal. No more than $5000."

Knowing there is a fee shifting provision if liability is established, that is, if there is liability and some damages awarded, defendant must also pay plaintiff's attorneys fees and costs, I asked counsel, "what is your best net case, that is, what will you spend to defend and limit damages to $5000?"

Counsel said nothing for a minute or so and then responded, "I suppose we will spend $50,000 to defend the case."

"And what about plaintiff's costs and attorney's fees," I asked. "Does not the defendant have to pay them if the jury enters a verdict for the plaintiff?"

"I guess so," answered counsel.

"And what do you estimate those costs and fees will be?"

"I suppose no less than what defense costs will be," responded counsel.

I then asked the $64,000 question. "If you have to pay your own defense costs and attorney's fees, and those of the plaintiff, isn't your best net case $105,000? Costs and attorneys' fees for both sides of $100,000, plus the verdict of $5000."

"I guess you are correct," said counsel.

"Well, that being the case, if I can settle the case for $30,000, would not it make sense to pay it and save $75,000?"

"When you put it that way, I guess you are right."

The case settled for $25,000.

A Cost Driven Case

Many times the cost of litigation exceeds the expected gain that a plaintiff might derive in litigating. Such was true in Spencer Supply Company vs. The Tri-State Purchasing and Panther Supply, Inc. Tri-State was the purchasing agent for some 150 elementary schools in the tri-state area of Illinois, Indiana and Kentucky. It was responsible for arranging the purchase of food supplies for cafeterias of its member schools. Each year bids for food suppliers was opened. The winning bidder earned millions dollars in sales each year.

For seven years straight, Panther Supplies, Inc. was the winning bidder even though on some items, it charged more than other suppliers. Spencer Supply Company began to suspect that there was a conspiracy between Tri-State and Panther to give the latter the cafeteria business. This was substantiated because an ex-employee of Panther became the purchasing director for Tri-State.

Spencer contacted a law firm in Chicago to inquire whether there was a cause of action under § 1 of the Sherman Antitrust Act. It was advised that the arrangement between Panther and Tri-State probably constituted a conspiracy to boycott Spencer from elementary school cafeteria market. Although it was advised that it was a close question, Spencer decided to move forward with a lawsuit and take its chances. A lawsuit was filed demanding $7 million in damages.

After some discovery was taken and motions for summary judgment resolved, the parties agreed to mediate and I was selected because of my antitrust background. After examining the case carefully, I concluded there was no antitrust violation or any other infraction of law. However, I was in a quandary as to how I could tell plaintiff's attorneys without losing their confidence in me. Without making any statement I gave counsel a leading opinion on the question and let them decide whether there was a problem or not. The opinion I gave them was *Expert Masonry, Inc. vs. Boone County, Kentucky*, 440 F.3d 336 (6th Cir 2006). As I suspected, after they read it, they indicated the case was no problem because the instant case was distinguishable. That is the response lawyers always make when faced with a difficult problem. In such instances I let the matter rest, for the attorneys are highly intelligent and they got the message regardless of what they were saying to me.

At this point, I changed my strategy. Rather than talk law I decided to play the psychological cost card – what will it cost to conclude the case through trial and appeal. And this worked.

First, I met with the defendant Panther. I ask counsel, "how much have you spent in defending the case to date?" Counsel responded, "close to $1 million."

I then asked the critical question: "how much more will you spend to complete discovery, try the case and conclude an appeal?" Much to my utter surprise, counsel said, "$2 million-$3 million."

I was certain costs would not be that high even in Chicago. Thinking through the issue I concluded that counsel exaggerated the cost to encourage his client to settle. His motivation was that if several million dollars were spent to defend a case concerning which there was no liability, the client might question why that was necessary. Therefore, to keep this valuable corporate client he pushed it to settle the matter presumably at less than costs.

Next, I met with the Spencer group and point blank asked them, "if I could settle the case for $1 million, would you accept it?" Counsel balked and said, "that's too low. We have to receive more than that, perhaps $1.5 million."

I then returned to the defense caucus with the Panther group and asked them if they would settle the case if I could get plaintiff down to $1.5 million or $1 million? After considerable discussion they indicated that they would go to $1 million. I was given authority to disclose this to the plaintiff with the understanding they would go no higher.

Returning to the plaintiff's caucus, I said, "Look here, I am pushing the defendant quite hard. If I could get the defendant to offer $1 million, will you in confidence accept? I would urge you to do so in view of the *Expert Masonry* case which I gave you.

Counsel for the plaintiff said, "that case is distinguishable. One million dollars is just too low, but we will talk about it." Ultimately, plaintiff accepted and the case settled.

I then met with the other defendant, Tri-State, which had been patiently waiting in the wings while I was settling the matter with Panther. In caucus, I was essentially speaking to the insurance carrier, which had $1 million in coverage. The policy, however, was a withering policy, that is, as attorneys' fees and costs were incurred, they were deducted from the coverage available. Because $250,000 had already been spent in defending the case, there was only $750,000 coverage left.

I first asked counsel, "how much will be spent to defend the case from this point on?"

Counsel said, "in excess of $1 million."

I then asked the critical question: "In other words, if we don't settle today we will exhaust the existing coverage plus an additional $250,000?"

Counsel acknowledged what I said was correct.

I continued: "If I could get the plaintiff to offer to settle for $650,000 would you pay it? You would save $100,000 on your policy. I know you feel there is no liability, and I cannot say I disagree with you, but to defend will cost you considerably more than the present coverage of $750,000."

After considerable discussion and telephone calls the adjuster agreed to pay $650,000. After all, as he pointed out, he would save his carrier $100,000 on the policy.

I then met with plaintiff, and pointed out that, "if you win a judgment against Tri-State, it will be uncollectible for Tri-State has no assets and the insurance money would have been spent in defense costs." It was an easy sale. Plaintiff agreed and that part of the case settled for $650,000.

By playing the psychological cost card and the consequences if the case were not settled, I was able to convince all parties that the only way they could benefit was if the case settled. Panther saved several million dollars off its projected costs to defend, and Tri-State saved $100,000

because the coverage of the policy would have been spent plus an

additional $250,000 in defense costs. Settling was the only possible

resolution. Thus Spencer collected $1,650,000 in a case where there was

no liability just because of the threat of cost of litigation.

B. The Need for Confidentiality

Mediation #41

The Fear of Disclosure – A Case of Herpes

The fear of public disclosure can be a strong psychological factor

in settling a case. For example, a church being sued for sexual abuse of a

child committed by a cleric may want the matter resolved without

publicity, or an insurance company may be willing to pay more to obtain a

confidentiality clause barring disclosure that female secretaries and male

salesman in an insurance sales office were carrying on in an

unprofessional manner because of the impact it would have on the

company's image, or, a woman sexually harassed in the workplace may

want confidentiality because the circumstances of the harassment might

prove embarrassing. In one case two police officers were sexually abused

by a cleric when altar boys and refused to have their cases even filed

because of concern that publicity might hurt their advancement on the police force. They settled for less than what the case was worth with a confidentiality clause.

The instant case involved Mary Joseph (MJ), a divorcee of two years. She had three daughters ages 14 and 15 and 19. She lived in an affluent area in a very conservative New England town near Boston. She decided to start dating because she was desirous of finding a marriage partner with whom she could spend the rest of her life. To begin the process, MJ went to the internet and received 300+ responses. She selected Milton Hutton as a good prospect.

Milton was 62 years old and a high school counselor. He had been divorced for 15 years. His two sons were 30 and 31 respectively.

Milton invited MJ out for a get acquainted dinner. All went well and a second evening was planned. After this dinner MJ consumed more alcohol than she was accustomed to. When dropping MJ off at her home, MJ invited Milton in for a cup of coffee. The children were not home and Milton suggested they go to MJ's bedroom. MJ stated that before going upstairs she asked Milton if he had any venereal diseases. He answered in the negative. Milton denies she made such an inquiry. Thereafter, they had unprotected sex. After this first liaison, Milton said he then told MJ he had herpes and was taking Valtrex to curb it. MJ denies he made such a disclosure at that time.

Over the next 30 days, Milton and MJ dated on a regular basis and had sex several more times. Milton told MJ he wanted to take the relationship to a higher level because he was falling in love. About this time, MJ got sick and went to her doctor who diagnosed her with a urinary tract infection and gave her antibiotics. When she mentioned this to Milton he wondered if she had herpes in that he was treating for it, but said nothing. Later he called her and raised the possibility that she might have herpes. She was shocked with the disclosure, and went into depression when her OB/GYN doctor confirmed that she had the disease.

Her depression turned to anger and she hired an aggressive plaintiff attorney, Don Hastings, to bring a lawsuit against Milton. Before suit was filed the lawyers on both sides agreed that mediation was a good alternative.

Milton's defense was that MJ cannot establish causal connection. She could have contracted herpes from her ex-husband or other sexual partners after her divorce. Further, he claims that he informed her of his herpes after the first encounter and she continued the relationship without being concerned. Milton's attorney planned to name MJ's first husband and other partners as defendants so they could be tested.

MJ asserts she asked Milton if he had any venereal disease before the first encounter and he answered in the negative. She emphatically denies Milton said anything about herpes until after she had the first outbreak. She further denies she had any relations with another man other than her ex-husband.

At the mediation, MJ would not sit in the same room with Milton. She was furious for what he had done. She felt she was a marked woman no man would want to marry. During most of the mediation she was weeping uncontrollably.

As I analyzed the case there were several issues that had to be addressed. First, who was telling truth about the first encounter. If MJ asked Milton about his health before they had the first encounter, Milton could be in serious trouble. If Milton was telling the truth that he told MJ about the condition after the first encounter and she continued the liaison without protection, this could be a problem for MJ. I decided to offer both polygraph tests. I was certain the one fabricating would decline to take it.

Second, there was an issue as to how much Milton could pay without facing bankruptcy. Apart from his IRA he had a net worth of $312,000:

Savings and checking – $25,000

Non-IRA accounts – $35,000

Mortgage equity – $52,000

He owed $32,000 on his car and there was $400,000 in his IRA account.

Third, it was clear to me that failure to settle and filing a lawsuit would be highly injurious to both parties because of the publicity, and this might be the strongest card I could play.

On the day of mediation, the parties were literally located in different buildings across a parking lot. I met first with MJ. She was quite attractive and clearly devastated by the whole affair. In one sense she wanted to punish Milton and didn't care how much money she received, and in another sense she wanted to keep the matter confidential because of the repercussions publicity might cause. She was also concerned that if her ex-husband learned of the matter, he would use it to gain custody of their daughters.

What I didn't anticipate was how aggressive her attorney, Don Hastings, was. He wanted to file suit because he was convinced he would get a verdict in the seven figures. He handed me five verdict reports where juries awarded plaintiffs in excess of $1 million each. I realized he was not concerned about the negative publicity the case would generate for the parties. He wasn't concerned about the collectability of any judgment. He wanted the publicity for himself. This would be the first case of its kind in Massachusetts and could generate considerable business if the verdict were large enough. His advice to MJ was for her to hold out for the last penny to punish Milton. He advised MJ to demand $1.5 million.

In the second caucus, I asked MJ if she would take a polygraph test concerning the facts in dispute. Without hesitation she agreed. At one point, I had defense counsel, Timothy Sargent, meet MJ. He was extremely impressed how devastated she was, especially when she broke down in tears.

In meeting with Milton and his attorneys, I found him to be a nice gentleman, rather conservative, probably sincere in his desire to marry MJ. He insisted he informed her about his condition after their first encounter. He did admit, however, that with three other women he told them about his condition before the first encounter. He had no explanation why he did not do the same with MJ.

It was at this point that I conferred with counsel to get permission to ask whether Milton would take a polygraph test. Sargent readily agreed because he was concerned that if the jury did not believe Milton, the verdict would bankrupt him.

Confronting Milton, I asked: "There is an important issue as to whether MJ asked about your health before the first encounter. Would you take a polygraph test to establish you are telling the truth?" He hesitated, and in that hesitation I knew he would not agree.

Then he said, "let me think about it and I will let you know." I looked at counsel and he gave me a knowing nod. Milton was lying.

I then gave Milton MJ's demand and he became angry. He started to get up as if to leave, and his attorney put his hand on his arm to restrain him. He said, "such a demand is ridiculous. I would rather go to trial because either way I am financially ruined."

I explained, "this is just the first demand and I have much to talk about on the other side. Please be patient and let me do my work."

Milton, after conferring with counsel, offered $50,000 to settle the case. He said, "I cannot go much above $100,000 without jeopardizing my financial future. I intend to retire in four years and a substantial verdict or settlement would eliminate that possibility."

Then, to everyone's surprise, Milton broke down and wept. He said, "I am becoming deeply depressed over this matter and I can no longer take the stress of a lawsuit. If the case goes to trial I will not only go bankrupt but I will lose my job at the school. I just cannot stand the pressure."

After this interlude, there was silence. No one wanted to speak. I finally spoke: "Milton, we will get the case settled at a level you can survive financially."

My next move was to convince MJ that the case had to settle because neither party wanted public disclosure. I played my trump card. I said to MJ: "Please consider the embarrassment public disclosure will have on you not only among your neighbors, friends and relatives, but also on your teenage daughters. The news would quickly flash throughout their high school and teenage girls can be quite cruel at this age." When I said this, MJ sat deep in thought. She clearly heard what I was saying. She then looked at her attorney as if she did not know what to say.

At this point, I explained Milton's finances, that he could not sustain a large judgment. MJ's attorney responded, they needed a verified statement of his finances. I pointed out that "to settle the case MJ would have to go below $300,000."

Hastings cut me off and said, "that is not possible."

After several more caucuses on both sides, I proposed the matter settle for $200,000. Both initially rejected my suggestion. Finally, Hastings said, "MJ will settle for $220,000 and not a penny less."

In confidence Hastings finally stated that MJ would go to the $200,000. Milton still refused to go above $150,000. A suggestion was finally made that the $50,000 difference could be made up by payments over a period of two years. When this was suggested both parties agreed. $150,000 would be paid immediately with the balance paid over two years. The case settled with a confidentiality clause being implemented. Although several psychological cards were played, the trump card was confidentiality. Neither side could survive adverse publicity and for different reasons.

C. <u>Mistake in the Law</u>

Mediation #42

<u>A Weeping Widow's Claim is Better Than a Blushing Bride's</u>

There are many types of lawyers a mediator faces. Some are most difficult and fight each step of the way. Others are willing to listen and cooperate. A few come into the mediation unprepared and expect the mediator to do all the work.

One of the most difficult lawyers I have dealt with, who is a friend, is never satisfied with any settlement. Whatever the settlement, favorable or not, he complains that he had to surrender in order to settle a matter. On occasion he has walked out of the mediation when he felt the defendant was not being responsive. Frankly, he is intimidating, and when asked to mediate for him I do so with reservations.

In one case, the attorney, we will call him Darren, asked me to mediate a wrongful death case. The decedent, Christopher Henderson, was driving with his father in a pickup truck, pulling a trailer that was hauling a new tractor made in Russia. They were traveling across Interstate 70 towards Kansas City, Kansas. It was 2 o'clock in the morning, the sky was clear and the pavement dry.

Defendant, Harry Doherty, left with his family on holiday from Terra Haute, Indiana, and was driving a conversion van. He was taking his wife and three children to Mount Rushmore and the Badlands of South Dakota. While the children slept, Harry entered Interstate 70 and came upon the Henderson truck. As he explained, he was awake, but was not

registering what was in front of him. With the Henderson vehicle going

35 mph (minimal speed limit is 40 mph), and one of the rear red lights out

on the trailer, he ran into it. The conversion van spun off into the median

and came to rest. No one, fortunately, was injured. The Henderson

trailer was pushed into the pickup truck, which jackknifed, causing

Christopher to fall out of the truck hitting the pavement and being killed.

He was not wearing a seat belt. His father was not injured.

Christopher was survived by his wife, Anna, and their daughters

Madison, age 12, Courtney, age 7, and Christina, age 5. Representing the

estate, Anna filed suit in federal district court in Kansas City, Missouri,

naming Harry Doherty as the sole defendant. The estate did not sue

Anna's father-in-law because the plaintiff (the estate) must be from a

different state than the defendant (father-in-law) to sue in federal court.

Both the estate and father-in-law were from Kansas.

Doherty, however, did name the father-in-law as a defendant,

which he was entitled to do in a third-party action. The estate then

amended its complaint and named the father-in-law as a defendant also.

Six months into the litigation, the parties decided to mediate.

As the mediation progressed, Darren made a high demand of $2.5 million, and was unwilling to compromise to any great extent. This I expected from past experiences. The insurance carrier offered $200,000, pointing out that policy limits were $500,000. Darren made it clear that he expected the defendant Doherty to contribute heavily out of his own pocket. This presented serious problems because he was not wealthy and worked in a meatpacking plant at an hourly rate. He did have some marginal farmland which constituted his entire estate, which was heavily mortgaged and used to build a college fund for the girls. He never finished high school because he had to go to work to support his brothers and sisters.

Attorney Darren had little sympathy for the plight Doherty found himself in. His goal was to recover as much as he could and had no reservations about going to trial. During the course of the mediation, it was clear that Doherty was deeply distressed and worried. At one point, he became ill and started showing signs of depression.

Although it was clear the insurance carrier would not consider paying more than policy limits, Darren held out for more. After six hours of negotiating, Darren reduced plaintiff's demand to $950,000 and suggested terminating the mediation if the carrier did not respond positively. He expected Doherty to pay an additional $400,000, which he clearly did not have.

During one of the breaks, I had a chance to talk to Anna. She was a delightful young mother, 32 years old, and seemed to be handling the loss of her husband very well. I said, "I know this lawsuit must be very difficult for you. I am doing everything I can to get it settled so you can go on with life."

Anna responded, "Yes, this has been a difficult two and one-half years since the accident. As soon as it is over, I am moving the family to Florida. I have a friend I am dating."

With this said it was clear that Anna wanted the matter resolved sooner than later. Her attorney evidently told her that it was inadvisable for her to remarry until after the lawsuit was resolved – a weeping widow will play much better before a jury than a blushing bride.

Examining the case closely, I found what I thought was a chink in Darren's armor. By naming the father-in-law as a defendant, even though named a defendant in Doherty's third-party action, the estate may have destroyed diversity jurisdiction – the estate and father-in-law were both from Kansas.

At this point I pulled Darren aside to have a heart-to-heart talk. I showed him a United States Supreme Court decision, which raised the question of diversity of citizenship, and if the defense raised the issue the court would be compelled to dismiss the case. I told Darren he had three options:

"First, you can hold out for more money and take the case to trial. This will take another two years. If you do this, the defense could try the case and try to win on the merits, and if it loses, raise the issue of subject matter jurisdiction for the first time on appeal and have the case dismissed for lack of diversity jurisdiction. In other words it would have a free bite at the apple.

"Second, you can dismiss the case now and file over in state court, where no diversity of jurisdiction is required. But, this would add another year to Anna's waiting period, and I feel this is not what she wants. In fact, you risk she might just remarry and not wait for the case to go to trial.

Third, you can follow the strong wishes of Anna and get the case settled now, so she and her little family can go on with life." Darren listened and finally concluded that settling was in fact in the best interest of his client. The case finally settled for $500,000, and Anna was most grateful. As expected, Darren complained that he had been strong-armed into settling, and perhaps he was.

Mediation #43

You Can't Win at Every Casino

Mediators can often draw on their legal backgrounds in a mediation. For example, when I was in practice in Chicago, I was primarily involved in antitrust litigation. I joined the Chadwell Keck law firm in 1963, which specialized in this area. One client that I was involved with was General Electric Company, which was sued by the federal government for fixing prices in the electrical industry. Of course, I was a minor bag-carrying associate for Mr. Chadwell and the other senior partners. But it was exciting because I traveled around the country attending meetings and participating in depositions.

One of the claims the government asserted was that General Electric, Westinghouse, and Allis Chalmers fixed prices on turbine generators for power plants. Much to my amazement, the government proved the three companies used the phase of the moon to bid on massive generator contracts. When the moon was full, or in the phase of the full moon, General Electric bid low and got the bid and the other two bid high; when no moon or the phase thereof, Westinghouse bid low, and so on. As it turned out an employee of General Electric was the only one who could figure out the bid on these massive pieces of equipment. Before bids were submitted, his pricing was submitted to the other two companies.

The defense was that no one was hurt, for the ultimate price was fair and there was no gouging. Ultimately, some top officers of the three companies pleaded guilty and served time in a federal penitentiary – the first time ever under the Sherman Act. One actually reorganized the prison library.

In another antitrust case involving Pabst Brewing Company, which acquired the Blatz Brewing Company, both of Milwaukee, the government attacked the merger as anticompetitive. The Chadwell firm represented Pabst. I traveled around the country interviewing owners of various beer companies, who were to testify that the merger would increase competition and not lesson it. It was an interesting assignment for one who does not drink alcohol.

On one occasion, after completing my interview, the witness wanted to go out to a bar for a drink. That was fine with me; however, when I ordered a Coca-Cola, the barmaid became irritated at me, which to say the least was embarrassing in front of the witness. I survived. At the trial, Mr. Chadwell allowed me to question one of the witnesses on direct examination. I was thrilled with the opportunity to show off my courtroom skills. I wrote up my questions carefully, rehearsed them with my wife, and prepared the witness. On the appointed day, I was ready. My witness was called, sworn in by the clerk, and I began. I got through my initial questions easily and then got to the meat of my examination. I was walking back and forth, pointing my finger to the ceiling and making earthshaking points that would save the world. I then happened to glance at the judge, a gray-haired gentleman, and found him fast asleep. He had not heard a single word my witness said. He was not even cognizant I existed. What a letdown, but that was the bane of my antitrust existence.

The mediation in question here involved the casino business in South Dakota. Under state law, any retailer can apply for a casino license and operate a so-called casino. They are nothing more than rooms filled with slot machines that played poker games. To operate a casino, an operator had not only to obtain a license, but had to purchase slot machines from state approved manufacturers.

Fifteen retail stores and gasoline stations applied for licenses but were denied. They then sued under § 1 of the Sherman Act, claiming that existing operators conspired with South Dakota to boycott them from the market. The complaint was filed in federal court and ultimately dismissed on summary judgment. On appeal to the Eighth Circuit Court of Appeals, the dismissal was affirmed.

The 13 defendants then turned around and sued the original plaintiffs to recover the $1.5 million, plus interest, spent in defending the action. They asserted malicious prosecution, abuse of process and common-law bad faith. Before the complaint was filed the parties decided to mediate the matter.

I traveled to Sioux Falls South Dakota for the mediation. I was informed that plaintiffs' counsel wanted to get the matter resolved because he was being paid at an hourly rate until the complaint was filed. Thereafter, he was working under a contingency fee.

The original plaintiffs (now defendants) offered to settle for $450,000. In the first caucus with the complainants, I immediately spotted a serious problem with their claim because of my antitrust background. I pulled counsel out into the hallway and explained there was a First Amendment defense I thought applied to the case. It is called the *Noerr-Pennington* doctrine. It provides that citizens, even if they conspire for illegal purposes, have the constitutional right to petition the legislature, petition the executive, and file a lawsuit. To overcome the defense, the plaintiff must show that in conspiring, the defendants subjectively and objectively had a frivolous and illegal purpose in mind. This is called a sham exception and most difficult to prove. I also noted that in this case, the original plaintiffs subjectively felt they had standing to sue. Therefore this defense would require the instant case be dismissed.

Counsel and I went to the law library and we dug up several United States Supreme Court decisions, which spelled out the defense. He was then satisfied that his case would be dismissed. He asked, what should we do? I responded, accept the $450,000, which was still on the table. He had to assume that the other side would sooner or later discover the defense. He agreed and asked me to explain it to his clients. Though disappointed they understood the risks and agreed to accept. The case settled.

This raises the ethical question whether I was required to disclose to the other side the fact that claimants could not succeed. The answer is, no. First, I was hired to get the case settled not dismissed. If I had disclosed it, the other side would have moved to dismiss the case. Second, I cannot do legal work for either side unless it will settle the case. This is my pledge of impartiality. And, third, if counsel continued prosecuting the case, he was going to lose at a significant cost to himself and clients. By disclosing his weakness, counsel was able to salvage something in the lawsuit.

Mediation #44

You Can't Trust Your Psychologist

The following is another case where mediator expertise assisted a lawyer in properly evaluating his case. Jody Dewitt was a nurse. She was married, but was having matrimonial difficulties. This led to depression and Jody visited a psychologist, Dr. Fenton Klein. He worked with Jody for several months, and there was improvement. Jody became attracted to the good doctor, and, as part of her therapy, to build her self-esteem, they began having an affair in his office. This continued for some time. As their relationship became closer, she started buying him presents.

One day Jody found out that the doctor was using the same therapy on two other patients. She became furious and suffered a relapse. She told her husband, and he insisted that she report Dr. Klein to the appropriate medical board. The doctor was ultimately suspended and permanently lost his license. He then moved to Ohio where he took on menial jobs to support himself. He was bankrupt and had no prospects of going back into the practice.

Again, at the insistence of her husband, she sued Dr. Klein and the psychology group with which he shared office space, on the grounds they held themselves out to be a partnership. Partners are liable for the negligence or torts of their partners. The group defended on the grounds that they were not a partnership but merely shared office space and a joint receptionist. Before spending money in pretrial discovery, the defendants, other than Dr. Klein, agreed to mediate the matter. Dr. Klein did not appear at the mediation and did not respond to the complaint, but defaulted.

At the mediation, plaintiff's attorney explained that they were pleading that Dr. Klein and the other psychologist were in fact a partnership. In the alternative, he contended that they were a partnership by estoppel, that is, they held themselves out as a partnership. They, (1) shared office space, (2) had a common receptionist, (3) had a sign listing the psychologists together as though they were partners, (4) shared the cost of furniture and other equipment, (5) were insured by the same insurance company, and (6) had a common telephone number.

Although the defendant psychologists had no inkling that Dr. Klein was having affairs with his clients, they recognized that a jury might punish them for the sins of Dr. Klein. They instructed their insurance carrier to settle the matter. The adjuster handling the case was not inclined to pay much money and was prepared to go to trial, which upset the defendant psychologists. It was finally agreed to mediate the matter.

Counsel for Jody demanded $500,000 to settle the case and the insurance carrier offered $20,000. Jody lowered the demand to $400,000 and the adjuster responded at $25,000. At this point the psychologists got angry with the adjuster for not acting in good faith. They put him on written notice that if the jury verdict exceeded policy limits of $1 million, the insurance carrier would be responsible.

During the course of the mediation we found a case which was right on point concerning partnership by estoppel. The Iowa Supreme Court stated that for partnership by estoppel to apply, it must have been in existence at the time plaintiff selected her psychologist, and that she relied on the appearance of a partnership when she selected Dr. Klein. The facts were that the instant partnership did not come into existence until six months after Jody selected Dr. Klein. In other words, Jody had no cause of action.

Jody's attorney recognized the problem and advised Jody to settle for whatever she could get. The case then settled for $38,000, costs of litigation.

Mediation #45

Work Comp Is Not For Everyone

When helping a party evaluate his or her case, the mediator has certain ethical responsibilities. For example, when the mediator discovers a potential ethical problem or malpractice infraction not yet identified by counsel, he is obligated to disclose it only to the party it will hurt by the disclosure. The mediator's pledge at the commencement of the mediation, not to assist one party over the other and remain impartial, means he should not disclose the problem to the party it will help. He has also pledged to get the matter settled. If, for example, in the South Dakota casino case, I had disclosed the *Noerr-Pennington* defense to the defendants, they would have thanked me, patted me on the back, and moved to dismiss the case. The case would not have been settled as I was pledged to do. By disclosing the *Noerr- Pennington* defense only to plaintiffs' counsel, I was able to get the case settled rather than dismissed.

This next case illustrates a further point. When the mediator discovers a malpractice situation, that is, counsel has made a critical mistake that would subject him to a malpractice lawsuit, he must be certain that the attorney discloses this to the client or the mediator should withdraw from the case.

Jonathan Tudor, was a nice young man, but mentally challenged. He learned to live and work on his own with guidance and support. McDonald's hired him as part of a program to help the handicapped. Because he could not drive, he was picked up each day near his home by another McDonald's employee and driven to and from work. The employee was compensated for his gas expense.

On the day in question, Jonathan climbed into the bed of the pick-up truck. As the truck gained speed, it turned a corner too sharply and Jonathan fell out hitting his head on the pavement. He suffered a mild closed head injury. He obtained an attorney, Frank Hillman, who filed a lawsuit against McDonald's.

Before discovery was taken, the matter was mediated. During caucus with Jonathan and his attorney, I learned that Jonathan had been transported to work and back on a regular basis. I then pulled counsel into the hallway and asked whether he could sue McDonald's in a separate tort action, "Wasn't this covered by workers compensation?" Counsel did not think so. If work comp applied, a person cannot sue his or her employer. The person must rely entirely on work comp for compensation.

At this point, we did some quick research and found a case which provided that when a person was transported to and from work by the employer on a regular basis, the only relief is to file a claim under the Workers Compensation Act. There is no independent claim to sue the employer in a tort action.

I asked Jonathan's attorney, "did you consider filing a work comp action rather than suing McDonald's?"

Frank hesitated a moment, and then rather sheepishly said, "I considered this possibility, but realized that the time for filing had lapsed."

Without saying anything, I knew counsel was concerned about a legal malpractice action being filed against him by Jonathan because his lawsuit against McDonald's would have to be dismissed.

After a lapse of what seemed like five minutes, I took Frank into the hallway. I said, "Look Frank, I think we have a problem here. As I see it we have three options: you can proceed ahead with the lawsuit and hope the defense does not detect our problem; you can inform Jonathan of the malpractice problem and hope he will waive it; or you can withdraw from the case, inform your insurance carrier and wait to be sued. If we continue the mediation, ethically you will have to inform Jonathan, or I will have to withdraw as mediator."

As a precaution, I suggested that another lawyer review the matter to be certain it was in Jonathan's best interest to waive his claim. He did so and Jonathan made clear that he wanted to get the matter resolved immediately, that he would waive his malpractice claim because the lawsuit was making him nervous. A fair settlement resulted.

Again, I used my expertise to get the matter resolved. I also maintained my ethical responsibility not to disclose the malpractice concern to the defense for had I done so the case would have been dismissed rather than settled.

CHAPTER 8

DEVELOPING A STRATEGY FOR SETTLEMENT

The primary function of the mediator is to develop a strategy for settling the case, particularly in the more complex and difficult cases. To do this, the mediator must encourage the parties to think wholistically: how could the needs and concerns of both, not just their own, be met. The following cases illustrate how strategies were developed to accomplish the parties' goals.

Mediation #46

The Bleak House

In December 1990, I was contacted by a law professor in Kansas City to mediate an antitrust case that had been in the courts for over 20 years. He had been appointed by the federal district court as a special master to try the issue of damages, liability having been established. The professor explained they were looking for an antitrust lawyer with mediation experience and a former judge to act as co-mediators. A number of teams were interviewed. I was matched up with former Iowa Supreme Court Justice Mark McCormick. I think the team from Iowa was chosen because as Iowans we could be counted on to be impartial and nonjudgmental. In other words, we were as pure as the new driven snow.

Mark is one of the brightest most intelligent lawyers I've ever met. Today he is a named partner in the Belin McCormick law firm, one of the top law firms in the Midwest. He has the marvelous talent of looking at a matter from a legal perspective and then going to the heart of it to resolve it. I was thrilled with the opportunity to work with him.

In the first week of January 1991, Mark and I traveled to Kansas City to meet the special master, Ted Henke. He was friendly and open; however, he felt that settling the case would be very difficult but he wanted to give it a try. I was flattered to be given the opportunity to work on this case. Mark had no mediation experience but was relying on me to set up the format.

Mark and I received thousands of pages of transcripts and documents to be reviewed before the first mediation session. The first session was set at the law school the middle of January. We arrived at 10:30 AM and were immediately escorted to Henke's office. I had a special interest in the University of Missouri School of Law, Kansas City, because Patrick Kelly, an alumnus of Drake Law School, had been dean of the school. As it turned out he recommended me as a mediator.

Ted Henke was very much the professor type. He was of medium build, balding with a distinguished black beard. Although his language was earthy at times, he displayed a clear intellect as he explained the case to us. The longer he talked, however, the clearer it became that he wanted the case settled so he would not have to go to hearing and decide the matter.

This 20-year-old case began in the early 1970s, when three Midwest milk cooperatives, Mid America Milk Cooperative (Mid-America), Associated Milk Producers, Inc. (AMPI) and Central Milk Producers Cooperative (CMPC) decided it was desirable to keep the National Farmers Organization of Ames Iowa (NFO) from entering the milk distribution business. Milk cooperatives are farmer organizations that contract with farmers to purchase their milk and then process and sell it wholesale into the market. At the time, NFO was a relatively new cooperative and was a threat to the established milk cooperatives.

Legal action began when Mid-America commenced a lawsuit against NFO, charging it with price-fixing in an effort to foreclose it from entering the market. NFO filed a counterclaim naming AMPI and CMPC as additional defendants, charging them with conspiracy to boycott NFO from the market. After years of discovery, the case was tried before

Judge Oliver of United States District Court for the Western District of Missouri. He ruled against everyone and dismissed the complaint and counterclaim. On appeal, the Eighth Circuit Court of Appeals, in opinion authored by Judge Heany, affirmed the ruling as to the dismissal of plaintiffs case but reversed as to the dismissal of NFO's counterclaim, ruling that it had established a violation of § 1 of the Sherman Act, and was entitled to an award of damages. On remand, Judge Oliver heard further evidence but refused to award NFO damages. In the second appeal, Judge Heany, in pointed language, stated that Judge Oliver had not followed the court's ruling, and gave specific directions for the award of damages and attorneys' fees and costs. (From this point on, I refer to NFO as plaintiff and the other corporations as defendants.)

Professor Henke informed us that the attorneys in the case were mostly from Washington D.C. The significance of this was their hourly rates were considerably higher than those in Kansas City. Indeed, eastern lawyers, at the time, were charging as high as $350 per hour while Kansas City rates were $200 per hour or less. (As of 2014, lawyer fees are as high as $1500 per hour.)

As we walked to the courtroom where the first session was to be held, I was nervous because I was supposed to be the mediator expert and I had never faced such a challenge before. When we arrived at the courtroom, which was quite spacious, it was full with participants. Each cooperative had 50 to 60 board members, and most were present with their lawyers.

Professor Henke introduced Mark and myself to the group. He spent the first hour explaining the process and how he viewed the case. Of course, he did not say what his award of damages was going to be, but by the way he analyzed the case the clear message was that it was going to be a substantial amount. Once this was completed, the group broke down into two caucuses, one for the plaintiff, which Mark handled, and the other for the defendants, which I directed. Previously, I had explained to Mark the format to be followed so he felt comfortable with the process.

The defendants met in the jury room, an octagonal shaped room with a large round table in the middle and comfortable armchairs surrounding it. Personal introductions were made and I met the key players in the mediation. I first met Don Barnes from Washington, D.C. He struck me as being very bright, an expert in antitrust law, and a lawyer I could trust. As I became better acquainted my first impression proved accurate, but I also learned that he would not push his client towards settlement. He was going to help as much as he could, but he was political enough not to displease those who paid the bills. It had to be a slow process, with the milk cooperative board he represented making up their own minds in their own time. Still, I enjoyed being with Don because he was affable and had a good sense of humor.

Next, I was introduced to Major Park, a Kansas City lawyer, who at first was rather quiet. Later I found he was a major player on the defense side in shaping the settlement and gaining support for it. When things looked bleak, which was not infrequent, I turned to Major Park for encouragement and hope. He was always calm and willing to consider new approaches.

Then there was Solomon Bude who was a whole other story. Saul was 75 years old at the time and a very brilliant lawyer, who truly knew more than the judges deciding the case. In fact every time we met, Saul would make brilliant arguments as to why defendants would win each legal point discussed. The only problem was the appellate court had already rejected each of Saul's well-thought-out arguments. It became a matter of routine to remind him that the arguments he was making had already been rejected; yet he persisted. I soon realized Saul took his losses in the Court of Appeals rather poorly, so much so that he was unwilling to admit the fact that he had lost on the issue of liability and all

that was before the court at this time was how much defendants had to

pay. Early in the mediation, Saul dominated discussions as he dominated

the case for 20 years. Because of his intransigence and unwillingness to

recommend a substantial payment of money to settle, it was necessary to

isolate him from center of decision-making.

Sitting around the table, in addition to the attorneys, were three

or four representatives of each of the three defendant milk cooperatives.

I quickly learned that each was elected to his respective farm board and

therefore was sensitive to the feelings and opinions of his constituents.

Of course, each was a farmer and had lived for 20 years with the burden

of this litigation. They were angry at NFO for sustaining the lawsuit all

these years and they were upset at paying millions of dollars in attorneys'

fees. And now the plaintiff was asking $23 million in attorneys' fees and

costs in addition to treble damages for the losses sustained.

For two and one-half hours, I asked questions about the

defendants' case, it strengths and weaknesses. Saul could identify no

weaknesses in spite of the fact the defendants faced a potential judgment

in excess of $30 million. The other lawyers more realistically appraised

the case. When we discussed what the first settlement offer should be, a figure $8 million was agreed upon. I tried to persuade them that a figure in excess of $10 million would have more impact on the plaintiff and give a better signal the defendants were serious about settling the case. After lunch break the defense continued discussing the case without my being present.

Thereafter Mark McCormick and I compared notes and decided to meet next with the plaintiff and it's attorneys. The purpose was to get a settlement demand that I could take back to the defendants. After several hours of discussion, I was authorized to give a figure of $29,500,000. Mark and I then met with the defendants and we disclosed the figure.

Saul's reaction was to terminate the mediation as a waste of time and money. It was at this point I realized he was opposed to the mediation in the first place and was there only because the judge had ordered it. "Gentlemen," I observed, "this is only plaintiff's first demand; they will come down. We need to go back with an offer that will keep it at the table. I hope you will put in excess of $10 million on the table."

At this point it was time to break for dinner. Ted Henke took us to dinner and afterwards Mark and I went to the Holiday Inn, where defendants were staying. It was located one mile from the law school campus. When we arrived everyone was waiting. Don Barnes was the spokesperson.

"Dick and Mark, we have discussed our first bid thoroughly and you're authorized to take a figure of $10,500,000 back to the plaintiff." After some discussion, I expressed my appreciation for exceeding $10 million, for I felt this would give a positive signal to NFO.

Mark and I drove to the Ritz-Carlton Hotel, the most expensive hotel in Kansas City. The plaintiff and its attorneys were housed in a large suite, the most expensive the hotel had. As we entered the room where the parties were waiting, we were met by David Donahoe of Washington, D.C., of the law firm of Aiken, Gump, Strauss, Haver and Field. Dave was extremely bright and articulate antitrust lawyer. He was as friendly and cordial as he was intelligent. I soon learned that Dave had carried the burden, almost single handedly, of winning the case in the Circuit Court of Appeals after the District Court had ruled against plaintiff on two occasions. I must add that through the entire mediation process, he was the one person on the plaintiff's side who never gave up hope that the mediation process would work even when things looked bleak. Dave was the person I called on the plaintiff's side for new ideas.

Discussion continued about what a counter offer should be. Mark and I were finally asked to leave the room so they could decide on a new figure. As Mark and I waited in the hallway, we agreed that we had been well received and this was encouraging. Mark then observed: "Based on everything I have heard in my discussion with the plaintiff group I don't think they will go below $23 million."

I responded: "I don't think defendants at this point will go to $20 million. That's the way it always is in the beginning. In fact, Mark, there'll be a number of times when you will be sure the mediation has failed; we just have to be persistent and exercise extraordinary patience."

We were called back into the room and given the figure of $27,800,000 as plaintiff's response. By the time we completed our discussions, it was late, and we returned to our Days Inn motel. We were scheduled to meet again with the defendants at 8 AM the next morning. Mark and I discussed our strategy for the next day and then retired.

Arriving at the Holiday Inn conference room the next morning, where defendants and their attorneys were gathered, we were asked to wait while they discussed other matters. Forty-five minutes later, we were ushered into the room and seated.

Mark began by stating, "we have a new demand, but, this is not their final offer, so we need to consider it and decide on a response. They are now offering to settle the case for $27,800,000."

"That's outrageous," shouted one farmer representative seated at the end of the table. Saul Bude then chimed in, "I told you we were wasting our time. I am here only because the special master ordered it, but we are never going to get this settled."

Mark snapped back in a low firm voice, "Saul, you know the mediation process – NFO is still posturing and its demand tells us nothing at this point. Now we simply have to be patient and work through this." What I thought of saying was better left unsaid, so it was.

For several hours the matter was discussed, some wishing to terminate the mediation, cooler heads wanting to push on. Finally, by 11:15 AM a new offer was proposed and agreed upon by all present. Mark and I proceeded back to the Ritz-Carlton Hotel.

When we entered the NFO suite, everyone seemed relaxed and in a friendly mood.

Once again, Mark began the conversation and informed the NFO group, that, "defendants have raised their offer to $14,200,000, which is a substantial increase."

Bob Brown responded, "I thought the defendants were going to act in good faith. As far as I am concerned we can just leave." His face showed that he was both frustrated and angry.

Dave Donahoe said nothing and there was a long silence. Finally, Dave asked, "what would you like us to do? Are you looking for a new demand?"

I responded: "Look, we know the defendants will increase their offer. The simple fact is that there is a great deal of posturing going on among defendants. Because there are so many interests involved they have to move slowly. No one wants to be the bad guy and jump too high, too fast. We must be patient."

There was more silence, and Mark was about to say something when Bob Brown went to the window, turned and looked at the group. "I'm just not certain where this is getting us. I just can't waste time like this."

"Bob," I said, "what we need to do is go back with another demand. This will permit Mark and myself to get a feel for where the defendants are willing to go. We're not going to get the job done in just two days."

After further discussion, Mark and I were asked to leave the room. As we stood in the hallway, Mark said, "I don't think we're going to get this settled; the parties are just too far apart."

"Mark, this is the way it always is. You have highs and lows. After all, we are not going to undo in two days what has taken 20 years to create."

After an hour we were called back into the room. Bob Brown got up from the sofa and said, "this is our final offer."

I immediately interrupted, "Bob, please don't say that; don't dig in. Give us a chance to do our job."

As I said this, I happened to look at Dave Donahoe who winked, so I said nothing more. Bob picked up again and said, "we are willing to go to $26,500,000, but defendants must make a major move."

After discussion, Mark and I headed back to the Holiday Inn. We concluded this was as far as we could get at this time. Defendants in particular needed to think about the process and consider the consequences if they did not settle. We gave them the new offer and asked them to set another date for the mediation. After some telephone calls to the plaintiff's room, it was decided we would meet again at the Kansas City Airport Holiday Inn in two weeks.

During the next week, I learned that NFO wanted to pay off their mortgage on their new facility in Ames, Iowa. This was quite helpful news for it gave the plaintiff a motive for settling at this time.

At the next mediation session, Mark and I first met with the defendants because NFO made the last offer. Some 30 representatives and attorneys were at the table or sitting along the wall. Mark began the session summarizing the progress made and expressing his pleasure with the moves both sides were making.

Ultimately, it was decided that defendants would offer $16 million, but this was getting close to their limit. I remarked, "at some point, Mark and I would like to know in confidence where you're willing to go. This will not be disclosed but will help us determine the progress of the mediation."

There was a long sustained silence and then I asked: "in confidence, could you tell us whether you'd be willing to settle for a figure more than $20 million." I held my breath for this was the first time we tried to sound the defendants out.

One farmer representative responded: "I would never agree to such a figure. I would rather have the court order me to pay $30 million, then to voluntarily pay $20 million to those − − −."

Mark immediately asked "why is that?" The farmer looked around and noted that most of his colleagues were agreeing with him. He looked at Mark and said, "we are elected to the board of our cooperatives, and if we agreed to pay such a sum to those −−− we would never be a reelected, none of us."

After some further discussion we headed up to Dave Donohoe's room. His entourage did not have the presidential suite this time. We presented defendants new offer and no one responded. I expected a tirade from Bob Brown, but he said nothing. Dave looked at the two farmer representatives and then each of the three other lawyers. Finally he said, "let us confer alone if this would be alright." It was agreed they would call us in Mark's room where we would be conferring.

In Mark's room, Mark sat down and looked up at me. "This case is just not going to settle. I don't think NFO will go below $24 million, at least not at this point."

There was a long lull and then I responded, "I don't think the defendants will go above $20 million if that. Maybe we need a new strategy. What if we put a mediator's figure out there and try to get both sides to accept it? It has to be a figure which will push both sides. This will take the farmer representatives off the hook because the mediators are setting the figure and not the plaintiff."

Mark responded, "sounds like a good idea. It sounds as though the defendants want to be told what the settlement should be so it will not appear they acquiesced. What do you think it should be?"

I thought a moment and then responded, "$21 million. My rationale is that the defendants' maximum figure is probably $20 million and NFO's $22 million."

"I don't think NFO will go below $23 million under any circumstances. That's my gut reaction. I think our settlement figure should be $22 million," said Mark.

"Mark, you're probably right, we need to push them hard. Two things we have going for us. Dave wants to settle badly inasmuch as NFO needs the money now to pay off the mortgage on its new national headquarters. And Dave's law firm is carrying a $1 million outlay of costs, and I am sure the firm would like to get this paid off now, not three years from now."

We talked further and Mark finally agreed to $21 million. It was also agreed that before we put the figure on the table we would ask the "walkaway" question, and if their response was favorable then we would give them the figure.

After nearly an hour we were called back and Dave gave us a new figure of $26 million. This did not seem like a big enough drop to respond to the $16 million put on the table by the defendants.

"Dave," I began, "could you in strictest confidence give us some sense of the range of your bottom figure. It would help us immeasurably because right now we're so far apart I'm not certain it is worthwhile continuing. Let me ask it in a different way. If the defendants were to come up to $20 million, would you reject the figure out of hand or would you at least consider it? In other words, would you just walk away?"

Dave looked at the farmer representative who was executive director of the NFO. Dan Jensen had a weather-worn ruddy face, large powerful hands that I did not like to shake because the grip hurt mine. He was heavyset and spoke with a slight Iowa farm drawl. However, as I got to know him better and found he had a good sense of humor and enjoyed telling jokes.

Dan thought a moment and then said, "I can't speak for the others, but if $20 million was put on the table I would not walk away. I wouldn't accept it because the settlement has to be more than $20 million or $21 million, but I would keep talking."

This told me a great deal. First, it confirmed that NFO wanted the settlement very badly, and second they would probably go below $23 million; how much below I was not certain. I looked at Mark to see if he read Dan the same as I did. He nodded just slightly and I said, "Mark and I have been talking and we have concluded that we should put a figure on the table that probably neither side can accept at this time. That makes it a good settlement figure. In other words, it is probably less than what you will accept and more than what the defendants will pay."

I hesitated to see if I was getting a reaction. All present were listening intently waiting for the figure. "The figure we would like to put on the table is $21 million."

I hardly had the words out of my mouth when Bob Brown blurted, "it's not enough; we just can't accept that. We might as well terminate the mediation."

Dave held up his hand and said firmly, "we want to at least discuss the figure. We could never agree to it because it is below our authorization. We would have to discuss it first.

Mark then spoke up. "Dave, why don't you and Bob discuss this with the board of NFO. We know it is below your expectations, but I can assure you it is above the defendants authority by considerable amount. All we ask you to do is talk about it with your people. If it is rejected, so be it. Defendants probably won't agree to it any event, but let's at least try."

Dan interjected once again and said, "we will talk about it, but I can't promise anything." Then he turned to me and said "go talk to defendants and see how they react. If we need you, would you be willing to come and talk to the NFO board?"

"Of course we will," Mark said.

I added, "that is a superb idea. As a matter fact, we should make the same offer to the defendants."

We left the room encouraged for the first time in several days. Once we rejoined defendants, Mark said, "Dick and I, as your mediators, are putting a mediator's figure on the table which we're asking both sides to at least consider. We are not asking for a response, but only that you will agree to give it consideration. We think the case should settle for $21 million, and —" Mark could not finish the sentence for several people spoke at once. The only words I heard were "impossible" and "it won't sell." Strangely enough the lawyers remained silent and even some of the key players, who had great influence.

After the room quieted down, I added: "gentlemen, I would like to make the following proposal. Each of you should ask your respective boards if Mark and myself can meet with them and make a presentation, explaining how we arrived at $21 million and why it is a good settlement figure. In that way we can take the heat off of you and your lawyers." As I said this, several of the parties started nodding their heads indicating consent and several even had expressions of hope.

Saul Bude then said, "how do we know NFO is acting in good faith and will do the same?"

I looked at Mark and responded, "let me suggest that we get everyone together, without the attorneys." Maybe we can have a heart to heart conversation to clear the air. Arrangements were made to do this at a time set in the afternoon.

The NFO group sat on one side of the conference table and the defendant farmers on the other side. Mark and I sat at one end. First, no one said anything and then Mark stated: "Gentlemen, we thought that after 20 fruitless years of litigation you might wish to face one another and try to settle this matter."

One of the defendant farmers, a heavyset individual with a firm but warm face said: "I have been in this matter since the beginning, and I cannot believe that we have been fighting for 20 years. We're all milk farmers and we have paid millions of dollars in attorneys' fees and for what –" and his voice trailed off.

An NFO farmer responded: "it don't make no sense for this to continue. The price of milk is lowest in years, and instead of doing something about it we just fight each other, which only depresses prices even more. We have to settle and work together to raise prices."

The discussion lasted over two hours with everyone agreeing that a settlement had to be found. As Mark and I drove back to Des Moines, we felt encouraged, but this was dampened when we turned on the radio and learned that our warplanes had just started bombing Iraq, kicking off the Gulf War.

In the next two weeks arrangements were made for me to meet with the three defendant boards and for Mark and myself to meet with the NFO board.

In preparation for my presentations, I worked up a damage sheet which outlined what potential damages could be. It was not my job to say what the special master was going to do for I did not know. As a matter of fact, Ted Henke did not know at this time himself. I did know it was going to be on the high side. My job was to outline the risks defendants faced if the matter was decided by Professor Henke. It was more difficult discussing NFO's risks because both Mark and I felt it was in a good position to get considerably more than $21 million.

I was scheduled to meet first with the defendant Mid-America at the Omaha International Airport. I arrived the night before and had a meeting with Wayne Hoecker, who was associated with Major Park and was counsel for the co-op. As I got to know Wayne better I realized he was the man behind the scenes and yielded considerable influence in ultimately resolving the case. He understood precisely the arguments I was making and agreed with my approach.

At 9 AM I arrived at the conference room, but had to wait 35 minutes while the 50 person board discussed other business. Wayne finally invited me in and introduced me to the board. The board members sat at tables arranged in a square. The podium was at one end. I handed out copies of my four damage estimates with a note at the top stating: "Highly Confidential To Be Returned After Meeting." I explained my role as mediator and how I was impartial and nonjudgmental. Then I explained what Professor Henke was doing and the risks defendants were facing in not settling the case. Next I explained that the mediators had come up with a settlement proposal of $21 million. When I mentioned the figure several of the board members said spontaneously, "never."

I stopped for a second, and looked at the board members who had spoken. Then I said, "I can understand your feelings. It's a lot of money. But look at the memorandum I handed you which, by the way, is highly confidential and must not be disclosed to NFO. I've outlined four scenarios of what the special master could do in awarding damages. As you can see, he could easily award $41 million, which is almost twice what we are proposing."

There was absolute silence as board members looked at my worksheet. "Quite frankly," I continued, "Professor Henke could easily award $30 million or more. The likely range is $28 million to $32 million."

One member raised his hand, and I acknowledged him. He said: "I don't understand how we can be made to pay so much money. NFO started this thing and has carried on the lawsuit all these years in bad faith."

Wayne walked up to the lectern. "Let me correct the record. We filed the original lawsuit and NFO counterclaimed against us."

Another member spoke up, "is there any possibility that if we do nothing they will get tired of this and finally give up?"

Again, Wayne responded, "no, that is not a possibility. We either settle now or pay in three and one-half years."

Another member asked, "wouldn't it be better to use our money now and wait three years or so before paying. At least we will have the use of the money?"

"That is a possibility," I responded. "However, we will pay so much more, for once the District Court enters judgment, interest will start to run, and interest on $28 million could be a considerable amount of money."

There was more discussion and I finally left. Wayne and I talked a few minutes and he felt the meeting generally went well. He added, "I think they will support your proposal, but we won't know until the next mediation session."

The following week I met with the AMPI board at the Kansas City International Airport. Once again, Mark was unable to join me because of other business. I made my proposal, only this board was more vocal and hostile towards me and my plan. Don Barnes was there, but he did little to support what I was proposing. In thinking about it later, I recognized that Don was not about to antagonize his board. If the settlement failed, he had to continue living with them and representing them in the lawsuit. I understood this. When the meeting concluded, Don said he did not know what his board would do.

On Friday of the same week, Mark and I drove up to Ames, Iowa , where NFO's new headquarters was located. I was informed the building was built in anticipation of receiving the judgment in this case, only the board had not realized there would be such a delay in receiving their money.

The NFO building is one-story with an atrium like entranceway. We were taken immediately to the spacious boardroom. It had a large conference table with very comfortable plush chairs around it. Mark made the presentation and we answered questions. Only a few of the directors were there but had full authority. The consensus seemed to be the $21 million was not enough but they would discuss the matter.

After we left, Mark was disappointed and again felt the matter would not resolve. I certainly agreed the meeting was not terribly encouraging, but also felt that Dave, who was present, was working behind-the-scenes to get NFO to move. To say I was hopeful is inaccurate, but I was not willing to give up.

The next session at the Kansas City International Airport was scheduled the following week. At the last moment Mark was unable to go so I went by myself. When I left my house, it was extremely foggy, but, as I headed south on I-35 the fog eased some. However, 40 miles north of the airport I hit the worst fog I've seen since my days in college when I traveled New Hampshire highways in winter. I literally could not see the road signs and could barely see the white line along the side of the road. I missed several turnoffs but finally made my way to the Hilton Hotel where the mediation was to take place.

The next morning, I met first with the defendants. I expressed my regrets that the CMPC board, which Saul Bude represented, was unable to meet with us. Saul's comment was that it had little money to contribute to the settlement because it was a cooperative made up of other cooperatives and therefore had no way to accumulate funds. As Saul spoke the others expressed a frustrated silence, so I dropped the issue.

After further discussion, Don Barnes said, "here is our final offer. We will put a total package of $18 million on the table. We want you to take this back to NFO."

"Don, please don't say this is the final offer. Just say it's the best you can do at this time. However, I feel it is a significant offer so let's see what NFO will do with it."

Immediately I left the conference room and went to Dave Donahoe's room. When I got there only Bob Brown was present with Dave. Bob got on the phone to call the others. I presented the defendants new proposal and there was considerable discussion. I was asked to leave the room and I retreated to my own room and waited for them to call. About an hour later I was called back, and David spoke.

"Richard," he began, "we want you to take this offer. We will accept an offer of $21 million cash or credit plus an agreement to permit NFO to handle the culling of cows from the herds of members of Mid-America and AMPI. The value of this would be a guaranteed $1 million for a total package of $22 million. In fact, if we are permitted to cull more cows, then the defendants can reduce the cash amount or credit to be paid. In other words, if we culled $2 million or $3 million worth of cows this could reduce the cash payment to $20 million or $19 million."

"What in heaven's name does 'culling cows' mean?" I asked.

Dave, being a city boy, looked at Bob Brown, who was no better qualified to answer. He looked at Ernie Erickson, one of the two farmer representatives at this session. In a decided Iowa drawl, Ernie said, "cull cows means removing nonproductive cows from the herd and selling them at market. Every farmer has several cows he has to cull every year because of age or sickness."

"I know nothing about this," I said, "but this seems like a very imaginative way to resolve the matter. I'm anxious to see what the defendants will say to such a creative plan."

I left the room with high hopes. When I presented the plan to the defendants, several opposed it, but several of the leaders thought that such a plan could work. It was agreed to take the plan back to the respective boards to see what their reaction would be. I informed the plaintiff group of this and they got upset for this meant another delay. Bob Brown thought this was a stall and wanted to terminate the mediation. Dave Donahoe prevailed and defendants were given 10 days to respond.

Ten days was not needed for each board rejected the concept in five days. I informed Dave of this and his response was, "don't get discouraged, Dick, we will get the job done. I will talk to my people and see if we can come up with another plan."

For the next week I was in constant contact with Wayne Hecker, Major Parks and Don Barnes. We worked up a new proposal whereby Mid-America and AMPI would each contribute $10 million, immediate payment of $8 million and a note for $2 million for a total of $20 million. And CMPC would contribute $1 million.

When Saul heard the new proposal he immediately rejected it saying that CMPC could only pay $200,000 and no more. It was finally decided for Mid-America and AMPI to settle alone and let NFO continue the suit against CMPC. Saul's response was that he would dissolve CMPC and never pay a penny because it has no assets which could be attached. Needless to say, we came to another logjam.

Another mediation session was scheduled at the Minneapolis International Airport. The meeting was set to begin at 1 o'clock in the afternoon on a Thursday, so I drove up there in the morning. However, I remember that trip very clearly because my back started hurting. It was so bad I could hardly sit in the car to drive the distance. When I met first with the defendants, I could barely sit down in the chair and had to pull myself out of the chair to stand. Everyone remarked about my discomfort and I joked that I must have hurt myself while exercising, which was not true.

This first day turned out to be the absolute low point in the mediation. The defendant representatives were angry with Saul for taking the stand he was concerning his client. At this point they could agree on nothing. I finally decided to meet with the NFO group, which was housed in the penthouse suite. They even had a hostess sitting at a desk outside the door. She was there to make arrangements for their meals and to assist in faxing material, if necessary. I must say I was impressed, but also wondered what this cost, but did not ask.

When the NFO group learned that the defendants were in disarray, they were ready to leave immediately. Needless to say they were very upset. Dave finally prevailed and suggested they come up with one last plan. I left the room while they worked on it.

Once back in my own room I could do nothing but lie on my bed and pray that my back would get better. I recognized that it was the result of stress and animosity generated by the anger of the parties trying to resolve the lawsuit.

Dave called me back into the room and presented me with two plans. "The first plan is the defendants will pay $16 million cash by June 1, 1991, and execute notes for $5,400,000, amortized over four years, gross guaranteed at 13 percent interest. If the defendants wish to allow

NFO to cull their cows, they would be credited at five dollars per cow. Plan two is $200,000 cash by May 1, 1991, and $16 million cash paid by June 1, 1991, and notes for $5,750,000, five year amortization at 9.75 percent interest."

I thanked Dave and presented the plan to the defendants, and there seemed to be renewed interest. They figured out that at 13 percent interest, the first plan would cost them $22 million. It was suggested that they could borrow funds at a lot less than 13 percent and pay off the entire $21 million. I was requested to go back to NFO and see if they would lower the interest rate. They wanted a rate of 6 or 7 percent. NFO finally agreed, after calling headquarters, to 9 ½ percent.

When the meeting broke up, everyone, for the first time, even Saul, began to feel that there might be a light at the end of the tunnel. As a matter fact, Dave gave me an ad ripped out of a magazine to give to Saul. The ad said: "how to make yourself judgment proof," and Dave added the words: "To Saul, catch me if you can, from D. Donahoe." When I saw this I knew we were almost there. Needless to say all defendants agreed with Dave's note.

Over the next two weeks the plan was finalized and Mid-America and AMPI worked out an arrangement with CMPC to help it pay its share of the payment. The deal was done.

When the matter was finally resolved I began to realize the full potential of mediation. Even the most difficult case can be resolved if the parties really want it and will work to get there.

Oh, by the way, as I hit the highway after the Minneapolis mediation session my back cleared up almost immediately. This confirmed my thought that it was simply the stress and tension caused by the struggle going on.

Although Dave promised me dinner if the case settled, I never heard from him or the other attorneys again. Ed Henke did visit Mark and myself when he was passing through Des Moines. He was very pleased with the settlement even though he would no longer receive $175 per hour, which was a lot of money in those days.

In this mediation several strategies were used: First, we established a mediators' figure of $21 million and asked each side to consider it. This strategy was initiated when a farmer said "we would rather be ordered by the judge to pay $30 million than voluntarily pay $20 million." I inquired why, because the $10 million difference was a lot of money. He responded, because "to *voluntarily* pay that much money would anger our members and we would not be reelected to our boards." Mark and I felt that our putting out a settlement figure would be more like a judge doing it and more acceptable to the membership.

Second, recognizing the sensitivity of the mediators' figure, Mark and I agreed to meet with the membership of each co-op and personally defend the figure. Any anger or criticism expressed would be directed at us and not board members or the attorneys. We acted like a lightning rod.

Third, we worked out a strategy to handle Saul Bude, who was trying to discredit us and the mediation process. The strategy was not to attack or belittle him, but allow him to do what he wanted. His negativity began to work against him until he isolated himself. He then was no longer a factor in the negotiations.

And fourth, we developed a strategy of planting a seed of what might occur if the special master decided the matter. We strongly suggested on many occasions that in our opinion, the special master was likely to award between $28 million and $32 million. This realization slowly sunk in and was instrumental in obtaining compromise from the defendants.

A word about planting a seed as a strategy. Essentially, what a mediator does when planting a seed is use time-tested "used car salesmen" techniques. A used car salesman knows that if he can get a customer thinking about a new car long enough, he will buy. He will encourage the customer to take the car out for a drive or even take it on a short trip well knowing that familiarity breeds a sale. The same strategy is used by the mediator. The longer the parties think about the proposal, the easier it becomes for them to accept it.

I must confess that I am helpless when buying a used car. I cannot negotiate for myself, which is strange for a mediator to admit. In fact, when buying a used car (I try to buy a car with less than 15,000 miles and then run it up to 100,000 miles in two or three years), I have my wife accompany me. I tell her that I want her to be firm with me and not let me go over $20,000 plus the trade-in. Each time the used-car salesman asks what I want to spend and he fills out his sheet, marking down the $20,000. He has me initial it. He then supposedly takes this offer to his boss to see if he can get him to accept. And, invariably comes back saying the boss will come all the way down to $24,000. When I insist that all I will pay is $20,000, he tries again. This time he comes back and says, "good news, the boss will agree to split the difference." I now have my heart set on the car, and I give in and the car is mine, and I end up paying much more than the $22,000, with the tax and all the add-ons.

The lesson to be learned from used-car salesmen is, one, place a settlement figure on the table for the parties to think about, not necessarily accept initially; two, give them every reason to continue thinking about it; three, the longer they think about it the more sure you are they will accept; and, four let them test drive the idea by suggesting what might happen if they allow the matter to go to trial.

I've employed the used car salesman approach on many occasions and the strategy works. I often say I hope I don't sound like a used car salesman. Some say I do. One party happened to be a used car salesman and he didn't think that was funny.

A word about the title of this mediation, *The Bleak House*. Our case was mediated in its 21st year of existence. This is an unconscionably long time for a case to be in court. Even ten years is a long time. During the course of the mediation, two individuals asked me if I had read the *Bleak House* by Charles Dickens. It is a story about an estate in England that was tied up in the English Chancery Court for 17 years. At the end of the book, those who were to receive the money go to the court, but are told by their attorneys that there was nothing left – the corpus of the trust was used up in attorneys' fees. The parallel to the instant case is the length of time the matter was in the legal system. A caveat: as a result of the book Parliament reformed the Chancery Court to avoid a repeat of what occurred in the book.

Mediation #47

Last Clear Chance – The Domino Strategy

When there are multiple defendants, and one or more are not cooperating or trying to hold a settlement hostage unless they are let out with a minimum contribution, a common tactic used by mediators is to employ the domino strategy. Once the mediator determines one or more of the defendants is not acting in good faith, he might suggest the plaintiff negotiate only with those serious about settling. As each defendant settles, it puts more pressure on those holding out because, one, costs and expenses are shared by fewer defendants and, two, those settling often take their experts with them so that the remaining defendant or defendants must find their own.

The next case study illustrates the domino strategy.

Mark Lofton got into his two door Mercury Lynx automobile. As he pulled onto Highway 34 heading east towards Red Oak, Iowa, it was still dark at 6:05 AM this October morning. He flipped his bright lights on and could see as far as the lights carried, there being no fog or haze normally expected this late during harvest time.

Red Oak was only 13 miles away and Mark wanted to arrive early for work at the meatpacking plant where he worked on the production line. Mark, who was 31 years old, had trouble keeping a job very long although he was not a troublemaker and was fairly conscientious about his work. He either got sick at the wrong time, or the job was seasonal, or he was hurt from an accident; it was always something.

As he sat in his car he had the front seat pushed back as far as it would go to accommodate his huge body of over 350 pounds. Oh, how he had tried to lose weight but his appetite always got the better of him. Mark rubbed his eyes still fuzzy from sleep. He increased his speed to over 60 mph as there were no other cars on the highway. About 2 miles from Red Oak he started going up a rather long incline. As he reached the crest a car passed going the opposite direction. He was blinded for a moment because the driver failed to lower his bright lights. As Mark came over the crest he saw two flashing amber lights some 2000 feet ahead, but lost them as two more cars came towards him going west. Suddenly Mark saw two wagons filled with grain 75 feet ahead being pulled at 17 mph by a tractor. He slammed on his brakes, but it was too late and crashed into the rear wagon and rolled over three times off the highway. Two hours

later Highway Patrol was able to extricate Mark from the wreckage, and

he was rushed to the hospital in Council Bluffs.

Two years later the phone rang and I picked it up. "Mr. Calkins,

this is Shelly. Would you like a mediation in Council Bluffs for Thursday,

July 11, 1998? It's a bad one, a quadriplegic."

The drive to Council Bluffs is always pleasant as Interstate 80

traverses beautiful rolling farmland. As you approach the city from the

East you enter a very hilly and wooded area located in the bluff area along

the Missouri River. Directly across the river is Omaha, Nebraska.

As I came over the knoll to descend into the business area of the

city, I could see the skyscrapers of Omaha in the distance. Finding the

building where plaintiff's attorney was located, I parked my car, entered

the building and took the elevator to the third floor. Upon arrival I was

immediately led into a conference room where two insurance adjusters

and their attorneys were waiting.

Dave Malmo, plaintiff's attorney, came into the room and in a

very affable and matter-of-fact voice explained that Mark and his brother

had just left home and would be there in an hour. Dave apologized and

explained that he had specifically told his client to be there at 9:00 AM.

Mark and his brother finally arrived. Mark was in a wheelchair which his younger brother was pushing. Mark was very large, over 300 pounds, which was somewhat less than what he weighed at the time the accident. He did have some use of his hands and arms but was still classified as a quadriplegic.

After my usual opening remarks, Dave began his opening statement summarizing plaintiff's case. He stated: "The defendant, Francis Jensen, was hauling grain to Red Oak. He was pulling two overloaded wagons at 17 miles per hour. There were no lights on the wagons and they should not have been on the highway in the first place — they are not made for highway use. He was using them as trailers, which are required to have rear red lights."

Dave hesitated a moment, took a drink of water, and then added, "we are suing Kiwanee Wagon Manufacture because they sold wagons without rear lights. It knew farmers would use them on the highway as trailers and therefore they were required to have rear lights. The installation would only cost $18. For that paltry amount this tragedy would have been avoided." We are also suing the farmer, Francis Jensen.

David started getting emotional. "And look at Mark now. Need I say more."

After David completed his remarks, Tom Jackson, attorney for the farmer, Francis Jensen, looked at counsel for Kiwanee, Philip Dunlap, as to who should proceed first. Phil deferred to Tom with the remark, "You have the most exposure in this case," which Tom ignored.

"We recognize that this was a most tragic accident and we feel a great sense of compassion towards you, Mark, and we are here today to see if there is something we can do to help you so that you will not have to go through the pain and trauma of a trial. However, you understand that as competent lawyers we must forcefully argue our clients' case."

Tom stopped, looked at his notes and then continued.

"As you know, Mr. Jensen is a farmer, has been such all his life. It is his livelihood and his life. It's all he knows. What he did on the morning in question is what he has done for 20 years, and what all farmers do, haul grain to market. All over Iowa, wagons filled with corn are pulled to town for sale at the local grainary. We're all familiar with this process and we know it is done night and day. The question is was Mr. Jensen required to have lights on the rear wagon, in addition to the slow-moving vehicle sign which was attached to the wagon.

In the case of *Lyons vs. Lange*, 447 NW.2d 407, the court directly held that equipment being pulled by a tractor is not required to have rear lights so long as the tractor has flashing amber lights."

"Excuse me, Tom, but what court is that?" I asked.

Tom looked at the opinion and answered: "It's the Iowa Court of Appeals with Judge Habhab writing the opinion of the court. Here's a copy for you and Dave. In other words, we have a complete defense here. If plaintiff is going to win, he will have to get the Iowa Supreme Court to overrule the *Lyons* rule of law."

As I listened to this argument I was astounded that Iowa law seemingly permitted farmers to pull wagons on the highway without rear red lights, and at very slow speeds. This just did not seem to be good law, but when I reviewed the *Lyons* opinion that is exactly what it said.

Tom continued: "Let's review the facts of the case, because they favor my client. He hooked up two wagons to his tractor and drove out to Highway 34 and drove east towards Red Oak, some 3 miles away. Approaching town he went over a fairly high hill and was descending towards town. As he was traveling, some 15 cars and pick-up trucks going both ways safely passed him. In fact we were able to locate two drivers who will testify they saw the flashing amber lights of the tractor and were able to pass safely.

"When Mark came over the crest of the hill he was 67.18 feet above the level the tractor and wagons which were 2000 feet ahead of him. At that time he had to see the flashing amber lights on the tractor as he was looking down on them. He did not react but kept traveling at the same rate of speed, which Mark says was 55 mph, the speed limit. I think the record will show he was traveling faster than that.

"Although he saw the flashing amber lights, and he had to have seen the "slow moving vehicle" sign, he did not react until he was only 43 feet from the wagon, when he slammed on his brakes. By then it was too late. It is our position Mark was more at fault than my client and a jury will find that his comparative fault was more than 51 percent, which means he cannot recover. He failed to keep a proper lookout; he failed to stop within the assumed clear distance ahead; he was exceeding the speed limit; and he failed to wear his seatbelt."

Tom stopped and looked at Phil. Phil looked up and said, "well I guess it's my turn. Frankly, I'm not certain why we are in this case because we manufacture these farm wagons like everyone else. No manufacture today, much less 17 years ago when these wagons were manufactured and sold to Mr. Jensen, installed rear lights on them. They're built for use on the farm and not the highway."

Phil continued: "I have been a farmer all my life, although I also practice law. I can tell you that every farmer in Iowa owns a wagon like this and they don't have lights on them and they don't have to. The law doesn't require it. I think plaintiff's counsel is confusing wagons with trailers. A trailer is built for highway use and requires rear lights. A wagon does not.

"Now if my client is to be held liable, plaintiff must show that the wagons without lights were inherently dangerous and we knew that when we sold them to Mr. Jensen. We have a complete defense of "state-of-the-art." We are entitled to a jury instruction that if our wagons conform to the state-of-the-art in existence at the time they are designed, tested, manufactured and sold, we cannot be held liable, unless a defect or dangerous condition was later discovered making the product unreasonably dangerous. Our research to date establishes that no manufacture, even at the present time, puts rear lights on their wagons. If plaintiff has found a case otherwise we ask that you disclose it to us at this time."

Phil stopped and the Dave looked up from his notepad on which he was taking notes." Please, may I make a few remarks in response to what counsel have said?"

"Of course," I responded.

"First, let me respond to the argument that Mark had to have seen the tractor's flashing amber lights when he crested the hill. His testimony is that he did not. Isn't that true, Mark?"

"Yes, Mr. Malmo," responded Mark in a quiet, calm voice.

"Furthermore," continued Malmo, "the two witnesses that saw the amber lights cannot help you. One was coming from the east going west, and the other was in a pickup truck which was much higher off the ground than Dave's compact car. In other words, he could see over the wagons and see the amber lights.

"We have two witnesses. One we have not yet identified, but will do so now. Her name is Margaret Streeter and she will testify that she came upon Mr. Jensen and did not see his lights and almost ran into him. She was so upset that when she got to the edge of town she decided to turn around and go back and warn Jensen of the unsafe condition, but the accident occurred at that moment. We learned of her because the next day she went to the police station and gave her name and address and complained of the conditions under which Mr. Jensen was pulling his wagons.

"We have also learned that the wagons Mr. Jensen was pulling were overloaded and the grain blocked his view of the amber lights. In fact some of the grain was spilling on the highway."

"As far as Kiwanee Wagon Company is concerned we have three experts who will testify the failure to provide lights violates recognized standards in the industry. I will have the reports in three weeks and will provide them to you."

When David finished he was out of breath talking so fast. I asked, "is there anything more to be said at this time? If not, let's go into caucus. I'll meet with the plaintiff first. This will take about an hour."

At this point David Malmo, Mark and his brother, and Dave's partner, Fred McNamara, who entered the room during the middle of the opening remarks, went into another conference room. I followed and once inside we immediately began discussing the strengths of the case. Other than review the facts already mentioned in opening remarks, Dave noted that the strongest point he had was that Mark was a quadriplegic and his life was all but over. He could never marry, and he would always have to be cared for. He also noted that he had two witnesses who would testify that they could not see the tractor's lights and almost ran into the wagons. As far as Kiwanee Wagon Company was concerned, it had a brochure, put out by the company, which counsel highlighted. The brochure stated that their wagon was built "for every job on the farm, in the field, on the road, or off the road." In another place the brochure stated, the wagon "steers like a car; accurate trailing is assured with use of this unique autotype roller bearing system. Even at highway speeds the wagon trails straight as a shot."

Dave gave me time to digest this and then added: "you see, they advertised their wagon for road use and therefore they had a common-law duty to provide it with rear lights."

"May I keep this brochure to show to the defendants when I caucus with them?" Dave answered, "of course."

"Dave, what do you see as weaknesses or concerns in your case? I will keep this confidential and they will not leave this room."

"There are two weaknesses" Dave said "but they're not serious. One is that many on the jury will be farmers, and they likewise pull wagons on the highway without rear lights and have done so for many years. Also, Mark had an opportunity to observe the tractor when he came over the crest of the hill and did not keep a proper lookout. Of course, our response is the lights coming the other way partly blinded him. Other than that I do not see any problems."

Dave then reviewed in detail the damages Mark was claiming. Surgery and rehabilitation had already cost $180,000. Plaintiffs expert, a PhD from University of Nebraska, set forth in his report that lost earnings for Mark's life expectancy would be for $750,205; his medical costs would be $100,790 per year for the rest of his life or $4,216,046; and one time medical and rehabilitation costs such as modifying his home and car would cost $129,679. Total damages $5,000,930. "And this is conservative," added Dave.

"What are the policy limits of the two insurance policies?"

Fred McNamara spoke for the first time and said "$1,100,000 on the farmer and $1 million on the wagon manufacture."

"Dave what do you see a jury doing in this case, best case, worst case? I will keep this confidential also."

Dave looked at Fred and then said with little hesitancy, "we could get $10 million in this case with our worst-case being $1 million."

"Have they made an offer of settlement?"

Fred responded, "yes, they have, but we were insulted. They offered only $250,000 total."

I said "we need a new demand; one that will give them the right signal that we are earnest about settling the case today."

I was asked to leave the room while they discussed it. After 10 minutes they called me back and Dave said, "we have discussed the matter and agreed to make a new demand of $4,500,000."

I gulped realizing that this was going to be a very difficult mediation. "But Dave," I protested, "their combined policy limits are $2,100,000. How can you ask a figure that doubles that? I will have difficulty even getting a response from them."

"Look, Dick, they asked for this mediation. We feel our demand is not unreasonable. The bottom line is we want to end up at policy limits so we need to begin much higher. Now, that is confidential and you're not to disclose it."

I then entered the room where the defense teams were waiting. The insurance adjuster representing the farmer joked, "well, have you settled the case?"

"Almost," was my response. "Actually, this is going to be a difficult mediation. I need all the ammunition you can give me. Let's begin by going through the strengths of your case that I can take back to the plaintiff."

Tom Jackson and Phil Dunlap worked together in outlining their case. The new information I got was that Mark had had an affair with his sister-in-law, and his older brothers had threatened to shoot him. This was fairly well known in the community and several jurors hearing the case would surely know about it.

Next they stressed that Iowa law does not require rear lights on a wagon being pulled by a tractor with flashing amber lights. Finally, they noted that 15 cars and trucks had passed the defendant on the highway before the accident.

"There is another matter you should know," added Tom. "Mark was in a prior accident in 1984 and claimed total disability, which was denied by social security. He received benefits for three years, then he had to go back to work."

"Well, Tom, are you claiming that Mark is malingering in this case?" I asked.

"No, I am not. But the point is that he had problems in the past and milked the system for all it was worth. I think this will neutralize some sympathy for Mark."

"If you can get it in," I noted.

"We will get it all in; don't worry about that," snapped back Tom.

When I asked what a jury would do in a case like this, they responded that a jury in this area of Iowa had never awarded a $1 million verdict; however, they recognized that in this case the verdict could go as high as $2.5 million.

I then gave plaintiff's new demand of $4.5 million. They responded by raising their combined offer to $300,000. Kiwanee's attorney then added: "we think this is a fair offer and Kiwanee is not prepared to offer much more than our $100,000. The rest will have to come from my good friend, Tom Jackson."

Jackson, with irritation, said: "come on now. You are not mediating in good faith. We are not going to carry the burden alone. Why did you even come to the table?"

I returned to the plaintiff's caucus and presented defendants' new offer. Dave said, "that offer is an insult and we will not respond to it. Defendants are clearly acting in bad faith."

I responded, "please do not get discouraged. You must understand that this is just their opening bid. They will come up substantially, I'm sure."

Dave, who was rather reflective, finally said, "Dick, we don't believe you. We know you're doing your best. But an offer of $300,000 doesn't even get us started so what is the sense of our coming back with a counter offer?"

There was a moment of silence. Finally, I said, "what would you like me to do? I have to follow your instructions. What I sense is that Jensen's insurance carrier wants to get this resolved, but Kiwanee is holding back for whatever reason." I hesitated a moment and then added: "what if we negotiate with each defendant separately so at least we can settle with Jensen?"

Dave looked at Mark and then at me. "I like the idea," he said. Upon further reflection, he added, however, "wouldn't that leave an empty chair to which Kiwanee could point?"

I responded: "that is always a risk, but in this case I think it is minimal. Kiwanee is an out-of- state manufacturer and to try and blame a local farmer for what happened will not be very well received by a jury made up of Iowa farmers and rural town folks."

Dave then said: "why don't we instead concentrate on Kiwanee because we have a weaker case against it."

I responded, "I think we have a strong case against Kiwanee. For $18 added to the cost of a wagon this tragedy would never have occurred.

Further, don't underestimate the feelings local jurors will have against an Illinois corporation."

After further discussing the matter, Dave agreed to try and settle with Jensen first. He felt this might put more pressure on Kiwanee to cooperate if ultimately it were left in the case alone. I asked for a new demand for Jensen.

After conferring, David said: "Dick, to show our good faith we will settle our case with Jensen for $1.5 million. I want you to know we have very little room to move. Please understand this."

I nodded assent. I then returned to the defendants' conference room and asked to speak alone with Tom Jackson and the adjuster appearing on behalf of Jensen. When we were alone, I said, "gentlemen, plaintiff proposes to negotiate with you alone and then fight its battle with the manufacture in court. Plaintiff's counsel does not believe that Kiwanee is acting in good faith. Plaintiff has instructed me to give you Mark's new demand of $1.5 million.

"Is that a global or just us?" asked Tom.

"Just Jensen." I responded.

Tom and his client asked to confer alone, so I left the room and met with the Kiwanee group. Entering their conference room I said,

"David decided to negotiate separately with the Jensen group. He feels that you are not really interested in settling at this time. I hope you don't mind."

There was a prolonged silence. Then Phil said, "this is unacceptable. You're trying to divide and conquer, and we will not stand for that. If you don't get us back into the negotiations we will terminate the mediation."

I responded, "I understand your frustrations, but this is a decision Dave has made. I'm just the mediator. I'll keep you posted on what is occurring as the negotiations between the plaintiff and the Jensen group progress."

Kiwanee's adjuster was clearly angry and probably blaming me. But they really had no choice other than leave. They stayed and waited to see what happened.

I returned to the farmer caucus room. Tom said, "we are most serious about settling today. If we can get the job done, we will pay $400,000, but there's little room to move off that figure.

After further discussion, I returned to the plaintiff's conference room and disclosed the new offer. Dave said, "that is progress, but it's still way too low."

I asked for a new demand.

"We have been discussing this while you were gone, and we are giving you our final figure," said David. "You can give Tom and his adjuster a demand of $1.1 million."

I returned to the Jensen conference room and gave them plaintiff's new demand. Then I added, "the Kiwanee group is very upset at me for putting them on the shelf. However, I think it will loosen them up for they can no longer put the onus on you to settle this matter."

After 30 minutes more discussion the Jensen group agreed to go to $600,000. I asked, "could you tell me in confidence how much further you will go?" However, they declined to do so, so I returned to the plaintiff's conference room.

"Gentlemen, the farmer's carrier is making a new offer of $600,000."

David said, "it's still too low. It's unacceptable. They are nickel and diming us."

"David, I never heard of anyone calling an increment of $200,000 nickel and diming."

At this point I decided to put a mediator's figure on the table of $850,000. I explained it to both sides and asked them to think about it.

I was waiting in the hall while both sides considered my proposal. David then called me into their room and said that they would go to $750,000. At the same time they handed me a structured annuity proposal which placed $300,000 of the settlement into an annuity for Mark, which would generate $25,000 per year for life tax-free. This was presented to the plaintiff, and David said they would agree to go to the $850,000. They said they would go no further. The adjuster for Jensen finally agreed to pay the $850,000 and the matter was resolved.

Because the hour was late, the Kiwanee group agreed to meet a week later and try to resolve the claim against it. In the meantime, Dave found an expert who concluded that Kiwanee Wagon Company had violated state and federal safety standards. However, he could not find a wagon manufacturer that provided rear lights. He did come up with the 1974 American Society of Agricultural Engineers year book, which suggested that rear lights should be provided on farm wagons if they were to be used on highways at night.

When negotiations began again, plaintiff demanded $1 million and Kiwanee offered $100,000. Going back-and-forth, plaintiff lowered his demand to $700,000 and Kewaunee raised its offer to $300,000. I then suggested we split the difference at $500,000 and both agreed. The case was settled. All in all, Mark ended up with a total settlement of $1.35 million which was more than ample to take care of him, and his family for that matter, for the rest of his life. Through the whole mediation plaintiff hardly said a word. He seemed very patient and trusted his attorney implicitly.

The strategy of separating the two defendants worked. It is called the domino strategy. When one of several defendants is not cooperating, the strategy is settle with each one separately leaving the difficult one for last. Invariably, having been isolated they will acquiesce.

After I completed my tenure at Drake law school, I was approached by Chief Justice Ward Reynoldson, a good friend through my law school activities, who encouraged me to run for the Iowa Supreme Court. He was retiring and felt that with my academic experience, in addition to my years of practice, I would make a good candidate. I was deeply honored to say least and decided to make a run for it.

In Iowa, unlike Illinois, a commission made up of lawyers and laypersons screens all candidates and then nominates three, which are sent to the governor. He then makes the final selection. This is so much better than having judges stand for election, like political office, and require them to get party endorsement. I remember in Illinois when Jim Dooley, an outstanding trial lawyer, ran for the Illinois Supreme Court. He had to campaign for months to gain voter recognition. One day I was on a train from Wilmette to Chicago and Jim Dooley and entourage walked from one end of the commuter train to the other shaking hands and asking for votes. This was demeaning for such an outstanding lawyer and jurist, but more critically it leads to serious abuse, for campaigns cost money and lawyers and friends are expected to donate. Certainly, having lawyers contribute to such campaigns has the potential for serious corruption in the judiciary.

After my interviews before the commissioners, I was delighted to be one of three nominated for the Iowa Supreme Court, but deeply disappointed to be one of two rejected by Governor Branstad. Justice Bruce Snell, whose father had been on the Iowa Supreme Court, got the nod, an excellent choice. My disappointment lingered for several months but later faded as I got into mediation and found that as a mediator I had the greatest opportunity of all to serve. Sometime later, I had a justice of the Supreme Court call me and asked to go to lunch. He stated that serving on the court had isolated him from the bar and many of his friends, and he was thinking about retiring. He wondered if I could help him become a mediator so he could get back in circulation. (In spite of all I have just said, I would have traded with him in a second if offered the opportunity. It would have been wonderful for my ego.)

Being a mediator gives me the greatest flexibility and satisfaction in the legal field. Consider the fact that I only mediate cases where negotiations have broken down and the case cannot be settled. In fact many times attorneys will say there's no way this case can be settled, but they are willing to give mediation a last chance before trial. When you do settle, and over 90 percent do, they are amazed and the parties relieved and grateful.

———————

"Dick, Roger Stetson is on the phone," said Susan. Roger Stetson was chairman of the Alternative Dispute Resolution Committee of the Iowa Bar Association and was working hard to get mediation accepted by the Iowa courts, but was having considerable difficulty. The biggest problem seemed to be that many judges, including several on the Iowa Supreme Court, thought of mediation in terms of binding arbitration, which they felt infringed upon the courts jurisdiction. This is not the case, however, since mediation is totally voluntary and there can be no settlement unless all parties agree. Further, the mediator has no authority or power over the parties and therefore cannot make any binding decisions. Another problem was resistance to mediation by those lawyers and law firms that work on an hourly basis. If mediation settles a case, they lose hourly billing, so it is in their economic self-interest to take a case through trial. Contrariwise, plaintiff attorneys, particularly those being paid by contingency fee arrangements, readily accept the process. They recover the same contingency fee regardless of whether the case is tried (and they win) or it is settled through mediation. Therefore, if they can settle the case before they have spent too much time in pretrial discovery or before the case is filed, they come out ahead.

Roger Stetson was not only the leader to introduce mediation in Iowa but is the father of mediation in Iowa.

Mediation #48
All Is not Corn in an Iowa Corn Bin

I was asked to mediate a case in which grain in storage bins became contaminated by a pesticide. The facts are best summed up by a statement made by an employee of Escole Spraying Company given to the Iowa Department of Agriculture. He stated that on October 17, 1986, "I mixed a load of Aldrin in my truck to be used in two termite control applications. Part of the solution was used October 17, 1986, and the balance on October 24, 1986. I don't recall if there was any Aldrin left in the tank or whether I cleaned the tank prior to spraying an empty grain

storage bin for Dallas County Grain Company. I used the same stainless

steel 100 gallon tank and spraying equipment for the termite control jobs

and the grain company job."

At the beginning of the opening session of the mediation, counsel

for the Dallas Grain Company, Ben Hilliard, stated that even a tiny fraction

of Aldrin in a grain bin requires the state to shut the facility down.

Counsel also noted that the Federal Drug Administration (FDA) inspector

made spot inspections of the Dallas County Grain Company bins on April

13, 1987, April 22, 1987, and May 4, 1987. In the first inspection he took

grain that had spilled through a crack in the wall, and testing showed that

it contained significant amounts of Aldrin. The inspector noted that

Escole was the only company that had sprayed pesticides in the bins in

question.

Hilliard adjusted his notes and then continued explaining that the

inspector then took samples from two other bins and found small

amounts of Aldrin in one and none in the other. He further explained

that, of course, all grain had to be removed and disposed of from two of

the bins.

Later in private caucus I inquired whether the grain was destroyed or disposed of in some other way. Hilliard responded that it was sold to Egypt at distressed prices. They do not have the same concerns concerning Aldrin as the FDA has.

Hilliard then explained what his client's damages were. The total claim was $1,518,950. "How do we get there? Simple," said Hilliard. "We had to purchase $95,358 worth of corn in the open market to replace the damaged corn. We had to store it in Davenport, which cost us $80,730. We paid $18,156 interest on the loan to purchase the corn; we lost $42,750 drying income in 1987, and we lost $410,696 income because we could not accept any more corn into the two bins."

Sarah Paisley, senior attorney in the Johnson Law firm, representing the defendant Escole interrupted and asked, "Why could you not store future grain in the two bins once the Aldrin was removed?"

"I'm glad you asked," said Hilliard. "Since the Aldrin was discovered, three companies have tried to wash out the bins to remove the Aldrin, and so far no one has succeeded. Once it gets into a facility it's very difficult to remove. In fact the insurance company defending here has taken on the job of having the bins cleaned out and has failed. For two years now we've done everything we can and nothing has worked, and we continue to lose money, which we are entitled to recover."

Continuing, Hilliard stated, "I mentioned before the $410,000 lost income; in addition we're entitled to receive $350,000 in future lost income – which will result because of the projected unwillingness of depositors to use our facilities because of the fear that decontamination has not been totally successful. In this regard, the federal government is the largest depositor and it simply chose not to use us any longer because of our problems. We will have an expert at trial discussing this."

Hilliard stopped a moment and looked at his notes and then added, "there is another $21,360 which covers quality discounts on shipped corn. The fact that a substantial portion of the corn at the Dallas Grain Company facility was contaminated meant that we lost the ability to blend corn in order to meet quality standards for shipments."

"Finally, if we are unable to eliminate the Aldrin, and we have now been trying unsuccessfully for two years, the residual value of the business adds another $500,000 toward damages. Thank you for listening."

Sarah leaned over and spoke to the insurance adjuster in a whisper. Then looking at Hilliard and then me stated: "I don't know how familiar you are with green contamination, but I think Mr. Hilliard is going to have a difficult time proving Escole was responsible. After all, substantial time has lapsed between the time the bins were sprayed and the Aldrin detected. The amount of Aldrin detected was more than could have come from the spraying by my client. In other words, I'm suggesting that the corn could have been contaminated before it was stored and therefore there is no causal connection with our spraying. There were also other chemicals found for which we could in no way be held responsible. In my humble opinion plaintiff is going to have some serious problems trying to prove that we were the cause of the Aldrin when there were a number of other possibilities. We also feel that plaintiff has not done enough to get rid of the Aldrin and it has a duty to mitigate its damages. Finally, we do not think that Mr. Donnelly, who owns the Dallas Grain Company wants to continue with the business and is looking to get out because it looks like the federal government is drastically modifying its federal grain storage program. We think we can develop this possibility in discovery. That is all I have to say."

At this point I separated the parties in two separate caucus rooms. I then followed Hilliard and his client, Donnelly, into the former's office. It was located at the southeast corner of the 20th floor and had a superb view of the Raccoon River joining the Des Moines River. The intersection creates a triangle of land where the Iowa Cubs ballpark is located. In the far distance there were high ridges covered by dense woods interspersed with homes. People who visit the Des Moines area for the first time are always amazed at how hilly and wooded it is.

We sat down in Hilliard's office and he stated, "we think we have a very strong case. We have spent considerable time investigating and we have the complaint prepared, which will be filed next Monday at the latest."

"That is if we cannot settle today, I take it." I interrupted because I like the parties to think positively.

"If we don't settle today," echoed Hillard.

At the end of the joint session, the insurance adjuster offered to settle the matter for $200,000. Hilliard considered this an insult, and said "such an offer gives me an excuse to try the case."

I held my hand up in a gesture to calm Hilliard – "it's only their opening offer," I said. "They are bound to move up as we progress in the mediation."

As we discussed the strengths and weaknesses of the case, I inquired of Donnelly whether it was true that he wanted to get out of the grain business altogether because of possible changes in the government subsidy program. He looked at me for a moment and then said: "look, whether I want to get out of this business is not the issue. I have three people that run this business for me and depend on it for their livelihood; I must keep it going for them and I intend to do so."

"What about the argument that the two warehouses could be torn down and rebuilt for $100,000, is that true?"

Donnelly looked at me and then his attorney and said, "we will have to admit that our damage figures might be a little high for it is based on not being able to get back into the business for some time."

"How much do you feel that would reduce the damages?" I asked.

Donnelly responded, "perhaps $600,000, but that still leaves us with a valid claim of $900,000."

Other matters were discussed and I then asked what Hilliard thought a jury would come back with, best case, worst case. Before answering he asked to speak alone with Donnelly. I left the room. They called me back a few minutes later and Hillard stated that their worst-case was $700,000 and best $1 million.

"They have made an offer, as you know, to settle the case for $200,000," I noted. Donnelly responded that they would make a new demand of $845,000, a major drop from the prior demand. He added, however, that he would not go much further.

I was pleased with this new demand for I thought it signaled that the plaintiff wished to settle the case and was acting in good faith. I thanked Donnelly and went back to the conference room where Sarah and the adjuster were waiting. Sarah was looking out the window west and could see the governor's mansion along Grand Avenue, where many of the city's wealthy once lived. To have a south of Grand address meant you were one of the wealthy and elite.

After sitting down, I immediately asked what the strengths and weaknesses of the defense were. Sarah was prepared and began by saying that she felt they had a 50-50 chance on liability. "Remember, plaintiff has the burden of proof by a preponderance of the evidence that Aldrin entered the bins through our spraying. Furthermore, the jury is not going to get angry with us for we have done everything to cooperate in this matter. We paid for the purchase of some of the replacement grain and storage of it. We have assisted in removing the Aldrin and we did not have to do this."

Sarah continued, "we have some problems with Donnelly. He was too quick to agree with the government and shut down the bins and his business. He should have challenged the government's findings. Actually, we think this whole matter was a stroke of luck for Donnelly inasmuch as he was ready to shut down the whole operation before the government pulled the rug from under him. In other words, he wants to get out of the business. His bins are old and have little replacement value. The whole operations was not worth $200,000, and that is what we offered."

In answering my question as to the weaknesses or concerns in the case, Sarah stated, "Richard, the jury might just believe William Donnelly because he is a nice guy, a local businessman, that is the risk. Furthermore, he might convince them that he wants to continue his business, and if he does that, damages could be substantial."

I then asked what Sarah thought was Escole's best case and worst case in front of a jury. She responded that their best case was around $200,000, and worst case no more than $500,000.

I then relayed Donnelly's new demand of $845,000. I was asked to leave the room while the two spoke. When I was called back in Sarah said their response was $235,000.

There was a long pause on my part because I was concerned how Donnelly would react to such a small increase. I said, "by going up such a small amount, when Donnally dropped a third off his original demand, might be sending the wrong signal. I am concerned that he might walk."

The adjuster spoke for the first time, "that is all I'm going to go up at this time. If he walks, he walks, and he can file his case. I like Sarah and don't mind paying her rather than William Donnelly."

There was little I could do but thank the adjuster and return to Hilliard's office. I tried to cushion the new offer but without success. When I told him that the offer was $235,000, Donnelly said, "I told you those - - - would not negotiate in good faith. That's an insult. I'm ready to leave right now." Hilliard added, "this is really disappointing after the new demand we made."

Rather than terminate the mediation I asked if I could continue the mediation by telephone over the next few days. I felt that both sides were getting tired and frustrated, and giving them the chance to sleep on the matter might improve the negotiating stance of both. Both agreed.

The next day I called Sarah and stated that unless the adjuster made a substantial move the mediation would fail. I then asked her if she would tell me in absolute confidence where she thought her adjuster would go to get this matter resolved. There was no need to hold back at this point because unless the adjuster made a serious offer we would not get the matter settled.

Sarah hesitated a moment and then said, in absolute confidence, "I think the adjuster will go to $450,000 and perhaps a little more." This was the major move I was looking for, but I was instructed I could not disclose it. I then asked Sarah if she could get her adjuster to $500,000 if that would settle the case. She said she didn't know but that she would try. I asked her to do so and get back to me as soon as she could.

Later that afternoon Sarah called back and said that if Donnelly would make a demand to settle for $500,000, the adjuster would pay it. I thanked her for her hard work and said I would do everything I could to get the matter resolved at that figure.

I held off calling Donnelly for another day knowing the next day was his golf day. I was hoping that he would have a good round of golf because, being a golfer myself, I know that if he shot a good score he would be much easier with which to work. As it turned out, he did have an excellent day, one of his best scores that year, and he readily agreed to settle for the $500,000. Hilliard approved and the matter was resolved.

In this case I used three strategies. First, when I felt parties were becoming tired and frustrated, I put the mediation over a few days, during which time I could contact each by telephone. This gave the parties a chance to think about the matter in a quiet setting without my pushing them. This is called pillow talk.

Second, I put a mediator's figure on the table of $500,000, when I realized that the adjuster was close to the figure in any event. Sarah was quite helpful in encouraging her adjuster to go a little further in the bidding process.

Third, I recognized the benefits of golf and what a good score would do to the party negotiating. Of course, I took a chance that he would not have a good score but he did. Being sensitive to this possibility enabled us to get this matter resolved.

Mediation #49

All You Want to Know About Insurance

The more complicated the case, the more sophisticated the strategy needs to be. This was brought out in an insurance case which I mediated in Kansas City, Missouri.

Kirk Landry, age 52, was an entrepreneur in Kansas City, who had a number of businesses. He borrowed heavily from banks to fund his various enterprises. Two insurance salesmen talked him into using insurance as a means to raise money, as well as to protect his estate. The salesmen, Andrew Harty and James Donovan were independent agents selling for a number of insurance companies. Over 12 years Harty and Donovan sold Landry over $52 million of insurance. At one point, he was paying premiums of over $1 million per year. Unable to sustain these payments, a number of policies were sold and some allowed to lapse. When Landry unexpectedly died in October 2007, he did not have one penny of coverage to sustain his widow and estate.

Eight months before his death, in December 2006, Harty and Donovan approached Landry and encouraged him to purchase a $10 million insurance policy from Star Insurance Company, operating out of

Montréal, Canada. At the time, Landry had been ill and had gone to the hospital with gallbladder complaints. He then had his gallbladder removed. In applying for the policy, he was required to fill out a medical form. Knowing that coverage would be denied if the gallbladder operation were disclosed, Harty suggested he would fill out the form for Landry to sign. Landry consented. In the portion of the application describing applicant's medical condition, Harty put down that there were no medical problems, and the only contact with a doctor was Landry's annual physical examination. Landry questioned the omission of his true medical condition. Harty and Donovan explained, that Landry only had to live two years after the policy issued and then it became "incontestable," and the insurance company could not deny coverage. Landry seemed to have recovered satisfactorily from his surgery and the three felt confident he would live more than two years.

The application was submitted to Star Insurance Company, and the policy issued on December 29, 2006. At this time, Landry also had a $20 million policy with Albuquerque Insurance Company which was incontestable – more than two years had lapsed since it issued. A third policy, also with Albuquerque Insurance, for $5 million was incontestable but allowed to lapse in December 2006 – Landry failed to pay the premium. In March 2007, a reinstatement application was filed, which

also included false statements concerning Landry's health status. Again,

Harty and Donovan filled out the forms and Landry signed. As with an

original policy, two years had to lapse before the reinstated policy

became incontestable.

In March 2007, Landry was short of cash and could not make his

premium payments. Payment was also owed to his bank on a loan

previously taken out. Harty and Donovan suggested Landry sell his $20

million Albuquerque policy in a viatical sale. A viatical sale is made when

a buyer buys the policy at a discount, pays the premiums, and when the

insured dies collects the proceeds of the policy. In such a sale, the sicker

the person is the more value the policy has.

Oak Insurance Company bought the policy and paid $1.1 million,

of which Harty and Donovan received a $400,000 commission and Landry

received $700,000, which he paid on the bank loan. In the viatical sale,

Harty and Donovan again filled out the forms for Landry only this time

they disclosed the true medical condition because that gave greater value

to the policy in the sale.

On November 17, 2008, Landry suddenly died of unknown causes.

Star Insurance then investigated and discovered the falsification of the application. It, therefore, denied payments to Landry's estate and filed a lawsuit to rescind the policy on grounds of fraud. Albuquerque Insurance Company likewise rescinded its $5 million reinstatement policy on the same grounds.

Landry's widow ended up with no insurance coverage. She hired lawyers to seek relief. Landry was survived by his widow, two sons, and two daughters.

The attorneys retained by the estate counterclaimed against Star Insurance Company to enforce the $10 million policy, and brought an original action against Albuquerque Insurance seeking to set aside the viatical sale of $20 million and enforce the $5 million policy.

When I received the assignment to mediate the case, and read the material sent to me, I was overwhelmed. This was an extremely complicated case and I did not know how to approach it. I finally decided to meet with each of the attorneys for the respective parties and try to get a better understanding of the case. Over several days, I set up my premediation caucuses just with counsel.

I first met with counsel for Star Insurance, Bill Henry, in downtown Kansas City. Bill Henry was 45 years old, an excellent trial lawyer, friendly, well prepared and always wore a coat and tie. The law firm was in a converted bank building, three stories high, a landmark in the city.

I waited in the first floor reception area which was spacious and had comfortable chairs. A secretary got off the elevator and approached me. "Mr. Calkins would you follow me?" We took the elevator to the third floor, walked down a long hallway until we came to Bill Henry's office, a spacious corner office. I walked in and introduced myself to Bill, another partner, Sam Stevens, and an associate Jennifer Silvers.

I thanked Bill for allowing me to meet with him and we quickly got to the merits of the case. Bill said, "Mr. Calkins ..." I interrupted him and said, "please call me, Dick."

He continued, "Dick, our position is that Kirk Landry falsified his medical condition and that is grounds to rescind our policy. It is that simple. We are prepared to refund his $400,000 premium payment, but that is the most we will do."

I asked, "what is the Landry estate's theory of the case?"

Bill said: "They are contending that although the medical statement is false, it was filled out by the insurance agents and simply signed by the insured. They contend that Harty and Donovan were Star Insurances agents; therefore, knowledge of the false statement was attributable to Star Insurance. Our position is, and we will prevail on this, that Harty and Donovan are independent contractors, who sell for many companies, not just Star Insurance, that they acted as agents for the insured."

"Bill, is there anything pending at this time?" I asked.

Bill answered, "Yes, there is. Summary judgment motions on both sides have been filed and briefed and we are waiting for a date to be set for oral argument. The judge just informed us that he will put that off until after the mediation, should it fail."

"I understand your position, Bill, and – –"

Bill interrupted me. "We have just filed a new complaint against the Landry estate and Harty and Donovan as defendants. In this complaint we are pleading that they entered into a conspiracy to commit a fraud against Star Insurance."

"That is a serious charge," I noted, "but I understand where you're coming from on this. Is there any room for compromise?"

Bill answered, "we are prepared to return the premium, but will not pay any additional money. We also have a claim against the agents for their commission of $300,000 on the sale of the policy. Maybe we could wave that if we got out of the case."

Bill was firm as we discussed the matter. I didn't disagree with his position and felt that it would be most difficult to get any additional funds to settle the case. I thanked him and exited his office and the building.

I had lunch and then met with Ted Billups and Jerry Spruce who were from separate firms representing Harty and Donovan respectively. The same errors and omissions insurance company, Tri-State Insurance, appointed them to represent the agents. Ted was in his 60s and was a senior member of the bar. He was dignified, well-respected, wore a three-piece suit and started work every morning at 6 AM.

Jerry was in his mid-30s, very energetic, tall, athletic and spoke fast. Introductions had barely been made when Jerry jumped right into the matter at hand. He said, "Richard, we have a real quagmire here. Just yesterday the Landry estate filed an action against our two clients alleging that they negligently handled Landry's account, improperly advised him, churned his policies, allowed incontestable policies to lapse, encouraged him to enter the viatical sale on the $20 million Albuquerque Insurance policy – do you want to hear more?"

Ted Billups very calmly added, "as you probably know we have joined with Landry's estate in the motion for summary judgment. If Star Insurance loses and the policy is enforced, the estate's claim against us will fall away. If we lose on the summary judgment, we have both Star Insurance and the Landry estate fighting us. And frankly, what our clients did over the years does not look good. We have $8 million in Errors and Omissions insurance coverage; however, a jury looking at Landry's widow without a penny after purchasing so much insurance, could come down hard on us and award more than the policy covers, thereby making the personal assets of our clients vulnerable."

"Thank you, I appreciate both of your comments. I will keep what has been said confidential, of course."

"Of course," added Ted. "As long as Star Insurance remains in the case our clients are vulnerable."

"Why is that," I asked.

Jerry picked up the discussion.

"Under Harty and Donovan's insurance policy, there is an exclusion for fraud and conspiracy. As long as Star Insurance remains in the case, it will argue this and our client's personal assets are vulnerable because there is no coverage. You have to get Star Insurance out of the case, and then the $8 million in coverage kicks in."

I responded: "you two, as attorneys, are in a difficult situation, because you have clients whose interests are contrary to Tri-City Insurance, who is paying your fees."

"We know that," said Ted, "that's the nature of being insurance attorneys."

After more discussion, I felt I learned everything I could at this preliminary stage. I took my leave. The next day I went to the office of the attorney representing the Landry estate. He was in his 50s, had extensive litigation experience, yet he was not recognized as a leader in the bar. Quickly, I learned that Joseph Hinkerman does not make mistakes and it will be most difficult to get him to change directions. I asked him the theory of his case.

He answered: "Star Insurance sued the estate to rescind the $10 million insurance policy. It's sales agents, Harty and Donovan induced the insured, Kirk Landry, to buy the policy. They filled out the application, including the medical portion, which they falsified. They then had Landry sign it, explaining to him that all would work out fine. He only had to live two years and the policy was incontestable. Landry did not know what contestable meant. As agents of Star Insurance, their knowledge is attributable to the company and the policy is valid. It can't be rescinded. It's simple principal and agency law."

I noted, "and this is what you have raised in your summary judgment motion?"

"Yes, it is," responded Hinkerman, "and the court will rule in our favor."

We then discussed the merits of the motion and Joe was very confident he would win. So I left it at that.

A week later, I flew to Albuquerque, New Mexico to meet with counsel for Albuquerque Insurance Company. Arthur Hansen had a seven person law firm. He handled all types of litigation, traveling around the country trying cases. He was rarely home. He was very easy to talk to, had a good sense of humor and enjoyed telling jokes. He might best be described as a "good old boy." However, I learned long ago that those are the attorneys you have to look out for.

"Arthur, tell me about your case. Whatever we discuss will be kept confidential."

"Well, Richard, there are two aspects to the case. One is the viatical sale of the $20 million policy and the other is the reinstatement of the $5 million policy. As to the first, I don't know why they have even brought an action. A viatical sale went through. Landry received $1.1 million and paid off his bank. He wanted the sale and needed it for business reasons. And, it should not be overlooked that we paid the $20 million to the viatical purchaser upon his death, and they had paid only one premium of $50,000."

"As to the reinstated policy, the two years had not lapsed from the date of reissue and death. Therefore, we had a legal right to contest the policy. As you must know, he falsified the application form the same way he did on the Star Insurance policy about his health. That's grounds for rescission."

I asked, "when did Albuquerque Insurance learn of the false statements?"

"About one month after it was issued," he responded.

"When did Albuquerque Insurance rescind?" I asked.

"About one month after he died."

"One more question, did the company accept premiums from the time of issuance until the policy was terminated some 18 months later?"

"Wait a minute," Arthur said. "I think I know where you are going with this."

"No," I assured him, "I'm just trying to gather all facts before we commence mediation."

We had further discussion, and I took Arthur to lunch and that afternoon flew back to the Des Moines.

With the information I had gained, I sat down and analyzed the case to determine what my strategy would be. I concluded the following:

1. <u>The Landry Estate.</u>

First, it was in the estate's best interest to get Star Insurance out of the case. I was rather certain the latter would prevail on the motion for summary judgment because the insurance agents, Harty and Donovan, were not employees or agents of Star Insurance. They were independent contractors and sold insurance for any number of companies, including Albuquerque Insurance. They were paid commissions only on the insurance they sold. Further, when they sold a policy it was submitted to another agency, which then submitted it to Star Insurance, so Harty and Donovan did not deal directly with Star Insurance in any event.

Second, there was even a stronger reason for dismissing Star Insurance. As long as it was in the case, the issue of fraud committed by Harty and Donovan in filling out the medical records remained in the case, and if Star Insurance prevailed on this issue, there was no insurance coverage for the agents – fraud and conspiracy were excluded from Harty's and Donovan's Tri-State Insurance Error and Omissions policies. This would be a potential loss of $8 million in coverage.

Third, the estate's best case was by far against the two agents. They acted negligently on several grounds, including selling Landry $52 million in insurance they knew he could not sustain; allowing many of the policies, that were incontestable, lapse (including the $5 million Albuquerque policy); advising Landry to falsify his medical condition to obtain the Star Insurance $10 million policy; advising Landry to falsify his $5 million Albuquerque reinstatement policy; and churning Landry's policies over the years, receiving several million dollars in premiums and allowing Landry to die without a penny of coverage for his widow and estate.

Fourth, a jury would be far more sympathetic to find for the widow and the estate against unscrupulous insurance agents than against Star Insurance, which Landry defrauded.

Fifth, the estate had little likelihood of prevailing against Albuquerque Insurance concerning $20 million viatical sale. The estate argued that the Albuquerque Insurance should not have allowed the viatical sale to go through inasmuch as it knew it was incontestable and

Landry needed it for coverage. However, as noted by the insurance company, Landry needed the viatical funds for business purposes and insisted on pursuing the sale. Also, Albuquerque insurance had already paid out $20 million to the viatical purchaser and should not be required to pay twice.

2. Insurance Agents Harty and Donovan.

It was in Harty's and Donovan's best interest to get Star Insurance out of the case. As long as it was in the case asserting fraud and conspiracy, they had no insurance coverage and would have to satisfy any judgment the estate might recover against them out of their personal assets. This would force both into bankruptcy. Even apart from the estate's claim, Star Insurance was seeking a return of the $300,000 commission paid them for the sale of the $10 million policy to Landry. This also would force them into bankruptcy. Their hope was that Star Insurance would settle and not require a return of the $300,000 commission.

3. Star Insurance.

Star Insurance's primary goal was to get out of the case and stop paying attorneys' fees. To this end, it informed me that it would waive the return of $300,000 commission and would refund the $400,000 premium paid to Landry. This was to be kept confidential until I had an agreement that it would settle the case. It was not willing to pay any extra money to settle.

4. <u>Albuquerque Insurance Company</u>.

It was clear to me that Albuquerque Insurance had little to be concerned about concerning the $20 million viatical sale for the reasons already discussed. As for the $5 million reinstatement policy, this was a different matter. I felt my approach had to be as follows: first, although Landry falsified his medical condition in the reinstatement application, Albuquerque Insurance learned of this one day after the policy issued. This occurred because in dealing with the viatical sale it received Landry's true medical condition. Second, in spite of this knowledge it continued to receive the premium payments until the time of Landry's death. Third, it seemed to me that this would constitute a waiver or estoppel. Recognizing this possibility, I decided to research the question before the mediation began.

The mediation commenced on April 8, 2010 at Billup's office. We had five conference rooms at our disposal. I met with all the lawyers first. All agreed that opening statements by each party would simply take too long and would further fracture an already hostile environment.

Generally, I like counsel to make opening statements, for it gives them a chance to speak to the party on the other side without interruption. However, in this instance I agreed.

I met with Bill Henry and Star Insurance first. They reiterated their position and I was certain that they would not pay more money other than the return of the premium and waive the $300,000 fee paid to Harty and Donovan.

I next met with Joe Hinkerman and his clients – Jane Landry, the widow, Tony Landry, the oldest child, Francis Landry Kevin, the oldest daughter, Mary Jean Landry Connolly, youngest daughter, and Frederick Landry, the youngest son. It was clear from the beginning that they did not like each other and they disdained their mother. The widow was heavy, hair was disheveled, her clothes plain and she was unattractive. She was angry because her husband, who had a mistress, left her without any means to support herself. She was looking for money, revenge, and blood.

As I walked in to the caucus room, Tony told his mother to shut up because she was always complaining. He added that it was no wonder dad couldn't take her any longer and dumped her for a younger woman. She broke down in tears and one of her daughters tried to comfort her.

I could see from counsel's expression that he had had it with the group. I asked him how he thought the summary judgment motion would come out.

He responded, "we have a good chance we will win and that will be the end of the matter."

We discussed the merits of motion; however, I did not suggest that they would probably lose. Too much money and time had been spent briefing the matter and Hinkerman might lose face in front of his clients. Instead I went through the pros and cons of dismissing Star Insurance. At first Hinkerman opposed even discussing the matter unless Star Insurance paid $2 million. I suggested that the estate's best case was against the two insurance agents – Harty and Donovan – who had $8 million in coverage, which was available only if Star Insurance was dismissed from the case.

After an hour of discussion, it was clear that Hinkerman was not willing to shift positions and give up his case against Star Insurance. I suggested they think about the matter, and zero in on Harty and Donovan.

One of the daughters interrupted the discussion and said, "you mean we would receive only $8 million and we would have to give up our claim for $10 million against Star Insurance? That doesn't make sense to me." Hinkerman gave her a frustrated look.

I left caucus room, took a deep breath and went to the next caucus, which was with Harty, Donovan and their attorneys. As I entered the room all conversation ceased and they looked at me with worried expressions. A representative from Tri-State Insurance was also present and he appeared to be indifferent about the matter.

It was apparent that there was a major conflict between the carrier and the two agents. In fact, Tri-State Insurance put the two agents on notice that it was proceeding with a reservation of rights – there was no coverage for fraud and conspiracy. Until Star Insurance was out of the case, it would not entertain putting anything on the table to settle the matter.

After considerable discussion, I asked to see the attorneys alone. Closing the door, I said, "gentlemen, I can see you are in a difficult situation. You're being paid by the carrier but you represent the two agents. Tri-State Insurance wants Star Insurance in the case, and Harty and Donovan want it out, so there will be insurance coverage for them."

Both acknowledge what I said. Ted then said, "how can we get Star Insurance out of the case?"

I responded, "the problem is not Star Insurance, but Joe Hinkerman. He is reluctant to give up his claim. And, he is dealing with difficult clients who are more prone to fight each other than to pursue a lawsuit."

Ted said, "what can we do to help?"

I answered, "perhaps you could talk to Joe and explain your dilemma, which also is his by the way, only he does not appreciate the problem."

The attorneys agreed to do this while I was caucusing with Albuquerque Insurance. It was after 2 p.m. and we stopped for a quick sandwich. I then went to my next caucus.

When I walked into the Albuquerque Insurance caucus room, Arthur Hansen was all smiles. In a slow Texas drawl, he said: "why, Richard, I thought you had forgotten all about us and gone home. If you had I would have understood because we do not even know why we are here. We have no exposure."

The Albuquerque vice president, Elbert Pendleton, nodded his head in agreement. We began discussing the case. I explained that I agreed with their assessment that there was little exposure concerning the $20 million viatical sale. However, as to the $5 million reinstatement policy, I had a concern. I explained the waiver point, that Albuquerque Insurance continued accepting premium payments even though it knew of Landry's medical condition and could have rescinded the policy.

Arthur interrupted me: "Now, Richard, you know how these big insurance companies are. That medical information came in on the viatical side of the company, and the boys in reinstatement never saw it."

"Arthur, I understand what you're saying, but will that fly in court? The bigger you are, the more you can hide behind your internal Chinese walls? I found a State Farm case where they made the same argument, which was rejected by the state supreme court. It held that if an insurance company is made aware of insured's medical condition, however it is learned, and it continues to accept premiums, it waives the right to rescind. Here's the case." Arthur looked at it and said, "I'm familiar with it. We will take that under consideration."

By the time we finished the caucus, it was time for dinner and all agreed to start at 8:30 AM the next morning.

The next morning, I met with Hinkerman and the Landry family. He had a good meeting with the Harty and Donovan attorneys and was trying to explain to his clients why they should settle with Star Insurance. Mrs. Landry was quite upset as always. She would not agree to give up her $10 million claim, because her husband had faithfully paid the premiums.

I spent some time slowly explaining the consequences of proceeding with a case against Star Insurance as now structured. I further explained that if we did not settle the case now it would take approximately three more years before it would be resolved.

When I said this Mrs. Landry went silent. Then she said "you mean, I won't have any money for another three years?" Then she went silent again.

I added, "and in three years we cannot be sure we will win. We could end up with nothing." Joe Hinkerman nodded his head in agreement.

After further discussion, it was decided to ask Star Insurance to pay an additional $200,000. It was a rich company and could afford to do so.

Although I knew what Star Insurance's response would be, I agreed to present the demand. After all the Landry estate was going in the right direction.

For the rest the day I went back-and-forth between conference rooms with new demands and offers. Mrs. Landry finally agreed to settle with Star Insurance on the terms it proposed. This brought Tri-State

Insurance into the mediation, and with Harty and Donovan pressuring it

to settle, it finally offered $3.8 million. Likewise, Albuquerque Insurance

offered $1.8 million to settle. This was a total of $5.6 million plus the

$400,000 premium returned by Star Insurance. The Landry estate

accepted. The matter was resolved. The strategy outlined above worked.

Mediation #50

Why Not Make Education A For-Profit Endeavor

One more example of the importance of developing a strategy to

settle a case involved several universities. For-profit universities have

been on the landscape for several decades now. A good example is

Phoenix University, which has students and campuses throughout the

world, and is the largest university in the world. It has purchased many

schools and turned them into profit centers. Small universities have taken

this lead and have expanded their campuses and student enrollments.

One such school is Lower Dakota University. It decided to join

with partner schools in the Far East, and expand its enrollment base. It

found that Asians, particularly Chinese, craved American degrees,

particularly MBAs. It therefore established campuses in the Far East and

offered courses leading to BA and MBA degrees from the university.

In 2001, Xavier Collins, president of Lower Dakota, and Milken Thompson, vice president, worked out a plan to expand its overseas operations. The plan called for partnering with schools in China, Malaysia, Thailand and India. The operation was a for-profit endeavor and projected income was dramatic. The plan was submitted to Lower Dakotas Board of Trustees which rejected it, feeling that the school had grown fast enough and needed to consolidate.

Collins and Thompson where most unhappy with the trustees' decision, and put the board on notice that if it did not reconsider the plan seriously they would resign. The board immediately accepted their resignations. The two then approached Nebraska Central University and offered the same plan. It's Board of Directors voted to approve the plan and hire both Collins and Thompson to run it. Money was poured into the project and partner schools in the Far East were lined up to participate.

Learning of Nebraska Central's plans, Lower Dakota filed a lawsuit in federal court to stop the project. It pleaded six counts: (1) breach of trade secrets, (2) conspiracy, (3) fraud and deceit, (4) intentional interference with contractual rights, (5) breach of fiduciary duty, and (6) breach of contract.

As in the Star Insurance Company mediation, I began by meeting with each party in premediation caucuses, to learn the facts of the case and work out my strategy. I first met with the president of Nebraska Central University. His attorney was present but said little. The president, Don Jacobs, played football at the University of Nebraska. With a degree of charisma he welcomed me.

I explained the purpose of the meeting. We had barely started when he explained that the school had dropped the program. It was causing too much conflict and now the lawsuit. The attorney, Oscar Simons, joined in and said there was no basis for the lawsuit particularly since the school dropped the project and terminated Collins and Thompson.

I pointed out to them that the complaint also asked for compensatory damages of $4 million for lost business opportunity. Oscar, who was short, rotund and in his 70s said, "bull –, that's ridiculous. They won't get one penny from us or anyone else."

I quickly realized I was going to get minimal cooperation from Oscar and the university because the former wanted to defend and bill as much time as he possibly could. I quickly wound up the discussion and took my leave. I then met with counsel for the plaintiff, Lower Dakota

University. David Aniston was senior partner in his law firm of 17 lawyers.

He was 71 years old, slim, balding, very energetic, one of the best trial

lawyers in the Midwest. He loved to try cases because it ignited his

"juices," as he was prone to say. We were good friends because his

daughter and my son were swimmers, so we saw each other at swim

meets.

We had an extensive discussion concerning the case. When we

finished he looked at me for a long moment, and then said, "you aren't

buying into my theory of liability, are you?"

"On the contrary," I answered, "I hope I didn't say anything that

gave you that impression. If anyone can sell this case to the jury, you can.

I do think it will be a challenge, however."

David smiled.

"David, all I'm doing now is getting an understanding of the case

so I can determine how to approach it. I learned this, neither Nebraska

Central's president nor it's attorney will be of any help to me. But that is

not a serious problem because the university is insured and the insurance

representatives will make all decisions concerning settlement. In other

words, we can literally ignore the president and his attorney for purposes of the mediation and concentrate on the adjusters. Have you had any contact with them?"

"No, I have not," said David. "They will be flying in from the East Coast the day before the mediation. They are two women. One is a vice president of the company."

"What insurance company is it?" I asked.

"Pennsylvania Mutual," was the response. It insures many universities and colleges."

I left with a few ideas as to strategy. I next met with Alex Crawford, attorney for Collins, and Michael Dempsey, attorney for Thompson. We met at Crawford's office, only a few miles from my own. The lawyers were middle-aged and had extensive trial experience. They were clearly the best lawyers on the defense side of the case. They explained that there were real problems with their two clients being in the case. First, insurance did not cover breach of contract and breach of fiduciary duty. Second, they had no money of their own, no separate insurance, so they were judgment proof. Any judgment against them was noncollectible. Third, the insurance company had held back paying them fully because their clients were not covered in two of the counts. They informed the carrier that if they were not paid in full, they would withdraw from the case.

This completed my premediation caucuses. I sat down and worked out my strategy:

First, Nebraska Central's president and his attorney were not players in the mediation. In fact, they probably would hinder resolution; therefore, they had to be isolated to a degree. The players were the two insurance adjusters for Nebraska Central.

Second, I had to convince the adjusters to pay Crawford and Dempsey (attorneys for the president and vice president) in full so they would remain in the case. The defense did not want to lose their best trial attorneys.

Third, I needed to impress upon David Aniston to gear his opening statement to the adjusters and not the defendant Nebraska Central and its president.

Fourth, I needed to convince him to drop the charges of breach of contract and breach of fiduciary duty against Collins and Thompson because there was no insurance covering those counts and the two were judgment proof.

One day before the mediation I met the two adjusters flying in from New York City. Linda Johnson was a vice president of Pennsylvania Mutual and Sarah Grimes was her assistant. I then drove them to their hotel in West Des Moines. We did not talk about case because I wanted to be a good host. Also I was trying to build some rapport and trust with the two agents.

The next morning I drove them to the mediation site. Before the mediation commenced, Oscar Simons, defense counsel for Nebraska Central stated, "let's forgo opening statements and go directly into caucus."

I responded that David had a few words and then Oscar could reply. Previously I had suggested to David that he make an extensive opening statement geared to the two adjusters. This was important because I felt that eastern insurance representatives would look down on Iowa lawyers and it was important for him to impress them with his adversarial skills.

David no more got started when Oscar interrupted stating again, "look, we are just wasting a lot of time. Let's get into caucus."

I motioned for Oscar to follow me into the hall. I said: "Oscar, David's remarks are not for you nor Nebraska Central; they are being addressed to the adjusters and this can only benefit you and your client."

Oscar said nothing and walked back into the conference room, sat down, and took out a newspaper. I could see that his client, Ben Jacobs, was also becoming anxious, so I pulled him out into the hallway and gave him the same speech. He confessed he did not understand what was going on.

David spoke for one and one half hours. From my perspective, it was well organized and a lawyer like presentation that I felt was having the impact I desired.

When David completed his opening statement, Oscar chose not to respond. I then went into caucus with David and Lower Dakota University. David agreed to dismiss the charges against Collins and Thompson for the reasons I urged. He then made a demand of $3 million. I then met with the two adjusters. After much discussion they made an offer of $750,000.

The day was then taken with my caucusing with each side and taking new demands and offers back and forth. Ultimately, the case settled for $2.25 million. Oscar was upset or so he pretended. He kept arguing that the University should pay nothing: it was a hold up. I was

convinced he would never try the matter, and if he did, David would make

minced meat of him. I concluded, Oscar was making a show of things

because, with the case settled, it was safe for him to do so. The insurance

company paid this much money in order to avoid the risks of losing, and

to save the costs of litigation, which would have been substantial. All in

all it was a good and fair settlement.

CHAPTER 9

APOLOGY AND FORGIVENESS

The most effective and yet most challenging tool the mediator can use is the apology and forgiveness. It is the most powerful tool the mediator has in his peacemaking arsenal. If it can be invoked, not only is resolution assured, but also conciliation, peace and healing. It is a tool that can only be used in mediation, because outside the context of mediation an apology would constitute an admission that could be used in court.

More and more, defendants, and in particular, insurance adjusters, recognize the value of the apology to an injured plaintiff. It tells the person the defendant does care and is concerned. And in the divorce context, an apology and forgiveness can be of particular importance to the ongoing relationship between the parties, particularly if there are children. The apology and forgiveness is not an act of surrender nor show of weakness. If both sides can be encouraged to see the humanity in the other, a major step has been taken towards peaceful resolution and healing.

The Amish church gives us an excellent example of forgiveness. When one of its members killed a number of little children, members rushed to the assailant's home to conduct a prayer of forgiveness with his wife and children, which brought healing to the entire community.

When Nelson Mandela was elected to the presidency of south Africa in 1994, after 27 years in a South African jail on terrorist charges, he faced the daunting challenge of how to unify the country split between blacks and whites. One of his personal bodyguards, Jason, requested more bodyguards to protect the president. So Mandella gave him four – the same white bodyguards who had protected his predecessor. Jason complained that "not long ago, they tried to kill us." Mandella responded, "reconciliation starts here" and added, "forgiveness starts here too; it liberates the soul. It removes fear; that's why it's such a powerful weapon."

President Lincoln was criticized for referring to the Confederacy in kind terms. A female critic asked him how could he speak so generously of his enemies when he should rather destroy them.

"Why madam," replied Lincoln, "do I not destroy them when I make them my friends?"

Mediation #51

Sexual Abuse Victim Finds Healing

Jamal Cranston, African-American, was the oldest of six children. He lived in the worst area of Chicago. He had no father and his mother barely survived on government support. She finally decided one of her children would have to leave the house. So 12-year-old Jamal was chosen. She approached Father Benson, a priest at the local church, and asked if he would take Jamal and be a father to him. Father Benson readily agreed and Jamal moved into the rectory. Almost immediately, father Benson put a wedding ring on Jamal's finger and called him his bride.

For the next six years, Father Benson sexually abused Jamal in every way imaginable. Jamal had nowhere to turn so he endured until he graduated from high school, when he went out on his own.

Twenty years later he appeared at a mediation, having made a claim against the church for the abuse he suffered. He now lived Atlanta, Georgia, had a wife and two children and had a good job. He appeared at the mediation wearing a coat and tie. He spoke calmly, was articulate, did not seem to be suffering as most of the other victims do. The case settled relatively quickly and Jamal seemed satisfied.

After, I pulled Jamal aside and asked, "Jamal, how is it that you appear to be in such control? You wear a coat and tie, have a stable family situation, have a good job. You don't seem to be suffering as all the others do."

Jamal looked at me and reflected for a moment. Finally, he said, "Mr. Calkins, I guess the answer is, I forgave Father Benson, who is now dead. In spite of everything, he was the only father I knew and I know he was a sick man. And I loved him as a father and I know in his own way he loved me as a son. And I also forgave the church, my family, and I regularly attend mass."

I sat there in wonderment, for I realized this was the power of forgiveness. It means survival and healing for those who are able to embrace it. Jamal's story gives me inspiration to continue my mediation work, for it is truly a glorious way to touch the lives of so many who are in need.

Mediation #52

Forgiveness Is A Glorious State of Mind

A case showing the power of forgiveness occurred in Iowa, when Jan Benedict was killed in a motorcycle – truck accident. Jan, who had become engaged to a young man in St. Louis, Missouri, was riding her motorcycle to St. Louis to attend the engagement party. She was riding south on a two-lane Iowa highway, when she came to a narrow bridge. The defendant, Leo Sanders, was driving a pickup truck with a wagon attached to its rear. Both arrived at the bridge at the same time: at that moment, the wagon, which was improperly attached, swung out and Jan was hit and instantly killed.

Mediation was held in Mason City and the Benedict family and Jan's fiancé were in attendance. An insurance adjuster attended on behalf of Sanders.

When everyone was seated, I began my opening remarks. Jan's father interrupted, "where is Mr. Sanders? We can't start without him."

"Mr. Benedict," I said, "the insurance adjuster is here on behalf of Mr. Sanders. He will negotiate the case and has full authority to settle."

By Mr. Benedict's expression it was clear he was not happy. He just sat there with his arms folded. Mrs. Benedict wept. After the opening session was completed, I went in to caucus with the Benedict family. Before I could sit down, Mr. Benedict exploded, "that…, doesn't even have enough remorse to attend. As far as I'm concerned, let's just go to trial."

I was caught off guard by his anger. I responded, "I don't know why he is not here. I'm going to talk to defense counsel."

I exited the room and went to the defense caucus. I announced that, "we are going to have a difficult mediation if we don't get Sanders here. The family thinks he doesn't even care about what happened. Can you reach him?"

Counsel for the carrier left the room and went to his office to get the number. He made the call and then returned to the conference room. "He's on his way." Thirty minutes later, Sanders walked into the office. I explained what happened, and then added, "anything you can say to comfort the folks will be deeply appreciated."

We walked in to the conference room and I asked Sanders to sit down at the table with the family. There was a long silence. Sanders looked at each member of the family and finally said: "I know how devastating the accident has been for all of you. There's not one day that goes by that I don't think about it and blame myself for what happened. I know you can't forgive me, but I want you to know I still get depressed thinking about it."

He stopped and looked down. He tried to say something more, but choked up. And he started to weep. The family quickly realized that he deeply felt the tragedy. This was what they needed and they were able to forgive him. Mrs. Benedict, with tears in her eyes, walked up to him and gave him a hug. I just stood there watching the power of forgiveness take place, and the case settled.

Mediation #53

The Tragedy of All Tragedies

Toby Zelinsky was a teenager and attended high school. He was a loner and not well liked by others. He spent his free time working in his garage rebuilding old cars. As soon as he got his driver's license he took a rebuilt 1938 Ford for a drive. As he drove down Elm Street, he saw three prekindergarten children playing in the parkway. He decided to "Buzz" them to give them a scare. He increased his speed, and, as he got close to the children, he misjudged the distance and ran into them, killing all three.

The parents of the children were devastated by the tragedy. Toby was convicted of manslaughter and sent to jail for six years. Subsequently, the parents sued Toby and his father. Because Toby owned the car, his father was dismissed from the lawsuit. Toby's father had purchased insurance for Toby on his car with $300,000 coverage. Early on, the insurance carrier offered to pay the policy limits. However, the parents rejected the offer.

At this point, the attorneys asked for mediation. Two years had gone by and the parents were still grieving. One mother in particular, refused to even consider settlement. She wanted to punish Toby for the rest of his life. She recognized that Toby had no money, and that a judgment would force him into bankruptcy. Her plan was to resist his being discharged in bankruptcy so she could attach funds he might earn the rest of his life. No one could talk her out of her plan for revenge.

Before the mediation, I spoke to the attorneys. They explained the situation and the need to get the matter resolved for the sake of the mental health of their clients. I made a decision to have Toby attend the mediation if possible. However, this was easier said than done because he was in the penitentiary.

I contacted state authorities and was able to work out an arrangement so Toby could attend the mediation. On the day of the mediation, the parents arrived early. We are all sitting in a conference room and no one was speaking. Then there was a knock at the door. I went to the door and opened it. In walked two state troopers, who must have been 6' 4"or 6'5" tall with Toby, who was 5'4" tall in front of them.

He had an orange jumpsuit on with handcuffs and a chain running between his legs. One of the officers was holding the chain.

They led Toby to a chair in front of the table and he sat down. A trooper stood on either side of him to his rear. He kept his head down and did not look at the parents.

Immediately the parents began screaming at Toby. Several mothers broke down weeping. Tears flooded the eyes of the fathers.

After 20 minutes, there was a lull and everyone looked at Toby. He kept his head down, and finally said: "what can I say." There were tears in his eyes, which he tried to wipe away. After further words from the parents, the mediation ended. Shortly after, the case settled for the $300,000 with each family receiving $100,000.

Although the parents could not forgive Toby, that was not asked, they did have a chance to vent, which was indeed therapeutic. They recognized that Toby was being adequately punished and they did not have to continue doing so. And although Toby did not apologize as such, his silence spoke louder than words.

CHAPTER 10

WORKING WITH THE DIFFICULT LAWYER

Most lawyers a mediator deals with are cooperative and make a real effort to get a case settled. There are some, however, who prove to be quite difficult and they have to be handled differently. Some get frustrated easily and threaten to terminate the mediation. Others, as a matter of strategy, simply hold out until they receive what they are asking. The following several cases discuss some of the difficult lawyers I have encountered and how I handled them.

Mediation #54

Let's Do The Charleston in Charleston, South Carolina

I was asked to fly to Charleston, South Carolina to conduct a mediation that involved the sexual abuse of three boys in seventh and eighth grade at a parochial school by their basketball coach. Examining the papers I received from the attorneys, it did not seem to be an overwhelmingly difficult case. The boys were rubbed in the genital area with their clothes on. To me that was a $75,000 to $100,000 case.

I landed at the airport and took a taxi to Billy Joe Thompson's office downtown Charleston. Billy Joe was probably the top plaintiff lawyer in the southeast. He was charming until he lost his temper. Then he could be quite difficult to handle.

I was led into Billy Joe's office, a pre-Civil War carriage house made over into a law office. He rose from behind his desk to shake my hand. He was 6'1", heavyset, with a full head of white hair. He had charisma.

"Richard, I'm so glad to meet you. I've heard so much about your good work; however, this is going to be a tough one. You are from Iowa, so put on your cowboy boots and let's get started."

Defense counsel and a representative of the church had not arrived yet, so Billy Joe showed me the antiques in his office. In one corner was a Confederate flag that had been carried in one of the battles. There was a framed Civil War revolver hanging on the wall. This desk purportedly belonged to General Longstreet, a Civil War general.

As we were talking, the church representative and insurance adjuster walked in accompanied by their attorneys. The church representative was Father Comito, the insurance adjuster Tilden Hermitage from Philadelphia, Pennsylvania, and the lawyer was Robert E. Lee.

Looking at Lee , I asked, "are you by chance related to the Civil War general?"

"No," he said. "I wish I was because I get asked that question every time I go south. Our last name is Lee, and my parents thought it would be cute to give me a Christian name of Robert."

Billy Joe said, "let me get my clients. They are in the other room." When we were all seated at a large conference table, we went around the room and introduced ourselves. Two of the boys involved were brothers and their mother and father were there on their behalf – they were 15 and 16 at the time of the mediation. The third boy was represented by his father alone.

After the opening session, I met in caucus with plaintiffs first. While discussing the case, the door opened and a 6'5" gentleman, in a white suit with snow white hair entered. Billy Joe looked up, and with a smile said, "everyone, we are honored this day. I want you to meet the Chief Justice of the South Carolina Supreme Court, C. Calhoun McGibbons."

Looking at the Chief Justice, Billy Joe gestured with his hand for him to sit in a chair at the table. He said, "now Bubba, I want you to listen to Richard. He is a mediator we brought in all the way from Des Moines,

Iowa to help us. You just listen to him for I know you can learn something just like we are."

We continued the caucus and I was instructed to take a demand of $1 million per child to the defendants. When I caucused with the defense, they agreed that the abuse had taken place, but that the boys had not been injured seriously, certainly not $1 million each. After 30 minutes they offered $75,000 per boy to settle.

I then returned of the plaintiffs' caucus. The Chief Justice had left and Billy Joe was sitting in his office alone. His clients were still in the adjoining conference room.

Billy Joe looked up and said, "well, Richard, what have they offered?"

I responded, "they started out low, but this is not a concern because this is the way it always begins in mediation. They offered $75,000 each."

Billy Joe just sat there with his face getting red. It was obvious he was trying to control his temper. "My good man," he said, "that is not a good faith offer." His voice started getting louder. "You go back and tell those people that this is not a satisfactory response; if they do not get serious, I will terminate the mediation. We will go down to $2.5 million total, but I expect a realistic response from the other side this time."

Before returning to the defense caucus, I tried to collect my thoughts and decide how I would approach the defense. I wanted the insurance adjuster to understand that he had to make a significant move to avoid termination of the mediation.

I walked into the room, sat down at the table, and looking at the adjuster, Tilden Hermitage, said, "as you may have guessed, I am having difficulty with Mr. Thompson. He has given me a new demand, but insists that we make a significant move. His demand now is $2.5 total."

Tilden looked at his attorney and shook his head. He said, "we're not going to get this done. I was afraid of this."

"Don't give up," I responded. "Many times mediations begin like this and still settle. It just may take longer. "

Without conferring with anyone, Tildon said, we will go to $100,000 each, but that is being generous. We do not have much more room to move."

I was concerned about this move because it was only $75,000 more total. I feared Thompson would not feel this was made in good faith.

With trepidation, I entered Billy Joe's office. He looked up expectantly. I said, "the adjuster only moved a small amount, but please do not get discouraged." I told him the figure.

Billy Joe just sat there. However, I saw his face become red again. "Mr. Calkins," he began, "this is unacceptable." His voice started to rise in pitch. "We have been here one and one-half hours and they have moved only $75,000 to $300,000, but I have come down $500,000. I won't stand for this." Now he was shouting, "I will give you 30 more minutes," tapping his watch, "and then you will be history. You can just get on your plane and fly back to Des Moines. I don't want to see you again."

I was stunned and did not know what to say. I could've responded that these mediations take time, 6 to 8 hours, and we are just getting started, or, plaintiff starts out high and defense low, but this is the way it always is, or, I was only the messenger so please do not blame me.

Instead, I followed the book. Don't defend yourself! I said, "Mr. Thompson, I understand your frustration and if I were in your shoes, I would feel the same way, and I would have said what you said, only more strongly." (The strategy with the difficult attorney is to agree with the person rather than defend. The latter only pours fuel on the fire).

Billy Joe relaxed slightly. He paused and then said, "Richard, get back to the other side and hammer them. I'm counting on you. But I'm going to hold you to the 30 minutes."

"I'm going to do everything I can, I promise you," I responded.

I left the room and sought out a room where I could collect my thoughts. The parties were so far apart that I was not certain what to do.

After considerable thought, the only thing I could think of was to use a mediator's number. I was certain the adjuster would not go to $1 million. Finally I decided to propose $750,000, which I was rather certain Thompson would reject, but it was the best I could do.

I went back to Billy Joe's office. "Mr. Thompson," I began, "I've given considerable thought as to how we can resolve this matter. I'm going to put on the table what I call a mediator's figure. It's a number which is going to be difficult for either side to accept and for that reason is probably a good one. I'm doing this in strict confidence. If one side accepts and the other side does not, there will be no disclosure. It will be kept confidential. Only if both sides accept will there be disclosure. Finally, I'm not asking you to accept the figure, only that you give it some thought." I stopped and observed that Billy Joe was looking at me intently.

"The figure I am thinking of is, " I almost gulped, "$750,000." Billy Joe hesitated, and in that hesitation I knew he would do it. If the party hesitates, looks up, looks at the client, these are all positive signs.

Billy Joe responded, "Oh , Richard, I don't know if we could go that low; however, we will talk about it."

The way he said this, convinced me even more that he would accept my proposal.

"Thank you for being willing to think about it. I will go to the other side to make the same presentation." I left the room and stuck my head in the defense caucus and asked to speak to Bob Lee , "a little 'lawyer talk,'" I added.

Bob and I went into another room and sat down at a small table.

"Bob," I began, "I have had a major breakthrough that I want to talk to you about before I meet with Hermitage. I put a mediator's figure on the table with Thompson."

"How much is it?" asked Lee, interrupting.

"750,000. So you can see it is a major drop from $2.5 million. He hasn't said he would accept, but he is thinking about it. If he does accept, do you think Hermitage will agree?"

"I don't know," said Bob. "It is a little rich; however, I would certainly urge him to accept, I can tell you that."

"Thanks Bob. That was my next question. Let's go back into the caucus room."

Bob returned to his caucus and I waited a few minutes before I knocked on the door and was admitted.

"Tildon," I began, looking at the adjuster, "I'm going to put a mediator's figure of the table that I'm asking both sides to consider. I think it will be difficult for both to accept; therefore, it probably is a good figure. In doing this, everything remains confidential. If you get to the figure and Thompson doesn't, there'll be no disclosure. You will not bid against yourself. Only if both parties accept will there be disclosure. I am not asking you to accept the figure only that you consider it." I hesitated a moment.

"The figure I am proposing is $750,000." Before I could get this out of my mouth, the adjuster was shaking his head, no. In my world that is a clear rejection.

Then Hermitage added, "we could not go much above $500,000." Although he rejected my proposal his statement turned everything around. What he was saying was that he would go to $550,000 or possibly $600,000, because at that level insurance adjusters work with increments of $50,000. In other words, it was highly unlikely he would only go to $525,000.

"Let me ask you this, Tildon. I will certainly tell Thompson you will not pay $750,000; however, may I also tell him that you would go not much above $500,000?"

Tilden thought a minute, and said, "yes, you may, if he first agrees he will go to $750,000."

I returned to Thompson's office. As I walked in, he said, "we will accept $750,000 if offered."

"Thank you," I responded; "however, the insurance company cannot go that high."

Immediately, Billy Joe's face started turning red. He was about to explode in anger, when I added, " Hermitage, that's the adjuster, did say that he could go, quote, not much above $500,000. That means to me they will go to $550,000 or $600,000."

Billy Joe's face relaxed. "Well," he said, "that's the kind of movement I was looking for. Why has it taken them so long?"

I asked, "would you consider something below $750,000?"

At this point, the father of the single boy stuck his head into the office. "May I talk to you alone, Mr. Thompson?"

I immediately stood up and exited the room.

A few minutes later, Billy Joe called me back into the room. He said, "the father wanted to terminate the mediation. It has been hard on his son and wasn't worth all the pain. He will accept $25,000 and walk. I told him that regardless of what happened with the brothers, I was certain the church would pay that. I explained where we were in the negotiations, but he still wanted to leave immediately."

"Billy Joe," I said, "I have a proposal. If I could get $300,000 for each of the brothers plus $25,000 for the other boy, would you accept?"

Billy Joe looked up and said nothing for what seemed like five minutes; however, this was a good sign. I said nothing and just waited. Then he said, "if you can get $300,000 for each brother and $25,000 for the other boy we will accept."

"Okay, "I said, " let me try." As I walked out of the room, Billy Joe said, "but not one penny less. Don't even come back if it is."

I returned to the insurance caucus. "Gentlemen," speaking to everyone, "I have good news, a deal you can't turn down." I was bluffing, of course, because Hermitage could easily turn down the new offer. I then explained the new figure and that one of the fathers wanted to end the mediation and accept $25,000. "If I could get the parents of the brothers to accept $300,000 each for a total $625,000 would you agree to pay this?"

Hermitage hesitated only a moment and said, "we will accept."

As I was leaving the room, I said I would do all I can to get agreement on the other side. Hermitages parting words were, "not one penny more."

As I closed the door, I heard laughing. I knew exactly why. Hermitage must have told the others that he knew how to work with mediators and he could get the case for less than $750,000 and he was right. As I read it, he would have gone to $750,000, and was bluffing, but that was not my concern. The case settled. That is all I cared about.

In this case, Thompson really became frustrated with mediation process and lost his temper. There are times when lawyers do this but are only acting to get a reaction out of the mediator. Their thinking is that when they do this the mediator will become worried about settling the case and therefore work harder to get it settled.

Other lawyers often begin with the line, I don't like mediation, I prefer to try cases. They are trying to get the mediator's attention also.

Some attorneys even accuse the mediator of being biased, favoring the other side. Their hope is the mediator will make a special effort to show his or her impartiality and favor the accusing attorney, which in itself raises the issue of bias.

Finally, there are lawyers who use, what I call, the Jerry Spence approach to negotiations. Jerry Spence is from Wyoming and one of the most successful trial lawyers in the country. He has a school in which he trains lawyers how to try a case and how to negotiate a settlement. The next case involves a Gerry Spence trained lawyer.

Mediation #55

Gerry Spence Rides Again

Harvey Conrad went into the construction business for himself. His primary focus was laying concrete sidewalks, driveways, and parking lots. On the day of the accident, he was laying a sidewalk. The defendant, Ready-Mix Concrete, dispatched one of its trucks to the site where Harvey was working. The driver, Phil Hancock, pulled out the chute at the back of the truck and concrete flowed to the area where Harvey was working. When he had enough, Harvey signaled for him to stop. Phil responded, and when the chute was clear of concrete, Phil folded it back and latched it to the rear of his truck. However, the latch did not hold and it snapped back to the open position, hitting Harvey in the head leaving him unconscious. He was rushed to the hospital, where he remained for a week. Thereafter, he went through extensive therapy for a closed head injury.

Within two years Harvey filed suit against Ready-Mix and the driver. Because his closed head injury kept getting worse he was unable to return to work. His doctors opined that he suffered permanent injuries and would never work again. He became depressed and began suffering post dramatic stress disorder, a medically recognized condition.

Because this was a serious case, Harvey's attorney, hired Malcom Chandler, a Gerry Spence trained lawyer from Denver, Colorado. Malcolm took over the case and resisted going to mediation when it was suggested. Finally, he consented, but made it clear that he did not have much hope of settlement.

The mediation was held in Sioux Falls, South Dakota. In the opening session, Malcolm made a demand of $3 million and the insurance carrier, represented by Ed Day, offered $350,000.

As the mediation progressed, I realized that Malcolm was not going to compromise very much. He repeatedly said he would not go below $2.5 million. I sensed, however, that the mediation was wearing

Harvey down. He stated he had a terrible headache and wanted to get the ordeal over with. He almost pleaded with Malcolm to compromise more but the latter would not.

I tried to give Malcolm reasons to compromise. I pointed out that Harvey was not wearing a hard hat as he was required to do. OSHA standards require all workmen in a worksite to wear hard hats. Malcolm answered, this applied only to employees, not independent contractors like Harvey. Ed Day interrupted and noted that when OSHA standards applied to employees it establishes negligence per se. For anyone else in the worksite it is only evidence of negligence.

Malcolm's answer to this was, "jurors do not worry about such niceties. No one wears hardhats doing this kind of work. In any event the jury will love him because he is such a nice person."

The more I argued with Malcolm, the more I realized he was not going to budge in spite of the law and his client's wishes. It was at the point I learned that Malcolm had been trained by Gerry Spence. When I heard this I sat up straight. So that is what the problem is, I thought to myself.

Gerry Spence lawyers will never settle the first day unless their outrageous demands are met. They will continue discovery, spend considerable amounts of money and take the case down to the time of trial. Then they will seriously negotiate. The theory is, the insurance carrier will either settle out of fear or exhaustion.

I explained to the defense not to be discouraged. It will just take some time. I told the adjuster "you have to determine if Malcom has earmarked the case for trial or not. Quite clearly, he can't try every case he has pending. If it is not so marked for trial, he will come around and get into a reasonable range. If it is, there's nothing that can be done other than pay the demand or try it. In this case," I explained, "I do not feel the case is marked for trial. The dollar claim was not large enough and the case itself would garner little publicity."

I kept in telephone contact with both attorneys and a month before trial Malcolm called me and said he would consider something slightly below $2 million. Ultimately, the case settled for $1,850,000. The only problem was, a huge amount of money was spent in discovery and Harvey was left in suspense for many months, which only added to his discomfort. All this could've been avoided if Malcolm had negotiated realistically at the time of the original session.

With the Jerry Spence lawyer the mediator must ask, is this a case the lawyer has earmarked for trial. He can't try every case. That depends on three things; one, is there a potential for a huge verdict; two, is there opportunity to receive positive publicity; and, three, is the defendant a target defendant that needs to be punished, like the tobacco companies. If none of these factors are present, the lawyer will look to settle at some point before trial. As in the instant case this was the conclusion I reached so I encouraged the insurance carrier to be patient.

Mediation #56

An Unusual Approach to Mediation

Frederick Hanley was an excellent trial lawyer of considerable reputation. He had a unique way to mediate. I mediated three cases for him and did not figure this out until the third case. In the first, a two-year-old boy was in the backseat of his parent's car unrestrained. The family had pulled into their church parking lot and the mother and father went into the church for a moment. The father left the car running to keep it cool on the hot summer day.

Teddy stood up in the backseat to look out the side window, which was down. Sticking his head out the window he started to climb out. His foot hit the up/down lever of the window raising it up. In the car model in question, pushing the lever down raised the window. As the window went up it caught Teddy in the neck and strangled him. When

Teddy's parents returned they screamed for help. Medics could not revive him and he died in the hospital of strangulation.

Hanley sued General Motors Corporation, manufacturer of the car, for an unsafe condition. He contended that the window should lower when a person pushes down on the up/down button. General Motors contended that, unlike today, all manufacturers made their windows operate the same way: it was a standard in the industry.

Hanley demanded $500,000 and General Motors offered only $100,000 and would not raise its offer. I did my best to get more pursuant to Hanley's instructions. General Motors threatened to name Teddy's parents as third-party defendants because of their negligence, leaving the motor running and the child unrestrained. Hanley would not lower his demand and GMC would not raise its offer. The mediation failed. Hanley spent a considerable amount of money visiting the GM plant looking at documents and hiring an expert. He finally gave up and accepted the $100,000.

Hanley then asked me to mediate a second case. This involved a six-year-old boy, Bobby Franklin, who darted out into a busy street and was hit by concrete mixer truck and severely injured. He made a miraculous recovery, except for his left leg, which required several surgeries. At the time of the mediation, the boy was able to walk without limp, but when he was older he would require another operation because the leg would not grow normally.

Hanley demanded $1 million and the insurance carrier for the concrete company offered $300,000. It finally raised it's offered to $500,000, which Bobby's parents wanted to accept. Hanley convinced them they would receive more if they were just patient. At trial, Hanley lowered his demand to $800,000 and then withdrew it because he felt he had the jury going his way. The jury returned a defense verdict, Bobby received nothing. The tragedy of this case was that Hanley could sustain the loss, but Bobby's parents could not.

Hanley then contacted me for the third case. I wondered why he would use me again when I failed twice. This time the case involved a grandfather ridding a lawnmower cutting his son's lawn. Without looking he started backing up and ran over his three-year-old grandson, who had crawled up behind him. The child survived but was badly injured.

Hanley sued the grandfather to reach his homeowners insurance policy. In this case, another lawyer was guardian ad litem for the child and was present at the mediation.

After several hours of mediation, the insurance company offered $300,000 and Hanley lowered his demand to $600,000 and stated that he would compromise no further. I was of the opinion that $300,000 was a fair settlement figure under the circumstances. The guardian ad litem, who said little during the mediation session, finally said he agreed with me. It was too much of a risk receiving nothing. Hanley disagreed and got into an argument with the guardian. The latter had the final say as guardian of the child. So the matter was resolved. Hanley was most unhappy.

It was at this point I realized what Hanley's modus operandi was. At each of these mediations, he had no intent to settle. He was using me, the mediator, to push the insurance carriers as hard as I could and then reject their final offer. He then tried to get more on the eve of trial. When I figured out what he was doing, I decided I had been too hard on myself for not getting the prior cases settled. Handley had no intent to settle. He was using me to negotiate. This was a misuse of the mediation process. I never mediated for him again.

Mediation #57

Young Female Lawyer Wins Out

Inger Johanson was an attractive woman, who graduated first in her law school class. She was editor-in-chief of the law review and was hired by the top law firm in Illinois. She was assigned to the Springfield office in the litigation section. After several weeks, the senior partner in charge of the office, Milton Hedrick, took a liking to her. She asked him to stop, but he thought she was just playing hard to get. Headrick was used to getting his way with female secretaries and considered Inger just another challenge.

The situation got worse and Inger contacted the home office in Chicago and complained. It sent a senior partner, Margaret Brenan, to investigate the matter. She took Inger aside and told her that, "boys will be boys; just ignore Hedrick and everything will be just fine."

Inger was not willing to accept this advice and finally quit. She contacted an attorney, who specialized in sexual harassment in the workplace, Stephen Hancock. Two weeks later she was hired by another law firm at about the same salary, but a better opportunity to make partner.

Hancock contacted the law firm in question and threatened to file a sexual harassment action under Title VII of the Civil Rights Act of 1964. He told the firm that Inger would settle for $800,000. The executive committee of the law firm met and discussed the matter. Their first reaction was this was blackmail. There was no way Inger had $800,000 in damages. She lost only two weeks of work, was hired by another firm at about the same salary, and clearly did not suffer any emotional distress. Cooler heads prevailed, and the firm offered to settle the matter for $100,000, which it felt was more than generous. The matter was then mediated.

Much to my surprise, Inger's attorney would not compromise off the $800,000. His position was that the Hedrick carried on like this with several other females in the office. Because of his position, it was difficult for them to stand up for their rights. They did not want to lose their jobs. Hancock was bringing the lawsuit to clear up the situation at the firm and was going to subpoena these other women. He explained that a jury, especially with women on it, would be angry and punish the law firm.

In confidence, the firm indicated to me that it would pay up to $300,000, but I could not disclose this unless I was certain it would settle the case. I finally informed Inger and her attorney, that unless they were willing to go below $400,000, we probably could not get the case settled at this time. Their response was they would not go below $600,000. However, I was not given permission to disclose this at that time.

I was relying on a mediation principle that "time works for you, not against you." I then put the mediation over for a number of months. However, I kept contacting the lawyers by telephone on a regular basis to see if any progress was being made. At one point I began to feel the attorneys were forgetting about the case entirely.

Two days before Christmas, I was driving down to Dallas, Texas to join my wife, Anita, and her family for the Christmas holidays. I was traveling south on Interstate 55 and was 20 miles south of Springfield, when I received a call on my cell phone. One of the attorneys in the case asked if I could come back to Springfield to give mediation another try. I was more than happy to do so.

The next day we met and worked for seven hours, and the case settled for $350,000. What changed was that the following day the case had to be filed – it had a two-year statute of limitations. Once the case was filed there would be considerable publicity and the damage would be done to the law firm. In other words, the case had value to the firm only if it could avoid the adverse publicity. Once filed, this was lost.

On Inger's side, she really suffered no damages and there was little likelihood that punitive damages would be awarded. Only if the other women joined the lawsuit was their value and they were not willing to jeopardize their positions with the firm.

The bottom line is that time worked for the benefit of all. And this brought about the settlement.

CHAPTER 11

THE PSYCHOLOGY OF FEAR

Mediators, without exception, use, what might be called, the psychology of fear. If the parties do not settle their dispute they face serious consequences. First, one such fear is the length of time it will take to conclude the matter if the parties choose to return to court. The mediator will establish this by asking counsel how long it will take to conclude pretrial discovery, trial, and the anticipated appeal. When the parties learn this could take three or four more years, this might just not be acceptable because of the stress and even depression they're facing because of the pendency of the dispute. Or, the plaintiff may be in debt and bill collectors are constantly harassing her, and four more years of this would be too difficult to bear. Settlement now would mean plaintiff could get out of debt and go on with life. Plaintiffs often face risk aversion for another reason. They may have been injured and therefore do not have the resources to support their families. Immediate settlement could change this dire situation.

When the mediator asks counsel how long it will take to conclude a case through the courts, and the attorney exaggerates the length of time, this signals the attorney also wishes to conclude the matter immediately and he is exaggerating the length of time to conclusion to get the client's attention.

Second, another fear is to point out the costs that will be incurred to go to trial. Litigation these days is extremely costly and to incur more debt for an outcome that may or may not be favorable is too great a risk. Indeed, there are some cases that are cost driven, that is costs of litigation exceed any realistic gain that they might obtain in trying the case.

There are also cases where there are fee shifting provisions, that is, if plaintiff wins at trial the defendant must pay the plaintiffs costs and attorney's fees in addition to their own costs and attorney's fees, thus dramatically increasing the exposure the defendant has. A number of federal and state statutes have these fee shifting provisions such as Title VII of the Civil Rights Act of 1964, § 4 of the Clayton Act (which applies to antitrust violations arising out of the Sherman Act), Fair Debt Collection Act, Gender Violence Act, Illinois Sexual Violence Act, the Nursing Home Care Act.

Third, another fear is that a party, no matter how good his or her case may be, may just lose before a jury. No one knows what a jury of 12 citizens will do. Lawyers recognize they lose cases they should win and win cases they should lose. My own experience is that cases I mediated which were unsuccessful and went to trial, more often than not came out

poorly for the plaintiff. Forty percent of those cases were defense

verdicts and 70% resulted in verdicts of less than $25,000. You can't

afford to try a case for $25,000.

Going to trial, especially when a significant offer has been made,

is rolling the dice. To roll the dice to get more leaves the party vulnerable

to receive nothing.

Fourth, there is the fear that if the case is filed and therefore

becomes a public record, it will injure the good name of one or both of

the parties, or in the case of defendant, generate more litigation against

it. Therefore, settlement now which incorporates a confidentiality

provision can have significant value.

Fifth, settlement has value. It means the parties can go on with

their lives and not be burdened with the albatross of litigation hanging

around their necks. Settlement is like a ton of bricks being lifted off the

parties' shoulders. It brings not only resolution but begins the healing

process.

Sixth, litigation interrupts the lives of the parties in that they are

required to attend depositions, answer interrogatories, produce

documents, and respond to motions filed in court. In other words, the parties are subject to the beck and call of their attorneys, which can divert many hours from business activities or normal living. Understanding the commitment litigation requires can be overwhelming.

Seventh, there is always the fear that after fighting for so many months and even years in court, a judgment may not be collectible because the defendant has become insolvent because of the costs of litigation or forced into bankruptcy.

These are all fears mediators use to get the parties' attention and willingness to compromise to get finality, certainty, and resolution.

Mediation #58

Victim Does Not Wish to Spend Her Golden Years in Litigation

Evelyn Steinhauser, a widow and grandmother, who was 75 years old, was walking on the sidewalk approaching the Norway Food Mart, where she was going to shop. Almost to the store, she had to walk around two rows of grocery carts lined parallel to the store front. As she did she tripped on a white plug that extended above the pavement by three quarters of an inch. The plug was round and about 1 inch in diameter. It had been placed there the day before by an employee of the store to plug a hole in the pavement.

Evelyn stumbled forward into the grocery carts severely injuring her right shoulder, cracking a rib, and hitting her head causing a concussion. Store employees came to her rescue and she was taken to the hospital.

Evelyn tried to settle with the insurance company insuring the store; however, they simply put her off and would not even pay her medical bills of $7500. In frustration she hired an aggressive trial lawyer, Judith Menke, who made a demand on the insurance company of $115,000. It responded with an offer of $25,000. Evelyn's attorney then filed suit. After several depositions had been taken, the insurance carrier requested mediation and I was retained.

After going through my usual questions in the first caucus with Evelyn, I asked counsel for a new demand. Without hesitation, she said, "$150,000."

This caught me by surprise for I expected her to demand something less than $115,000 already made. "Judith, don't you think it will make it more difficult to settle by increasing your demand. The defense will expect a lower demand, off the $115,000?"

"Mr. Calkins, we made that demand two years ago and we have spent an additional $20,000 in discovery. I think we are justified."

"Well, I will do as you direct, but we risk the defense walking out on us."

"That's alright," responded Judith. "We don't expect to settle the case anyway."

Usually a plaintiff attorney will raise the demand only if there is real justification, such as disclosure of additional injuries, or there are income losses not previously identified. The fact that money is spent in pretrial discovery is not justification.

More recently, however, I have not tried to talk an attorney out of raising the demand. He or she knows the other side will be unhappy and take it as a signal the party really does not want to settle. I have concluded that lawyers do this for several reasons. The lawyer may be having difficulty with the client who may not yet be ready to negotiate realistically, or the attorney wants to settle in a higher range, or the lawyer is testing the mediator to see how he reacts – if negatively he might conclude the mediator is pro the other side.

When I took Evelyn's new demand to the other side, they were most unhappy and refused to respond. Attorney, Troy Littleton, said, "we are not going to respond until plaintiff puts the $115,000 back on the table. That's bad faith raising the demand. Judith always does that and we are not going to dignify the demand with a response."

Realizing I was getting nowhere I decided to play a psychological fear. Returning to plaintiff's caucus, I asked, "Judith, how long will it take to complete pretrial discovery and try the case and exhaust the appeals."

Judith hesitated a moment because I think she understood what I was doing. However, she was candid and said, "it will take 3 to 4 years to complete the case." To this, Evelyn reacted in a way that demonstrated she was unhappy with the response. At that moment I determined that Evelyn did not want to spend her golden years in litigation, but with her grandchildren. Therefore I eased up convinced the case would easily settle.

Returning to the defense caucus I explained, "I am having a problem with Judith and Evelyn. You will have to be patient. However, I am confident the case will settle. If I can get Evelyn to drop to below $100,000, will you go up to $50,000?" Troy said it would.

This is a technique called bracketing.

Returning to the plaintiff's caucus, I explained, "I am changing directions. I know I can't get the insurance carrier to settle for $100,000; therefore, if we want to keep the mediation going, you will have to agree to go below $100,000. If this is not possible, then it is fruitless to continue the mediation." As I said this I was observing Evelyn. She was looking at Judith, silently pleading with her to agree. Judith asked to speak with Evelyn alone, after which they agreed to go below $100,000.

As I was returning to the defense caucus, I analyzed the case. Plaintiff would go below $100,000, which to me meant $90,000 or possibly $85,000. Defendant was willing to go above $50,000 which meant $60,000 or possibly $65,000. The gap was thus narrowed, possibly $20,000, and with this I knew the case would settle. And it did settle at $72,500 an hour later.

This mediation illustrates using the psychological fear of how long it will take to conclude the case in the courts. It was not that Evelyn was stressed over the pendency of the action or that she lacked funds to live on, but that she did not want to spend her Golden Years in litigation. She wanted to be with her grandchildren.

Mediation #59

Another Tragedy

Jamie Hicklin was 28 years old. She was married with a two-year-old daughter and twin girls six months old. She took her three children to the mall to shop. Afterwards, she got in her car and strapped the children in and started driving home. It was late in the afternoon and a winter storm blew up which turned into a blizzard, with high winds and icing conditions. She entered the interstate going 30 mph and drove some 10 miles when she came upon a semi-truck, which had jackknifed blocking the highway. She tried to brake but hit ice and slid into the semi. She dented a fender, but there was no more damage. She got out and carried one of the twins to the semi so she would be warm. As she returned to get the other two, a semi traveling 40 mph, slammed into the back of her vehicle and killed the two children on the spot. It was a horrible scene. As mediator, I was told if I did not have to look at the photographs of the children I should not. I decided not to.

Jamie retained a lawyer and sued both trucking companies for the death of her two children, and a bystander claim on behalf of herself as mother. Some discovery was taken including the depositions of the truck drivers, as well as a third trucker, who, prior to the accident, knowing the highway was blocked, tried to slow traffic down by driving down the middle of the interstate at 20 mph with amber lights flashing.

At the mediation, which took place two years after the accident, Jamie was fairly composed, although she did break down when describing the accident scene. Before the mediation started, the trucking company, owning the semi that jackknifed, paid Jamie $350,000. Therefore the mediation only involved the trucking company that crashed into Jamie's vehicle. The adjuster was present from Northern Insurance coming out of Minneapolis, Minnesota.

As the mediation progressed, Dan Harmon of Northern, offered $350,000, and explained that was his final authority. I was surprised at this because this was a most serious case, and when I heard the full facts I felt Northern was making a terrible mistake. Dan called for more authority but was denied. At this time Jamie was demanding $10 million.

The facts that developed during the mediation were that Dan Hemingway, a truck driver, was driving down the interstate about 10 miles before the accident scene. He learned that there had been an accident up ahead on his CB radio. He pulled into the middle of the interstate and put on his amber flashing lights to slow traffic down behind him. He slowed down to 20 mph. About this time, the defendant trucker, Felix Mattson, drove by him, driving on the shoulder at 50 mph. As he did, Hemingway held up his CB radio, trying to get Mattson's attention, but to no avail. Instead the latter gave him the "finger" as he drove by.

The attorney for Northern Insurance, Sam Monroe, made several weak arguments that, first, Jamie should not have traveled with the children in a blizzard; second, Mattson was not driving too fast for conditions; and third, had the first semi not jackknifed there would have been no accident. Later, the same attorney told me he did not want to try the case because the facts were so disturbing.

Plaintiff's attorney, Neil Phillips, a very successful trial lawyer, spoke calmly, making it clear that the $350,000 offer was an insult and that Sam Monroe, as attorney for the carrier, should have known better than to make such an offer. They would not have agreed to mediate if that was all the carrier was going to offer.

The mediation failed. I then asked permission to keep trying. All parties agreed, and I set up a meeting with the senior vice president at Northern Insurance, Bill Sanchez, so that I could make a presentation. To prepare, I asked plaintiff's attorney to put together a 30-minute video of the defendant truck drivers' depositions.

In caucus with the plaintiff, plaintiff's attorney Phillips informed me that his law firm had conducted a mock trial of the case. They hired a jury to listen to the facts, and members of the firm played the defense attorneys and an actor was hired to play the trucker who slammed into Jamie's car. The trial took three days.

Phillips stopped and looked down and then raised his head and looked at me. He said, "the jury returned its verdict – $13 million."

When he said this, I knew my mediation was in real trouble. Only something in that range would be accepted and I did not feel such a figure was realistic. The more I talked to Phillips, the more I realized he felt this was his big case to build his reputation. He was so obsessed, and that is the only word I can use to describe him, he couldn't sleep at night and every waking hour was spent thinking about the case.

Jamie was just as bad. When she heard the mock jury's award of $13 million anything less was an insult. In fact, she opposed making an offer of only $10 million at the end of the first session.

With the mediation failing, I made arrangements to travel to Minneapolis a week later to meet with VP Santos at Northern Insurance Company's main office. He was very professional and received me graciously. I then showed him the video I asked plaintiff's counsel to make in preparation for the meeting. First, it showed Dan Hemingway's video deposition. He was clean-cut and spoke slowly but barely audible. He explained how he tried to slow traffic down, and how Mattson drove around him on the shoulder of the highway going 50 mph. He explained how he tried to get Mattson on his CB radio to warn him of the accident.

Finally he explained how Mattson gave him the finger as he passed by. The deposition concluded with Hemingway explaining the accident scene. He actually broke down and wept. His testimony was compelling.

Next were excerpts from Mattson's deposition. He looked unkempt, had a beard and mustache and was very defensive, contending that he was not driving too fast for conditions. He was then asked what the "finger" meant. He answered. He was then asked if he ever used it on the highway. He answered in the affirmative. The next logical question was not asked, but the implication was clear.

Sanchez understood the gravity of the situation. He said he would get back to me in a few days, because he had to take the case to the "top." Later that week he made the following offer: they were willing to settle for $2 million. If this was rejected, they were willing to offer a high and low on any jury verdict. They would pay a low of $1 million and a high of $3 million. If the jury returned a verdict of less than $1 million, Jamie would still get $1 million, and if more than $3 million she would receive the ceiling of $3 million.

When I presented this to Phillips, without any thought he said, "rejected. This is an insult. I don't even have time to talk to Jamie about it, although I will. I know what her answer will be. I could never recommend this."

The day before the trial began, I spoke to the trial judge. He said this would be the worst case he ever tried. He added, "please keep trying to settle."

The first day of trial, I was present working in the hallway trying to get the plaintiff to compromise or give me a new figure somewhere in the range of that being offered, but to no avail. The trial went forward.

The jury had three truckers and one emergency room nurse on it. I did not feel they would be favorable for the plaintiff, although the truckers turned out more favorable than might have been expected.

Jamie testified, and just as the jury was leaving the court room, she got sick and threw up all over the floor. It was a very trying and demanding trial.

The jury came back and rendered its verdict. It found that total damages were $2 million. It allocated 25% of the fault to Jamie for being on the highway during a blizzard. It found the trucker that jackknifed, 35% at fault, and Mattson 40% at fault. In other words, Northern Insurance had to pay only $800,000. Jamie left $1.2 million on the table.

CHAPTER 12

SEXUAL ABUSE OF CHILDREN BY CLERICS

As indicated previously, I have conducted over 900 sexual abuse cases, mostly involving men of the cloth. This has included Seventh Day Adventists, Lutherans, and Catholics. It has also included people of trust in the YMCA, Boy Scouts, schools, day care centers, and orphanages.

Child abuse standing alone is tragic, but when committed by a cleric or church official the consequences are even more severe and lasting. What makes the abuse so tragic is that the child can tell no one because parents will not believe that a person who has sat at their table and was often treated as a member of the family could do such horrendous acts. When the child does say something he is punished by making such accusations. The child therefore lives with the shame throughout the formative years into adulthood. So often this leads the victim to smother the pain in alcohol and drugs, even as young as 10 and 11 years old. In reaching adulthood, the victim experiences substantial guilt, feeling they were the cause of the abuse. They also feel they were the only one abused and are surprised to learn otherwise.

When the person does come forward and sues, he is often attacked by the congregation believing the person has made false accusations against their cleric for financial gain. This compounds their suffering, all of which results in their becoming alcoholics and drug addicts. Many have committed suicide and any number have ended up in jail. Those who have married have not even told their spouses until they began receiving treatment.

Because 95 percent of the cases I have been involved in are with the Catholic Church, I will relate my experience to those cases. I have mediated abuse cases in Los Angeles, Orange County, California, San Francisco, Denver, Colorado, New Orleans, Louisiana, Charleston, South Carolina, Washington D.C., Albany, New York, Cleveland, Ohio, Chicago, Illinois, Davenport, Dubuque and Des Moines, Iowa. What compounds the injuries suffered by the children and the confusion they face when abused by a priest is the fact that the priest is God's representative on earth – he turns bread into the body of Christ, and wine into his blood. And he can forgive sin and assure the person will enter heaven. Thus, for the child to tell a parent what is happening at the hands of a priest is a sin in itself and treated accordingly.

The scandal in the Catholic Church has reached worldwide. All the bishops in Ireland were dismissed because they covered up the abuse. Other than in the U.S., few lawsuits have been successful. Although thousands of claims have been made here, I know of not one successful claim prosecuted in Latin America. Victims there have been reluctant to come forward primarily because of cultural concerns. To admit their manhood has been compromised is to lose face.

Jeff Anderson actually held a press conference in Mexico City announcing he was commencing legal action in Mexico against the Catholic Church. In the middle of his press conference, several thugs entered the room, physically grabbed him and took him to the airport. He was put on a plane to the U.S. and told that if he returned he would not leave a second time.

In the movie *Spotlight*, the Boston Globe identified 80 priests who had abused children of all ages in the Boston area. It ran a story of how the Archdiocese of Boston and its Cardinal covered up the abuse for many years. The movie received an Academy Award in 2016 for best movie. Mitch Garabedian, the lawyer portrayed in the movie, for whom I have done many mediations, has handled thousands of abuse cases and has many hundreds more still pending. In Davenport, Iowa, I mediated approximately 50 cases. Another 200 victims came forward when the diocese filed bankruptcy. I counted 45 clerics accused of molesting children in this diocese alone, and it is not a large diocese.

As pointed out in the movie, clerics pick the most vulnerable children as their victims. Children who have lost a parent, or the father is an alcoholic and beats the children, or has abandoned the family. They pick children who are loners and have few friends and then they groom them by plying them with gifts, alcohol and personal friendship so they feel wanted and important. Many times the cleric is treated like a member of the family and eats at the victim's table and sleeps over on occasion. They are loved and respected by the family and the family is honored and thrilled the priest shows so much interest in their son.

Jeff Anderson produced a documentary film *Deliver Us from Evil* which received an Academy Award nomination. Other movies discussing the problem include HBO's *Mea Maxima Culpa, The Magdalen Sisters, Philomena* as well as *Spotlight*.

Before discussing how cleric abuse cases are mediated it might be helpful to explain how pedophiles operate. First, there are different categories of abusers – pedophiles, ephebophiles, and predators. The pedophile abuses children, mostly boys but also young girls, as young as 3 years old as occurred in one daycare center. Ephebophiles abuse generally boys who have reached puberty and older. And the predator abuses children, teenagers and adults, male and female.

Second, each pedophile or ephebophile will have his own method of abuse. When an alleged victim describes an abuse outside the known pattern, the victim is suspect, that the person is making up the claim.

Third, unfortunately, the abuser is a sick person who cannot be healed through psychiatric treatment. Even where the abuser does all he can to stop the abuse, he cannot permanently be cured. Pedophilia is a disease with no known cure.

Fourth, the pedophile and, in particular, the ephebophile, does not believe he is doing anything wrong. With boys he feels it is normal, the dawn of manhood. Some Catholic priests make it appear to be a religious experience, while others threaten the victims with spiritual punishment should they reveal the abuse.

Fifth, some abusers are so conditioned to their mental makeup that they have passed polygraph tests because in their minds they have done nothing wrong.

Sixth, many times the abuser was sexually abused himself. In fact, some victims, upon having children themselves, are fearful they might resort to abusing them.

Unfortunately, it seems to be true, once a child has been victimized it is difficult for the person ever to recover and their suffering is lifelong. I know of three instances out of over 900 where I felt there had been a full recovery. One, described in Mediation #50, the victim, Jamal Cranston, an African American, whose mother abandoned him, asking a priest to be his father, was sexually abused for six years beginning in seventh grade through high school. The cleric put a wedding ring on his finger and called him his wife. Yet, in spite of the severe abuse, he appeared at the mediation in a coat and tie, was married with three children, had a good job and seemed to have fully recovered. Surprised at this, I asked him how he had survived, and he explained that he had forgiven the priest and the church. This was his salvation. And I concluded that forgiveness, as difficult as it is, is the only real cure.

One victim wrote a poem, which I set forth, with his permission.

When I think of what you did to me,
the emotions swell up inside,
a part of me was left behind
you took some of my pride.
The years of hurting, pain and tears,
took over much of my life,
it affected my family and my friends
my daughters and my wife
to stay above it all became a test for me.

Learning to bury it, hide it, not speak of it at all,
led me down some roads not chosen, there I took the fall.
I ran alone, alone I ran, not knowing where to go,

trying to find the place I belong, the place I'd never know.
While others say they shoot for the stars in search of their Dreams,
my life became a depression, of flashbacks, nightmares, and screams.

I was so afraid to say anything, that others would think less of me.

I decided that the time had come, for me to seek you out,
to know that others were safe from you, I wouldn't scream or shout.
I found you in a place of concern, with children all around,
I panicked and felt so all alone, as if my hands were bound.
You remembered me after so many years with such a matter of fact,
but your answers seemed so insincere, like it was all just an act.

The safety of others would become a quest for me.
And now as I struggle to reassemble my life in each and all its ways,
the months seem long, the years seem longer, a blur casts out the days.
The hope, the healing, I reach out for, is just a matter of time,
the strength I'll need comes from within, I can call it mine.
The parts you took, were only parts, like branches of the tree,
there's much that's left, like all the leaves, there's so much more to me.

I have decided you cannot have the rest of me because you never took the best of me.

Dennis Sobezak Survivor 2005

Filing civil actions against a church entity is a recent phenomenon because the church always had certain defenses which barred recovery. Although the cleric can always be sued for assault and battery, most were judgment proof, that is, they have no money to satisfy a judgement. Therefore, the only avenue of recovery was to sue the church entity or diocese. The defenses raised are: (1) the entity did not have notice the cleric was sexually abusing children, (2) the claim is barred by the applicable statute of limitations (the victim must sue within a certain number of years after the victim reaches majority), (3) the action is barred by a statute of repose (suit must be brought no later than the victim's 30th birthday), and (4) the institution is protected by charitable immunity for any wrongdoing of its officers or employees.

These barriers were broken for the first time some thirty years ago when attorney Jeff Anderson of St. Paul, Minnesota successfully sued a church entity in St. Paul. Thereafter, thousands of victims have recovered against churches around the country with billions of dollars paid in settlements and judgements. The Catholic Church alone has paid out over $3 billion. What I have learned is that when a church tries to defend against allegations of abuse, if the case gets to a jury, the resulting verdict is severe on the church entity. For example, 13 victims sued the

Archdiocese of Dallas and received a verdict in excess of $100 million, which the diocese could not pay. The matter was resolved by the diocese paying half that amount.

The Diocese of Davenport, Iowa, after successfully mediating some 50 cases decided to try one because it was running out of money, and more victims were emerging each day. It litigated a case it could have settled for $300,000. At the trial, plaintiff's counsel requested a verdict of $750,000. Instead, the jury award $1.5 million and two days later the diocese filed for bankruptcy protection. Ultimately, plaintiff only received a fraction of what the jury awarded because some 200 more victims came forward and made claims in the bankruptcy proceedings.

The Archdiocese of Los Angeles alone has paid out over $1 billion. Twelve dioceses and archdioceses have filed bankruptcy protection: Archdiocese of Portland, Oregon (filed 7/6/04), Diocese of Tucson, Arizona (filed 9/20/04), Diocese of Spokane, Washington (filed 12/6/04), Diocese of Davenport, Iowa (filed 10/10/06), Archdiocese of San Diego, California (filed 2/27/07), Diocese of Fairbanks, Alaska (filed 3/1/08), Diocese of Wilmington, Delaware (filed 10/18/09), Archdiocese of Milwaukee, Wisconsin(filed 1/4/11), Diocese of Gallup, New Mexico (filed 11/12/13), Diocese of Stockton, California (1/15/14), Diocese of Helena,

Montana (filed 1/31/14), and Archdiocese of Minneapolis, Minnesota (filed 12/20/14).

In the mediations I have done, a different format from that outlined in the cases described above has been used. Three steps are conducted: first, victims are given an opportunity to vent and tell their stories. Allowing victims to express their feelings and explain what happened and how the abuse has affected their lives is therapeutic and begins the healing process. One case mentioned is the executive who flew to Davenport for his mediation session and pointed a dagger at the bishop to express his anger at what happened. One thing we strive for is forgiveness on the part of the victim because if they can forgive, true healing is possible.

The second step in the process is to discuss noneconomic conditions. Many times these can be just as important as economic considerations. This might include (1) defrocking the clerics involved so they could no longer have access to housing or other facilities; (2) having the bishop write a letter of apology to each victim and family, if requested; (3) when there is an allegation of sexual abuse, suspending the pastor while an investigation is conducted; (4) having an investigation of all sexual abuse incidents conducted by an independent investigative agency; (5) announcing from the pulpit the names of the clerics abusing children; (6) publishing a public apology in a local newspaper by the bishop or church official addressing the victims and their families; (7) criminally prosecuting those offenders who can still be indicted; (8) allowing no cleric to travel alone with children under the age of 18 years, or staying overnight with a child without a proper chaperone; (9) establishing a church hotline, with the telephone number posted around the church and schools; and (10) permitting representatives of the victims to meet periodically with church officials to discuss current concerns.

The final step is to discuss financial remuneration. Many times, having agreed to noneconomic matters first, victims have an investment in the process so that they might moderate their demands so as not to lose what has already been agreed to.

In the cleric cases I have mediated, there have been only three I felt were bogus. There are two ways to determine if a case is legitimate. One, because pedophiles follow the same pattern with all victims, if there is substantial deviation in a particular case, it raises a red flag. And, two, the appearances and pain a victim suffers is apparent and when a victim is acting, it shows up immediately.

In one case, a 7 year old boy claimed a priest molested him. What he described, however, fit no pattern of abuse. Unfortunately, the case had been aired on *60 Minutes* television show and the parents were locked into following through with the claim. Eventually, the boy told his psychologist he made up the story to avoid being punished by his father. The church said it would spend $1 million to defend the priest because he was innocent of the charges. I was able to convince the parents that their son's story was not believable from a jury's perspective. The claim was dismissed and the church paid only out-of-pocket expenses of the plaintiff.

In a second case the so-called victim showed none of the signs of abuse. Although he cried, it just did not fit reality. When he refused to discuss what happened, it was apparent he was fabricating. He did receive costs of litigation.

The third case involved acts of abuse that did not fit the pattern of the cleric abuser. It was clear the so-called victim was making up a story. The case was settled, however, for less than costs of litigation.

In those cases which are actually filed, the key for the church is to get the case dismissed on a motion to dismiss or motion for summary judgment. These are granted if the court concludes there are no issues of fact in dispute and the case can be dismissed on the law. For example, if the court concluded there was no evidence that the church had notice that the cleric abused children, it can dismiss the case because this is an element that must be proven by the plaintiff. If the court determines there are issues of fact to be determined by the jury this is very bad for the church. Jurors, regardless of their religious preferences, are very pro plaintiff in these abuse cases and are not concerned with legal niceties as evidenced by the Dallas and Davenport, Iowa cases.

CONCLUSION

I recognize I have included several mediations I could not settle and they went to trial. I did so for a reason. It illustrates that when a reasonable offer has been made, plaintiff rolls the dice to go to trial. I have completed over 2000 cases with a success rate approaching 94 percent, which is acceptable (some mediators have a success rate over 97 percent). Of the 120 cases or so I have not settled and gone to trial, 40 percent resulted in defense verdicts. Plaintiffs received nothing and incurred the heavy costs of going to court. And 70 percent resulted in verdicts of less than $25,000. You cannot try a case for so little return unless the attorney is only seeking experience.

After two decades of mediating, I realize how much it has changed my life and made living it a happier more fulfilling experience. Mediation is indeed a noble calling raising the lawyer to a new level of societal acceptance. Lawyers now join others on the pedestal of the healing ministries.

However, there has been another side to the experience. Mediation has introduced me to a side of life I never knew existed. (My legal career before was limited to the sterile halls of antitrust, where no hugs are given for work well done.) Although many of the mediations

involved tragic circumstances, not all did. Some had lighter moments.

In one, I was mediating a case involving two adult women who

had been sexually molested by a cleric when children. When the matter

was amicably resolved, one of the women, who was attractive in a hard

sort of way, asked where I was from. I proudly responded the great city of

Des Moines, Iowa.

"Oh," she said. "That is the dullest city I have ever worked in."

I asked if she traveled quite a bit and she answered in the

affirmative. I then asked what she did. She responded, "I am an exotic

dancer in nude bars."

Catching myself, I asked, "In Des Moines?"

"Yes," she responded.

"Where?"

On another occasion an attractive woman in her 30s was suing

her ex-employer for sexual harassment under Title VII of the Civil Rights

Act of 1964. He insisted they have an affair. He was married and she was

single.

I was quite sympathetic to her cause until I learned she also was a

nude dancer and worked at her brother's bar in Des Moines. Then she revealed what her ex-boss was asking, that she join him and his wife in a ménage á trois. She added, she was quite popular in such arrangements because she was a single. I did not know what a ménage á trois was.

By the way, I never did find out where those bars are.